The American Revolution

The American Revolution

JOSEPH C. MORTON

Greenwood Guides to Historic Events, 1500–1900
Linda S. Frey and Marsha L. Frey, Series Editors

GREENWOOD PRESS
Westport, Connecticut • London

Library of Congress Cataloging-in-Publication Data

Morton, Joseph C.
  The American Revolution / Joseph C. Morton.
      p.   cm.—(Greenwood guides to historic events, 1500–1900, ISSN 1538–442X)
  Includes bibliographical references and index.
  ISBN 0–313–31792–5 (alk. paper)
      1. United States—History—Revolution 1775–1783. I. Title. II. Series.
E208.M9   2003
973.3—dc21   2003040836

British Library Cataloguing in Publication Data is available.

Library of Congress Catalog Card Number: 2003040836
ISBN: 0–313–31792–5
ISSN: 1538–442X

First published in 2003

Greenwood Press, 88 Post Road West, Westport, CT 06881
An imprint of Greenwood Publishing Group, Inc.
www.greenwood.com

Printed in the United States of America

The paper used in this book complies with the
Permanent Paper Standard issued by the National
Information Standards Organization (Z39.48–1984).

10 9 8 7 6 5 4 3 2 1

CONTENTS

Photo essay follows page 76.

SERIES FOREWORD

American statesman Adlai Stevenson stated that "We can chart our future clearly and wisely only when we know the path which has led to the present." This series, Greenwood Guides to Historic Events, 1500–1900, is designed to illuminate that path by focusing on events from 1500 to 1900 that have shaped the world. The years 1500 to 1900 include what historians call the Early Modern Period (1500 to 1789, the onset of the French Revolution) and part of the modern period (1789 to 1900).

In 1500, an acceleration of key trends marked the beginnings of an interdependent world and the posing of seminal questions that changed the nature and terms of intellectual debate. The series closes with 1900, the inauguration of the twentieth century. This period witnessed profound economic, social, political, cultural, religious, and military changes. An industrial and technological revolution transformed the modes of production, marked the transition from a rural to an urban economy, and ultimately raised the standard of living. Social classes and distinctions shifted. The emergence of the territorial and later the national state altered man's relations with and view of political authority. The shattering of the religious unity of the Roman Catholic world in Europe marked the rise of a new pluralism. Military revolutions changed the nature of warfare. The books in this series emphasize the complexity and diversity of the human tapestry and include political, economic, social, intellectual, military, and cultural topics. Some of the authors focus on events in U.S. history such as the Salem Witchcraft Trials, the American Revolution, the abolitionist movement, and the Civil War. Others analyze European topics, such as the Reformation and Counter Reformation and the French Revolution. Still others bridge cultures and continents by examining the voyages of discovery, the Atlantic slave trade, and the Age of Imperialism. Some focus on intellectual questions that have shaped the modern world, such as Darwin's *Origin of Species* or on turning points such as the Age of Romanticism. Others examine defining economic, religious, or legal events or issues such as the building of the railroads, the Second Great Awakening, and abolitionism. Heroes (e.g., Lewis and Clark), scientists (e.g., Darwin), military leaders (e.g., Napoleon), poets (e.g., Byron), stride across its pages. Many of these events were seminal in that they marked profound changes or turning points. The Scientific Revolution, for example, changed the way individuals viewed themselves and their world.

The authors, acknowledged experts in their fields, synthesize key events, set developments within the larger historical context, and, most important, present a well-balanced, well-written account that integrates the most recent scholarship in the field.

The topics were chosen by an advisory board composed of historians, high school history teachers, and school librarians to support the curriculum and meet student research needs. The volumes are designed to serve as resources for student research and to provide clearly written interpretations of topics central to the secondary school and lower-level undergraduate history curriculum. Each author outlines a basic chronology to guide the reader through often confusing events and a historical overview to set those events within a narrative framework. Three to five topical chapters underscore critical aspects of the event. In the final chapter the author examines the impact and consequences of the event. Biographical sketches furnish background on the lives and contributions of the players who strut across this stage. Ten to fifteen primary documents ranging from letters to diary entries, song lyrics, proclamations, and posters, cast light on the event, provide material for student essays, and stimulate a critical engagement with the sources. Introductions identify the authors of the documents and the main issues. In some cases a glossary of selected terms is provided as a guide to the reader. Each work contains an annotated bibliography of recommended books, articles, CD-ROMs, Internet sites, videos, and films that set the materials within the historical debate.

These works will lead to a more sophisticated understanding of the events and debates that have shaped the modern world and will stimulate a more active engagement with the issues that still affect us. It has been a particularly enriching experience to work closely with such dedicated professionals. We have come to know and value even more highly the authors in this series and our editors at Greenwood, particularly Kevin Ohe. In many cases they have become more than colleagues; they have become friends. To them and to future historians we dedicate this series.

Linda S. Frey
University of Montana

Marsha L. Frey
Kansas State University

PREFACE

In many ways, the eighteenth century ushered in the modern age. Several of the more important historic events of that exciting century were of such significance and magnitude that their impact has influenced nearly every facet of human life. For Americans, the Great Awakening (a religious revival) and the French and Indian War (1754–1763) brought about momentous social, economic, political, and religious changes. More significantly, the beginning of the Industrial Revolution, the American Revolution, and the French Revolution have profoundly influenced the lives of people everywhere, often in ways unanticipated and not fully understood even today.

For its part, the American Revolution (1763–1783) gave birth to a new world republic and a philosophy based on freedom, liberty, and equality for all free people. Although historically not always implemented even in the United States (witness the ill treatment of Native Americans; the exploitation of Blacks; the social, economic, and political subordination of women; and the all-too-prevalent racism and intolerance still seen today), the philosophical concepts articulated by the revolutionary leaders have become the model for positive change for people worldwide.

Although there is an abundance of excellent, informative, thought-provoking studies on almost every aspect of the American Revolution, every generation should reinterpret its history to reflect its own needs and ideals. Thus this book is offered as a fresh, concise, general survey of the events that brought about the birth of the American republic and the creation of an American revolutionary philosophy. Moreover, it reflects the continuing need for Americans to discover their historical roots: roots that can serve as an anchor as they undertake, at times somewhat hesitantly, to meet the challenges and opportunities of a new millennium.

ACKNOWLEDGMENTS

All books are collaborative endeavors. Numerous individuals, many in ways they themselves were unaware of, have aided me in the preparation of this manuscript. Since the secondary literature on the revolutionary era is particularly rich, I gratefully acknowledge the help of those historians who have preceded me in the study of this seminal period of American history. Also I gratefully acknowledge the contributions of the hundreds of university students who, in enduring my undergraduate and graduate courses on the American Revolution at Northeastern Illinois University, have added greatly to my understanding of the revolutionary epoch.

I am grateful to the editors of Greenwood Publishing Group, Inc. for their unfailing courtesy and valuable assistance in every phase of this work. Special thanks go to Kevin Ohe, Managing Editor, Print and Electronic Products, and the series editors, Professors Linda S. Frey and Marsha L. Frey. Marsha Frey was particularly helpful in saving me from egregious errors of fact and grammar. Every author should have the pleasant experience of working with an editor as considerate and as knowledgeable as Marsha Frey. In addition, thanks go to Marcia Goldstein of Greenwood Press and to the staff of House of Equations, Inc., for their valuable assistance during the production phase of this project and to copy editor Catherine Kirby for her careful editing of the entire manuscript.

I also thank Jill Althage, Reference Librarian at Northeastern Illinois University, for her generous assistance in obtaining primary source materials, and Esther Perica for her encouragement and the expert preparation of the index. My greatest obligation, however, is to my wife

Deanne who, uncomplainingly, endured having a recently retired old cur-
mudgeon professor sharing her domain all day long every day of the
week. Her encouragement and good humor made the completion of the
manuscript possible.

CHRONOLOGY OF EVENTS

1763

February 10–Treaty of Paris

May 7–November 28–Pontiac's Rebellion

October 7–Proclamation of 1763

November 5–December 1–Parson's Cause

December 13–December 27–Paxton Boys' Revolt

1764

April 5–American Revenue Act (Sugar Act)

April 9–Currency Act

1765

March 22–Stamp Act

October 7–October 25–Stamp Act Congress

1766

March 18–Repeal of Stamp Act

March 18–Declaratory Act

1767

June 29–Townshend Acts

November–January 1768–*Letters From a Farmer in Pennsylvania to the Inhabitants of the British Colonies*

1768

February 11–Massachusetts Circular Letter

June 10–Seizure of the *Liberty*

1769

May 16–May 18–Virginia Resolves and Association

1770

March 5–Boston Massacre

April 12–Partial repeal of Townshend Duties

1771

May 16–Battle of Alamance Creek

1772

June 9–Burning of the *Gaspee*

November 2–Committees of Correspondence

1773

May 10–Tea Act

December 16–Boston Tea Party

1774

January 30–Franklin dismissed as Deputy Postmaster General for America

March 31–May 20–Coercive Acts

May 20–Quebec Act

June 2–Quartering Act

September 5–October 26–First Continental Congress

September 28–Galloway's Plan of Union

October 18–Continental Association

1775

February 27–Lord North's Conciliation Plan

March 30–New England Restraining Act

April 19–Battle of Lexington and Concord

May 10–Capture of Fort Ticonderoga

May 10–Second Continental Congress

June 15–Appointment of George Washington as Commander in Chief of
    the Continental Army

June 17–Battle of Bunker Hill

July 5–Olive Branch Petition

July 6–Declaration of the Causes and Necessities of Taking Up Arms

August 23–King George proclaimed America in rebellion

August 28–December 31–Montgomery's Expedition against Quebec

November 7–Lord Dunmore's Proclamation

1776

January 9–Publication of *Common Sense*
February 17–Battle of Moore's Creek Bridge
March 17–British evacuated Boston
June 7–Richard Henry Lee's motion for Independence
July 2–Congress voted for Independence
July 4–Congress approved amended Declaration of Independence
August 27–Battle of Long Island
September 11–Staten Island Peace Conference
September 15–British occupied New York City
September 16–Battle of Harlem Heights
October 11–Battle of Valcour Bay
October 28–Battle of White Plains
November 16–British captured Fort Washington
November 18–December 20–Washington retreated across New Jersey
November 20–British captured Fort Lee
December 26–Battle of Trenton

1777

January 3–Battle of Princeton
September 11–Battle of Brandywine Creek
September 26–British occupied Philadelphia
October 4–Battle of Germantown
October 17–British surrendered at Saratoga
November 15–Congress approved Articles of Confederation

1778

February 6–Franco-American alliance signed
April 12–Carlisle Peace Commission
June 28–Battle of Monmouth Courthouse
July 4–George Rogers Clark captured Kaskaskia
December 29–British captured Savannah

1779

September 23–*Bonhomme Richard–Serapis* sea battle

1780

May 12–British captured Charleston
August 16–Battle of Camden
September–Treason of Benedict Arnold
October 7–Battle of King's Mountain

1781

January 17–Battle of Cowpens
March 1–Ratification of Articles of Confederation
March 15–Battle of Guilford Courthouse
October 19–British surrendered at Yorktown

1782

March 20–Fall of Lord North's Ministry
November 30–Preliminary Articles of Peace signed

1783

April 15–Congress ratified Preliminary Articles of Peace
November 15–British evacuated New York City

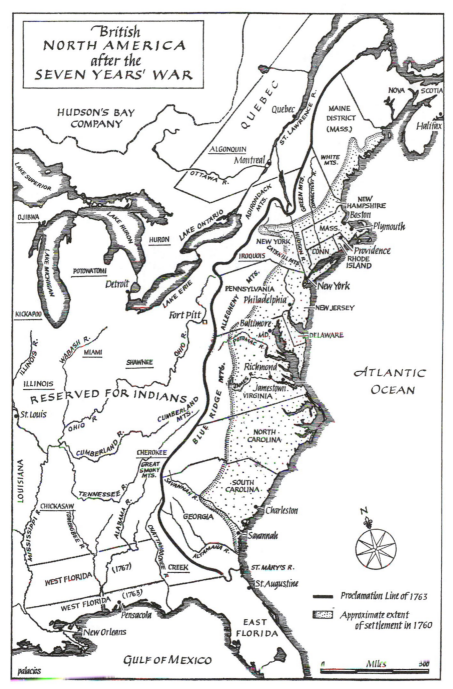

From *A History of the American Revolution* by John R. Alden, Copyright © 1969 by John R. Alden. Used by permission of Alfred A. Knopf, a division of Random House, Inc.

CHAPTER 1

NARRATIVE HISTORICAL OVERVIEW

The American Revolution (1763–1783) was a pivotal period in the history of the United States. During this tempestuous era, the thirteen English North American mainland colonies were able, against seemingly overwhelming odds, to secure their independence from Great Britain, to design a revolutionary philosophy the achievement of which is still today the hope and dream of countless millions throughout the world, and to create a government and society that implemented the revolutionary ideals of freedom, liberty, and equality. It is especially important in the early twenty-first century for Americans to be reminded of their glorious revolutionary heritage, which is today both envied and feared. It is envied by the downtrodden everywhere and feared by those who would deny others the basic rights articulated and implemented by the revolutionary generation.

A revolution can be defined in general terms as a series of events that bring about widespread, profound, and permanent change. Without question, the exciting events of the years 1763–1783 could truly be called revolutionary. Although there is disagreement as to a precise definition of the American Revolution, there is general agreement that the changes wrought during this time were widespread. In many ways, the American Revolution ushered in an age of democratic revolutions. The French revolutionaries, the Russian revolutionaries, the Chinese revolutionaries, and many of the leaders of the twentieth-century independence movements in Africa, South America, and Asia have used the political philosophy so convincingly and engagingly set forth by Thomas Paine, John Dickinson, Thomas Jefferson, and other authors and statesmen of the Revolutionary era to explain and justify their own revolutions and/or independence movements.

There is likewise consensus that the changes of the late eighteenth century were profound. The democratic era inaugurated by the American Revolution has changed the views many hold about the nature, structure, and philosophy of government. Moreover, it has given the oppressed and exploited everywhere a model and a hope for a brighter future where freedom, liberty, and equality prevail. Finally, the revolutionary changes carried out by the Founders are permanent. Always in theory and usually in practice, the United States is even today the political, economic, and social embodiment of the significant revolutionary transformation first proclaimed over two hundred years ago.

What is generally referred to as the American Revolution was actually a multifaceted series of events taking place in a relatively short period. It was, of course, a war for independence from Great Britain. In addition, it was a civil war in which the British were pitted against the British and Americans against Americans. It became, after 1778, another in a series of worldwide conflicts between Great Britain and her longtime Bourbon enemies, France and Spain. Moreover, it was during the Revolutionary era that a political, social, and economic philosophy was articulated that greatly challenged existing views and has had ever since a profound influence worldwide.

Although there is general agreement that the American Revolution brought about widespread, profound, and permanent changes, there is little agreement as to whether these changes were, in their total impact and influence, revolutionary or evolutionary. On the one hand, it is obvious that the American revolutionaries drew heavily on their European (especially British) heritage and on their colonial experience as they conducted the War for Independence and created a new national government, new state governments, and a new American culture. To the extent that they did retain much from their past, the American Revolution can be considered evolutionary, or at least a conservative revolution. However, the overwhelming evidence suggests otherwise. As with most wars, the War for American Independence accelerated social, political, economic, and cultural changes. It is also apparent that many of these changes were under way before the Revolutionary era and would have taken place even if there had been no American Revolution. On balance, however, the American Revolution was revolutionary. In many areas, the Revolution witnessed the overthrow of the old order politically, socially, economically, and religiously. Although the Revolution began as a protest movement against alleged British tyranny, it soon broadened to become one also against other traditional forms of authority, be they religious, economic, social, or political. Historian J. Franklin Jameson cogently and concisely stated the case for considering the Revolution a broad, revolutionary social movement when he wrote:

> The stream of revolution, once started, could not be confined within narrow banks, but spread abroad upon the land. Many economic desires, many social aspirations were set free by the political struggle, many aspects of colonial society profoundly altered by the forces thus let loose. The relations of social classes to each other, the institution of slavery, the system of land-holding, the course of business, the forms and spirit of the intellectual and religious life, all felt the transforming hand of revolution, all emerged from under it in shapes advanced many degrees nearer to those we know.[1]

The political changes were particularly profound. Although retaining much of the governmental structure of the colonial period, the revolutionaries established new republics (state and national) that stressed the sovereignty of the people. The glory of the Declaration of Independence is that it remains the best, concise statement of an American revolutionary philosophy with which the revolutionaries created republican governments still envied and emulated today. Although the United States has not always adhered to the lofty principles of the Declaration, the philosophical concepts of that charter of liberty continue to be the goals of most Americans.

In implementing the high ideals of its most famous founding document, the revolution's leaders broadened economic opportunities, enlarged the suffrage, abolished many of the symbols of aristocratic rule, and weakened the hold of the established churches. Thus in many areas of American life, the Revolution was an early reform movement.

In declaring "that all men are created equal," the revolutionaries, perhaps for many unintentionally, inaugurated the first antislavery movement. There were, during this period, the first serious debates about the morality of the institution of slavery. In the colonial period, the Society of Friends (Quakers) was the only group in America that questioned the morality of slavery. During the Revolutionary era, the Quakers were joined by others who saw the inconsistency in championing political independence from British oppression on the one hand while condoning the existence, in point of law and practice, of an institution in which thousands

were systematically denied their natural right to freedom and independence. Although not successful in abolishing slavery (that would only come
with the ratification, in 1865, of the Thirteenth Amendment to the Constitution of 1787), the first antislavery movement that emerged during the
latter years of the eighteenth century was a revolutionary, necessary first
step in the freeing of all slaves.

The transformation of thirteen colonies into largely self-governing
republics was revolutionary in its impact. Actually, with the official creation
of a national government in 1781, there were fourteen new world republics established based on the sovereignty of the people—certainly a revolutionary concept. During the Revolution, eleven of the thirteen states drew
up state constitutions. (Connecticut and Rhode Island merely amended their
colonial charters.) A few of these governing charters were conservative in
that they permitted a mercantile elite (in New England and the middle states)
and a planter aristocracy (in the South) to retain their economic, social, and
political dominance. However, even these conservative state constitutions
contained, in most cases, provisions for broadening the suffrage, for creating weak executives, for granting most political power to the elected legislatures, and for frequent elections. The more democratic state constitutions
(especially the Pennsylvania Constitution of 1776) created governments of
limited powers. Also, most state charters contained comprehensive bills of
rights that were designed to protect citizens from arbitrary state governments.
These ideals reflected the democratic beliefs that governments were, at least
potentially, despotic and tyrannical and that the people needed constitutional
protections from possible arbitrary rule. Limit the power given to government, and the potential for repression and despotism is correspondingly
limited. The credo of many revolutionaries was: the less government the
better. At the national level, the Articles of Confederation reflected the prevailing revolutionary mistrust of strong government by creating a weak central government.

In 1763, the thirteen mainland colonies were only a part of a powerful, worldwide British empire. All had been founded as charter colonies
(in which the crown chartered a private company to found, finance, and
govern a new world settlement) or proprietary colonies (in which a single
individual or a small group was granted a royal charter to found, finance,
and govern a colony under a feudal landowning arrangement). Thus it was
private initiative and private financial capital that founded the new world
settlements. When the colonies became well established and prosperous,

the monarchy took over their administration, making them royal colonies (in which the crown and the Privy Council governed the settlement directly). Thus by 1763, of the thirteen colonies, there were two charter colonies (Connecticut and Rhode Island), three proprietary colonies (Delaware, Pennsylvania, and Maryland), and eight (New Hampshire, Massachusetts, New York, New Jersey, Virginia, North Carolina, South Carolina, and Georgia) crown colonies.

Virginia (Jamestown) was not only the first British colony established in the Americas; it was the largest, most populous, and most influential. It was the first founded as a charter colony, first to become a royal colony, first legally to establish African slavery, first to wage war against Native Americans, and first to have a representative assembly. By the time the English arrived in the spring of 1607, the Native American population of the region had been largely decimated by disease and tribal warfare and thus was neither strong nor numerous enough to repel the European invaders. After a perilous beginning of internal bickering, Indian warfare, and underfinancing from London, Virginia (a crown colony after 1624) became by the early eighteenth century the most important of the mainland colonies. Locally governed by an emerging planter elite, Virginia became a prosperous agricultural society. By 1763, there were four distinct regions. In the Tidewater area with its numerous tidal rivers flowing into the Chesapeake Bay, a landed gentry primarily of English heritage ruled politically, socially, and economically. Motivated primarily by economic considerations and sustained by a large bound labor force (indentured servants and black slaves), this talented American aristocracy produced an inordinate number of Founding Fathers. Out of this plantation-owning, slave-owning Virginia gentry came, just to name the more prominent, George Washington, Thomas Jefferson, Patrick Henry, George Mason, James Madison, James Monroe, John Marshall, Edmund Randolph, Peyton Randolph, Richard Henry Lee, and George Wythe. The resultant racial and class dichotomy, however, produced an economic, political, and social stratification that became ever more evident during the revolutionary period.

Just to the west of the Tidewater region was the Piedmont. The third and fourth regions were the Great Valley and the Trans-Appalachian West. Inhabited primarily by subsistence farmers and hunters, these three areas were settled by English, Scot, Scotch-Irish, and German settlers, most of whom came Up the Valley (i.e., in a south-southwestern direction) from

Pennsylvania. The emerging settlements of these three western regions were often in political conflict with the Tidewater over issues of land policy, taxation, legislative representation, and frontier defense.

Most of the New England colonies were founded before 1750. Motivated by religious as well as economic considerations, English immigrants (mostly Puritans) flocked to the rocky, inhospitable shores of Cape Anne, Massachusetts Bay, Narragansett Bay, and Long Island Sound to establish New World settlements where religious freedom and economic opportunities could be enjoyed by most whites. Particularly during the 1630s, many immigrants to New England were escaping discrimination and/or persecution in England and often seriously disagreed with the English government and the Church of England over governmental policy and religion. Thus New Hampshire, Connecticut, New Haven (absorbed into Connecticut in 1662), Plymouth (annexed by Massachusetts in 1691), Rhode Island, and especially Massachusetts were from their founding often at odds with the mother country. That much of the impetus for American independence emanated in New England (especially in the Bay Colony) should not be surprising. These hardworking, God-fearing seventeenth-century New Englanders nurtured a society that gave rise to the independently-minded colonists who overwhelmingly favored independence from Great Britain in the late eighteenth century.

New York and New Jersey were both initially founded by the Dutch in the first quarter of the seventeenth century. Taken over by the English as a result of a decisive victory in the Third Anglo-Dutch War (1672–1674), these two colonies (but especially New York) became the most cosmopolitan of English mainland settlements, attracting immigrants not only from the United Provinces (the Netherlands) and the British Isles but also from many other western European countries. The Dutch influence and culture are still evident especially on Long Island, in New York City, and up the Hudson River. The Dutch patroonships (large landed estates along the Hudson River) produced numerous notable families such as the Livingstons, Morrises, Schuylers, and Van Rensselaers. These families supplied many revolutionary and early national period leaders. Originally founded by Sweden in 1638, Delaware was taken over by the Dutch in 1655. The Dutch possessions in turn were seized by the English in 1674. Throughout the period after the founding of Pennsylvania, Delaware was overshadowed by its powerful neighbor, often sharing a single governor but always maintaining a separate legislative assembly.

Founded by Cecilius Calvert, Maryland was the first proprietary colony. As the second Lord Baltimore, Calvert founded Maryland in the 1630s to be a New World haven for persecuted English Roman Catholics. Although always in the minority, Catholics ruled Maryland until the Protestant revolt that accompanied the English Glorious Revolution (1688–1689). However, in 1715 when the Lord Proprietor converted to Anglicanism, political power was returned to the Calvert family and Maryland reverted to being a proprietary colony until 1776. Economically, Maryland followed the example of Virginia in becoming an agricultural colony with tobacco as the staple crop. This tobacco culture of colonial Maryland gave rise, as it had earlier in Virginia, to a plantation-owning, slave-owning landed gentry, who dominated the colony politically, socially, and economically.

Pennsylvania was founded as a result of a proprietary grant by King Charles II to William Penn in 1681. Patterned after the Maryland grant, the Pennsylvania charter gave the proprietor almost absolute political power, generous boundaries, and the authority to established a New World refuge for the oft-persecuted Quakers. As a convert to the Society of Friends (Quakers), William Penn in turn granted to his early settlers a charter that allowed for religious toleration and a generous land policy by which actual settlers could acquire land (a headright) for a nominal annual quit-rent (rent paid in lieu of feudal service). The well-planned Pennsylvania metropolis of Philadelphia became the port of entry for most eighteenth century white immigrants (especially the Scotch-Irish and German) and the largest city in British America (second only to London in the British empire).

The original 1663 Carolina proprietary grant was given by the newly restored (1660) monarch to eight prominent Englishmen, most of whom had supported the exiled Charles II during the turbulent period of the English Civil War in the 1640s. The northern region grew slowly whereas the southern part with its ideally situated port of Charles Town (Charleston) became prosperous primarily on the labor of Black slaves who cultivated rice and, after the 1740s, indigo along the coastal area. In 1691 the two regions were given separate governors and in 1729 royal charters, which organized the area into North Carolina and South Carolina as royal colonies.

Unique among the mainland colonies, Georgia was originally a trusteeship founded in the 1730s by the British government to serve as a buffer

zone between English South Carolina and Spanish Florida and by its idealistic trustees to be a philanthropic enterprise of small farmers. The early
trustee regulations outlawing slavery and alcoholic spirits and restricting
the size of landholdings gave way by the mid–eighteenth century, and
Georgia became a royal colony in 1752. Georgia was the last mainland
colony founded and the only one whose founding was financed in large
part by the royal treasury. Economically, Georgia, with its major port at
Savannah, followed the lead of neighboring South Carolina in develop-
ing rice as its staple crop.

By 1763, there were thirteen separate English mainland colonies. It
should be noted and indeed emphasized that these thirteen separate colonies, in many cases distinctly different, were founded at different times,
by different people, for often slightly different reasons. Up to the revolutionary period, there was frequently a great deal of jealousy, rivalry, and
open animosity between these separate political entities.

During the Colonial Period (1607–1763) there had been several
major attempts to bring together these disparate colonies into a colonial
union. The first, the New England Confederation, was established in 1643
in response to perceived threats from the Dutch, Native Americans, and
the French to the four New England colonies of Plymouth, Connecticut,
New Haven, and Massachusetts. Rivalry, jealousy, and the arrogance of
Massachusetts led to its demise in 1684. The second attempt at colonial
union was the Dominion of New England (1685–1688). Organized by
King James II to include all of the New England colonies, as well as New
York, New Jersey, and Pennsylvania, this union was established to prepare
the colonies militarily for the anticipated war with France and to ensure
more efficient enforcement of the Trade and Navigation Acts. It collapsed
in 1688 when word was received of the Glorious Revolution in England
that resulted in the overthrow of King James II and the installation of
William III and Mary II as constitutional monarchs. By the early eighteenth
century the mainland colonies had returned to their former status as individual political entities frequently at odds over boundary disputes, defense policies, and religious issues. The last serious attempt at colonial
union came in 1754 at the Albany Congress. The impending war with
France prompted the British government to advise the northern colonies
to conclude a treaty of alliance, or at least an agreement for Indian neutrality, with the powerful Iroquois Confederacy. The threat of war also
prompted Benjamin Franklin, a Pennsylvania delegate, to draw up a plan

that called for a union of all mainland colonies (except Georgia). The British government rejected the plan because it granted too much power to the colonies, and the colonies rejected it for leaving too much authority in the hands of the government in London. However, the quasi-federal governmental system proposed by Franklin in 1754 in which political authority was formally divided between the mother country and the colonies influenced the state and national constitution-makers of the Revolutionary era.

By the beginning in 1754 of the French and Indian War, Great Britain governed a far-flung empire, which included almost thirty colonies in the Americas alone. Therefore the thirteen North American mainland colonies were only a part of the First British Empire, the Empire that collapsed as a result of the War of American Independence.

Britain governed her worldwide empire under the theory of Mercantilism. Mercantilism can be defined as an economic system that has as its primary goal economic self-sufficiency. To implement this highly nationalistic goal, Britain created an integrated commercial empire consisting of the mother country and numerous dependent colonies. The mother country would manufacture the finished goods and the colonies would furnish the raw materials (e.g., lumber, naval stores, and furs) not available in Britain and provide overseas markets. The ideal was that both the mother country and the colonies would benefit from this commercial relationship. However, if one component had to suffer, it would not be Great Britain.

The major facets of theoretical Mercantilism included the accumulation of gold and silver (Spain's acquisition of these precious metals from Central and South America in the sixteenth century had made her the most powerful country in Europe and the envy of, and the model to be emulated by, her western European neighbors), the adoption of policies by which the mother country consistently exported more than she imported (i.e., created a favorable balance of trade), and the maintenance of a large navy to protect the empire and a large merchant marine to facilitate trade. Also necessary would be the establishment in law of labor systems, which would supply cheap labor, particularly in the colonies. Thus the time-honored, exploitative apprentice system of the old country would be transferred in slightly altered form to the colonies as indentured servitude. Probably close to half of the white immigrants who emigrated to what became the United States came as indentured servants. Indentured servitude became the dominant labor system in the seventeenth century. By the eighteenth century, however, African slavery had replaced indentured ser-vitude as the major labor system. These two labor systems, in the case of the British colonies, furnished much of the labor needed to subdue the wilderness of North America and to create viable settlements. Finally, Mercantilism called for the adoption of protectionist policies that, at least in theory, would benefit both mother country and colonies by protecting them from foreign competition.

To implement theoretical Mercantilism it was thought necessary to create a regulated, centrally controlled commercial empire. In the case of England, beginning in the mid-seventeenth century, Parliament passed the first of what would be a series of Trade and Navigation Acts. These mer-cantilist enactments regulated and controlled all trade in the empire and subordinated colonial interests to those of the mother country when they were at variance.

There were in general three groups of Trade and Navigation Acts:

1. Bottoms acts: provided that trade within the empire must be carried on ships where the owner, the captain, and most of the crew were English (this would include the colonists). The first bottoms act was passed by Parliament in 1651 and was aimed at the Dutch, who had heretofore controlled much of the trade within the English Empire. This act precipitated a series of wars (1652–1654, 1664–1667, and 1672–1674) with the United Provinces in which England acquired the Dutch colonies in North America.

2. Enumerated articles acts: provided that most major colonial exports could only be shipped to English ports. By the mid–eighteenth century, these included rice, naval stores, tobacco, and furs. Particularly beneficial to the colonies was the stipula-tion that these articles could not be produced or grown in Britain itself.

3. Prohibition of colonial manufacturing: by 1763, Parliament had passed three specific acts curtailing colonial manufacturing. These included the Wool Act of 1699 (primarily enacted against the Irish), the Hat Act of 1732, which regulated rather minutely the colonial hat industry, and the Iron Act of 1750, which greatly limited the manufacturing of finished iron products in the colo-

nies. These manufacturing prohibitions were designed to protect British manufacturing from colonial competition.

These Trade and Navigation Acts were intended to create and maintain a commercial empire, which by 1763 had become the largest and most powerful in the Western world. In studying the coming of the American Revolution, the question must be asked: to what extent did these acts constitute a cause for colonial discontent and thus become a motive to seek independence from Great Britain? There is little evidence, except in a few isolated cases, of serious colonial opposition to these trade regulations before 1763. For one thing, rarely were these acts strictly enforced. The first British Empire was loosely and inefficiently governed. The vast distances from London militated against effective enforcement of laws in the colonies, laws which were enacted by those who often had very little knowledge of or concern for colonial affairs. Moreover, colonial opposition, often subtly applied, convinced many that vigorous enforcement was not in the best interests of either the mother country or the colonies. Customs collectors were often negligent in the discharge of their duties or were susceptible to colonial bribery. It appeared that when enforcement caused economic hardship among the colonists or was burdensome, these laws were openly and successfully circumvented. Many colonial fortunes (especially, although not exclusively, in New England) were made by smuggling, bribery, or other noncompliance with these commercial enactments. It can, therefore, be stated with almost complete certainty that the British Trade and Navigation Acts were not a cause for the War of American Independence.

The colonial policy followed by Great Britain to govern what would become a worldwide empire was often one of "salutary neglect." Especially during times of relative peace and stability, Britain essentially ignored her colonies if they were prosperous and if they appeared to have acquiesced in the loosely enforced Trade and Navigation Acts. The period between the Treaty of Utrecht (1713) and the outbreak of war with Spain (The war of Jenkins' Ear—1739) is often referred to as the era of "salutary neglect." It was during this long period of relative peace (i.e., absence of a declared war) that many of the mainland colonies became almost autonomous political entities. Most notably, many colonial lower houses of assembly gained political power and even supremacy through the power of the "purse string." Governors of Royal and Proprietary colonies became dependent upon the locally elected assemblies not only for their salaries but also for appropriations generally. To put it more succinctly, this was the period when imperial interests (as represented by the governor and his appointed officials) diverged more sharply from provincial interests (in most colonies represented by a local mercantile or planter elite in the lower houses of the legislatures). The "neglect" that allowed for this virtual autonomy was caused in part by the indifference of the Hanoverian British kings George I (1714–1727) and George II (1727–1760) to colonial affairs.

To govern this empire even inefficiently, Britain established a number of committees, councils, and agencies, headquartered in faraway London. Originally, newly founded colonies were regulated through royal charters that spelled out in general terms how power was to be distributed between the mother country and the new settlements. In addition, the mother country attempted to govern through the formal instructions given to newly appointed governors. Also in the pre–Civil War period (1607–1642), the Privy Council and various Parliamentary committees exercised at least nominal control over the growing empire. However, this experimental governmental arrangement was found to be exceedingly inefficient, especially during the era of the English Civil War and the Protectorate of Oliver Cromwell. With the restoration of the monarchy in 1660, the government in London became more active in colonial affairs. In 1675 Parliament established the Lords of Trade. It was composed primarily of English merchants whose main concern was to facilitate commerce in the empire. With the failure of the Lords of Trade to enforce trade regulations, King William III, in 1696, established the Board of Trade. As an advisory body to the Privy Council, this Board became the primary agency in London for overseeing the empire. It was charged with supervising all trade, all fisheries, and the English poor laws. Most important, it was also to administer plantation or colonial affairs. With a membership ranging from eight to fifteen, this Board was overworked and inefficient. By 1763 there were at least a dozen major agencies that in one way or another were concerned with various aspects of colonial governance. In addition to the Board of Trade, the home government relied upon the Privy Council, the Treasury, the Commissioners of Customs, the Post Office, the Admiralty, the Navy Board, the War Office, the Bishop of London, and the Secretary of State for the Southern Department to regulate and govern this vast empire. This plethora of agencies resulted in a great deal of confusion, duplication of effort, and inefficiency. Thus at the beginning of the Revolutionary era, most mainland colonies had achieved relative autonomy in local and provincial matters. With the ancient enemies (France and Spain) finally and decisively defeated in the Seven Years' War (1756–1763), many colonists began to question the need or desirability of a close imperial connection with Great Britain. To be sure, nobody espoused independence from the mother country at this early date. Rather what most colonists wanted was a continuation of the prewar policies of "salutary neglect," of relative nonenforcement of trade and navigation acts, of allowing local colonial control in most provincial matters, and of military intervention only during times of war and extreme social and economic unrest.

One of the most important themes of the colonial period was the longtime imperial rivalry between Britain and France. From the founding of their first North American colonies, England (Virginia 1607) and France (Quebec 1608) were in almost continual conflict. In the four intercolonial declared wars fought between 1689 and 1763, Britain came to the aid of her beleaguered North American colonies with financial aid and direct military assistance. These four declared wars were interspersed with almost constant skirmishing between the French and their Native American allies in what became Canada, and the British and their colonists along the Atlanta seaboard to the south. These colonial conflicts are sometimes referred to as the "Second Hundred Years' War." Confusingly, each of these confrontations has two names. Thus there was King William's War (in Europe, the War of the League of Augsburg—1689–1697), Queen Anne's War (in Europe, the War of the Spanish Succession—1702–1714), King George's War (in Europe, the War of the Austrian Succession—1740–1748), and the French and Indian War—1754–1763 (in Europe, the Seven Years' War—1756–1763). This series of worldwide conflicts between England and France was continued after 1763 with the War of American Independence (after 1778) and the wars of the French Revolution and of Napoleon Bonaparte. The first three colonial contests ended indecisively with neither side gaining the sought-after goal—mastery of North America.

It was, however, during the fourth colonial war (French and Indian War) that Great Britain, with significant help from her mainland colonists, decisively defeated her Bourbon enemies and thus gained control of most of North America. With the signing of the Treaty of Paris (1763), the French menace to the British seaboard colonies was finally removed. The colonists now wanted a return to the peacetime status of "salutary neglect," or at least of former inefficient imperial government. As shall be seen, it was not to be!

In evaluating Great Britain's Old Colonial System (i.e., the empire before 1763), there were clearly beneficial as well as detrimental aspects to colonial membership. On the positive side, the colonists, at least most white settlers, had inherited British law and governmental structures and practices. Most colonists enjoyed more freedom and liberty than did their European counterparts. There were in addition the economic benefits of guaranteed markets for most staple crops, bounties on such exports as indigo, banking and insurance services, and lax enforcement of navigation laws. Of great benefit to the colonies was the protection of the British navy against incursions of the French, Spanish, Dutch, and pirates. Moreover, during wartime Britain furnished much-needed financial aid and troops.

On the negative side, membership in the empire resulted in the colonies becoming ever more economically dependent on the mother country. The imbalance in trade (the colonies imported more than they exported), the manufacturing restrictions, the indirect export and import duties, the quit-rents (rent paid in lieu of services) especially in the proprietary colonies, and land policies that generally favored British investors at the expense of the colonists led to an economic exploitation that, although not clearly recognized or resented by most colonists, hindered colonial development.

The year 1763 represented a watershed in British colonial administration. Through emigration, conquest, and diplomacy, Great Britain had established a worldwide empire, which was the envy of the other western European powers. However, colonial success also prompted a desire for revenge on the part of recently defeated and humiliated European rivals. The Bourbon powers of France and Spain especially were eager to regain lost territories and prestige. With victory over her ancient foes, Great Britain, however, was confronted with a host of new problems, which called for new policies and a closer, more effective and efficient regulation of colonial economic life, particularly colonial trade. Under the terms of the Treaty of Paris (1763), Great Britain added Canada, Cape Breton Island, the vast territory between the Allegheny Mountains and the Mississippi River, and East and West Florida to an already sizeable worldwide domain.

The major problem faced by a war-weary Britain was indebtedness. With a debt of some 140 million pounds sterling, the British people were heavily taxed just to service this staggering amount. British ministries looked to share the burden of taxation with the heretofore undertaxed (certainly untaxed to raise revenue) colonists. Moreover, there was the problem of how to govern the newly acquired lands of French Canada and Spanish Florida. The adoption of new Indian policies was particularly urgent, especially after Pontiac's Rebellion erupted in 1763, rolling back white settlement to the east of the Allegheny Mountains. Only Fort Detroit and Fort Pitt west of the mountains were able to hold out against determined Indian sieges. In attempting to solve these vexing problems, British ministries in the 1760s and early 1770s adopted new policies that signaled a significant shift in colonial administration from that of "salutary neglect" to one of tighter, more efficient control.

During the American Revolution, American nationhood was achieved. The colonists created a viable republic that was conceived in a period of political unrest and even violence. (The War of American Independence was after all a violent, bloody affair.) This republic, so conceived, was dedicated to the proposition of freedom, liberty, and equality for all (originally at least all whites). The American Revolution secured, in theory and usually in practice, these rights not only for the colonists but also for future generations.

Note

1. J. Franklin Jameson, *The American Revolution Considered as a Social Movement.* Princeton: Princeton University Press, 1926, 9.

CHAPTER 2

THE ROAD TO REVOLUTION

The Road to Revolution (1763–1775) was a rocky, frequently muddy or dusty, poorly marked roadway full of potholes, hairpin turns, and obstructions that made for an eventful journey from triumph (Treaty of Paris, 1763) to what many thought by 1775 was the inevitable clash of arms (Battle of Lexington and Concord).

In 1763, the British colonists in North America proudly rejoiced in the decisive victory over the French and their Spanish and Indian allies. As an integral part of the victorious British Empire, they looked forward to a period of prosperity and of expansion into lands formerly claimed by the French and Spanish. These goals could, it was hoped, be realized under a complacent British government that would return to the prewar policies of allowing the colonies almost complete local political autonomy with a minimum of regulation over colonial commerce and defense. With the large influx of non-British immigrants and the significant increase in the number of settlers born in America, the colonists began to think of themselves as being different from the people of Great Britain. They were, in fact, becoming Americans.

However, 1763 ushered in a period, in both Britain and the colonies, of political unrest and instability rather than the hoped-for one of peace, stability, and mutual prosperity. Britain, for her part, was faced with the problems of heavy indebtedness; the need to formulate new colonial policies for recently acquired Canada and Florida; the immediate necessity, given Pontiac's War that broke out on the colonial frontier in 1763, to adopt new policies regarding relations with Native Americans; and finally, the need to redefine imperial-colonial relations.

What Britain needed was statesmanship to cope successfully with its manifold problems. What it got instead, however, was political mediocrity and instability. When George III became king in 1760 upon the death of his grandfather, George II, he was a politically inexperienced twenty-two-year-old. Although he readily accepted the role of a constitutional monarch, he took time learning to be a capable king. Eventually, he did become an effective, conscientious ruler. By 1770 he was able to assemble a ministry that he could control and manipulate. However, during the 1760s when statesmanship was needed, Britain was saddled with an inexperienced king and a series of weak ministries. In the absence of clearly defined political parties, there emerged numerous political factions each headed by a leader or small group concerned primarily with gaining political power, land, patronage, and titles. This political instability in Britain only exacerbated the growing crisis in colonial relations.

In addition to political incompetence and inexperience, the British government attempted to come to grips with the manifold problems caused by the long, weary, expensive Seven Years' War (1756–1763). With each attempt to solve a problem with legislation or a new policy, Britain alienated yet another segment of colonial society. For example, the outbreak of Pontiac's War along the colonial western frontier prompted the young king to issue the Royal Proclamation of 1763. This far-reaching proclamation established the Appalachian Mountains as the dividing line between colonists and Native Americans. From the British point of view, this policy was at least a temporary solution to end the bloody conflict. In addition, the proclamation created three new provinces: Quebec, East Florida, and West Florida. British laws and British institutions were given to the former French colony of Quebec. Two colonial groups opposed the proclamation. Frontier settlers largely ignored the provision of no settlement west of the mountains. Because the frontiersmen were underrepresented in the colonial assemblies and therefore had little political power, their opposition was of little consequence. However, the opposition of land speculators meant that many prominent, politically powerful colonists were angered by the provision that called into question or even annulled existing western land titles. Among those speculators who opposed this proclamation were George Washington, Benjamin Franklin, and the Virginia Lees. Starting in 1763 with the Royal Proclamation, every time Britain attempted to solve a problem with a new policy or new law, there was increased colonial opposition.

Another example of British actions invoking colonial opposition was the Parson's Cause of late 1763. It involved the disallowance by the Privy Council (the king in council) of a Virginia law that regulated the salaries of Anglican ministers. A 1662 Virginia law had stipulated that the salaries be paid in tobacco. Because of the failure of the tobacco crop (because of a severe drought), the Virginia Assembly in 1755 (reenacted in 1758) commuted the salary into currency at the rate of second per pound. Upon petition of the Anglican clergy in Virginia, the Privy Council in Britain disallowed this act. The clergy then sued for back pay, claiming that they had been paid (actually underpaid) under the provisions of an act that was now disallowed. This dispute resulted in the celebrated case before the Hanover County court during which the young Patrick Henry first came to public notice when he held that the king had violated the contract between ruler and subjects, thereby waiving "all rights to his subjects' obedience." This famous case demonstrated growing colonial opposition to the established Anglican Church (considered to be an arm of the British government) and to unbridled monarchical authority.

The December 1763 frontier uprising in Pennsylvania known as the Paxton Boys' Revolt was not only another illustration of colonial hostility to unrestrained authority but also an indication of the kind of political unrest that often precedes armed revolt and revolution. A frontier mob from Paxton attacked a group of peaceful Conestoga Indians and then marched east towards Philadelphia to demand frontier protection. At the last minute Benjamin Franklin was able to deter the angry rabble from entering the city by extending the promise, later fulfilled, of greater frontier representation in the Assembly. This confrontation, although more indicative of east-west sectionalism within the colonies than a dispute over British policy, did show discontent on the part of many colonists towards autocratic political authority. More ominously, it showed that violence or the threat of violence could be politically effective.

With the coming of peace, a new ministry in London embarked upon a program that further angered many colonists. Faced with a debt of some 140 million pounds sterling, Chancellor of the Exchequer, George Grenville in 1764 inaugurated the Grenville Program with the introduction of the American Revenue Act (commonly known as the Sugar Act). This was the first act passed by Parliament for the specific purpose of raising revenue in the colonies. Earlier laws that might have produced revenue were enacted only to regulate trade. This act was essentially an amendment to the Molasses Act of 1733, which had taxed foreign molasses coming into the colonies. Although the Sugar Act reduced the tax rate on molasses, it added several new taxes on foreign refined sugar, and on non-British textiles, coffee, and Spanish wines. Colonial merchants opposed this external tax, designed to raise approximately 45,000 pounds sterling annually. Because merchants, especially in the middle colonies and New England, were an influential, but conservative, group in colonial society, their opposition to the new British policies of raising revenue in the colonies and of tightening the enforcement of existing trade and navigation laws was particularly noteworthy. It showed that the initial anti-British movement in the colonies was anything but revolutionary. Colonial merchants only wanted a return to the policies of "salutary neglect" that had characterized British rule before the outbreak of the French and Indian War in 1754. The Grenville program also included the establishment of a vice-admiralty court in Halifax, Nova Scotia, with jurisdiction over most of North America. Colonists opposed vice-admiralty courts because they were in essence military tribunals that denied the long-established British right of a trial by a jury of peers to the accused.

As part of his overall program to strengthen Britain's control over its far-flung empire, Grenville pushed for passage of the Currency Act of 1764. This parliamentary act extended the provisions of a 1751 law that had prohibited the issuance of legal-tender paper money in New England. The new act extended this prohibition to all of the mainland colonies. Aimed primarily at Virginia, this law angered many influential Tidewater planters who were perennially in debt to British merchants and who therefore favored inflationary laws that would lessen their actual indebtedness. As a deflationary measure, this act seemed to favor British creditors at the expense of colonial debtors and therefore caused great colonial resentment.

Led by Massachusetts, Americans began actively to oppose the Sugar Act and Currency Act. At a Boston town meeting, held in May 1764, many criticized what they considered to be taxation without representation and urged united colonial action to protest these infringements on what many Americans considered their traditional rights as British subjects. Soon thereafter the Massachusetts House of Representatives established a Committee of Correspondence to begin a dialogue with the other mainland colonies. In Boston, merchants initiated the first nonimportation agreements; that is, they agreed to boycott certain English luxury imports until such time as the detested Parliamentary Acts were repealed. Although initially ineffectual, nonconsumption, nonimportation, and nonexportation agreements would become, in time, effective weapons against alleged British tyranny.

It was, however, the passage of the Stamp Act that brought about the first major crisis in Anglo-American relations. As the first direct (internal) tax levied on the colonists, this act was designed to raise approximately 60,000 pounds sterling a year. This figure, along with the 45,000 pounds sterling to be garnered from the Sugar Act, would be approximately a third of the 300,000 pounds sterling Britain felt was needed to maintain an appropriate civil and military presence in America. The act levied a tax on business papers, legal documents, newspapers, almanacs, pamphlets, playing cards, and dice. It also included several other repugnant provisions. Payment of the tax had to be in scarce British pound sterling, violators were to be tried in vice-admiralty courts (courts without juries), and authors of pamphlets and broadsides criticizing British actions had to sign their publications, thus opening up the possibility of official retribution and legal action. This act directly affected lawyers, printers, clergymen, and merchants. In fact, this law affected a larger segment of the population than any previous Parliamentary enactment. Opposition to the Stamp Act was so widespread that many colonists, who after the commencement of armed conflict in April of 1775 would remain loyal to Great Britain, openly opposed the imposition of the hated stamp duties.

Universal resistance to the Stamp Act precipitated a crisis, which only abated when Britain revoked the onerous act in March 1766. Passed in March 1765 after little debate, the act was to become effective November 1, 1765. The effective date came and went with only a few stamps ever being sold. Although stamp distributors were appointed for most colonies, by November all had been persuaded to resign their commissions, frequently under conditions of extreme intimidation by local Sons of Liberty. Resistance to the Stamp Act took many forms. Legal opposition included piously worded petitions from colonial legislatures, with Virginia taking the lead with Patrick Henry's famous resolutions that asserted the rights of Virginians (and hence all Americans) to the ancient, traditional rights that belonged to all British subjects. Specifically, they proclaimed that only Americans could tax Americans. Because the colonists were not represented in either house of Parliament, Americans claimed that Parliamentary taxation was a violation of the unwritten British constitution.

Among the many pamphlets and broadsides published in opposition to the Stamp Act was the cogently written *The Considerations on the Propriety of Imposing Taxes in the British Colonies, for the Purpose of Raising a Revenue, by Act of Parliament* (1765). Written by the prominent Maryland lawyer Daniel Dulany the Younger, this widely distributed tract expressed what was probably the prevailing colonial view of the time that Parliament could regulate colonial trade with *external* taxes even if they incidentally produced revenue, but denied to that body the right to impose *internal* taxes of any kind. Dulany also advanced the idea that the colonists were not virtually represented in Parliament (the British contended that the colonists were virtually represented). Moreover, he maintained that they could not be actually represented in a legislative body thousands of miles from their shores. Virginian Richard Bland in his *The Colonel Dismounted: or the Rector Vindicated* (1764) had made the same argument. He maintained that the colonists' most cherished birthright as Britons was to be governed by laws enacted by legislatures in which they were actually represented.

Further opposition to the Stamp Act came in June of 1765 when the Massachusetts Assembly proposed the calling of what became the Stamp Act Congress. The twenty-seven delegates from nine of the thirteen colonies (New Hampshire declined the invitation; Virginia, North Carolina, and Georgia were prevented from sending delegations because their royal governors refused to convene the colonial legislatures to elect delegates) drew up the moderate "Declaration of Rights and Grievances." Written by Pennsylvania delegate John Dickinson, this declaration represented the views of the conservative majority who, while determined not to infringe upon the traditional powers of Parliament or of the Crown, nevertheless claimed that the colonists were entitled to all the rights enjoyed by British subjects in the mother country. The minority faction favored petitioning only the crown and ignoring Parliament, alleging that Americans did not hold their rights from that body. In petitions sent to the king, the House of Commons, and the House of Lords, the delegates urged repeal of the currency act and the revenue acts—particularly the Stamp Act with its provisions for imposing an internal tax and for expanding the jurisdiction of vice-admiralty courts. Declaring their loyalty to the crown and subordination to Parliament, the petitioners stated in simple terms the prevailing American view in 1765: they claimed all the rights of British subjects in Great Britain. They also denied by implication the British claim that the colonists were virtually represented in Parliament. Instead they advanced the doctrine of actual representation in which only Americans directly elected by Americans could impose taxes upon Americans.

The Stamp Act Congress was significant for at least two reasons. First, it was the first important step towards colonial union. Previously, the colonies more often than not argued over boundaries, frontier defense, and commerce. That nine colonies could act in unison in the face of alleged British oppression was a surprise to many in the colonies, including many colonists and many in London. Second, the delegates met for the first time men with whom they later carried out a revolution and established the new American republic. Prominent among the delegates were James Otis, Jr. of Massachusetts, William Samuel Johnson of Connecticut, Robert R. Livingston of New York, John Dickinson of Pennsylvania, Thomas McKean of Delaware, and Christopher Gadsden and John Rutledge of South Carolina. These men, in shedding their localism, were becoming Americans rather than Massachusetts men or South Carolinians. This fostering of American nationalism was a necessary first step leading to independence.

Particularly in Boston but also in New York City and other ports, artisans, small merchants, and laborers resorted to violence to protest the stamp levies. Various groups styling themselves The Sons of Liberty (the name was taken from a speech in Parliament by Isaac Barre in which he used the term to identify those colonists who openly opposed the Stamp Act) sprang up in New York City, in several New England towns, and in Charleston, South Carolina. Sometimes these rowdy bands were called committees of correspondence, committees of safety, or Whigs. Whatever their designation, these groups, starting in 1765, often used physical intimidation to achieve their increasingly radical goals. Although frequently led, at least originally, by prominent merchants and political agitators (e.g., John Hancock and Samuel Adams in Boston, John Lamb and Alexander McDougall in New York City, and Christopher Gadsden in Charleston), these secret societies were responsible for much of the violence and property damage against British officials following passage of the Stamp Act. For example, The Sons of Liberty were undoubtedly culpable for the late August 1765 sacking of Lieutenant Governor Thomas Hutchinson's Boston mansion, for forcing most of the stamp distributors to resign their commissions, and for enforcing the nonimportation agreements. In the Stamp Act riots, the laboring classes joined the merchants and gentry in the anti-British movement. The increased involvement of colonial craftsmen and laborers in the anti-British movement suggests that the coming American Revolution, although initially only a protest movement against British policies, was becoming, at least in small part, a class conflict and was therefore revolutionary.

Other forms of opposition to the Stamp Act included new, more stringent nonconsumption, nonimportation agreements. Often enforced by the Sons of Liberty, these trade embargoes led to a drastic reduction in British exports to America. As a result of these economic hardships, London merchants and over twenty-five British towns petitioned Parliament to repeal the unpopular Stamp Act.

When the Grenville ministry fell because of a regency bill dispute having nothing to do with colonial affairs, the incoming government of the Marquis of Rockingham pushed for repeal. After extensive Parliamentary debate during which the colonial agents resident in London were called to testify before the House of Commons sitting as a committee of the whole, the Commons voted for repeal (March 4th), followed by the House of Lords (March 17th). As the best-known American agent, Benjamin Franklin gave testimony before the Commons that was perhaps most telling when he claimed that the use of British troops to enforce collection of the stamp duties could precipitate rebellion. Ominously, on the same day the repeal bill received the royal assent (March 18th), Parliament passed the largely ignored Declaratory Act, which asserted that Parliament retained the right to pass laws for the colonists "in all cases whatsoever." Thus while the crisis was temporarily averted with the repeal, the constitutional issue of who had the right to tax the colonists remained unresolved. In the Declaratory Act, Great Britain steadfastly maintained that the mother country had the right to govern (and this would most certainly include the right to tax) the colonies. Just as adamantly, the colonists asserted that only Americans could tax Americans. Americans generally considered the repeal of the Stamp Act a victory for the colonists and ignored the ominous implications of the Declaratory Act.

With the repeal of the Stamp Act, the new British ministry of William Pitt (with the Chancellor of the Exchequer Charles Townshend as the active leader because of Pitt's real and imagined illnesses) still faced the problem of heavy indebtedness. The mercurial Townshend took note of the distinction made by some Americans between external (indirect) taxes, which they considered burdensome but constitutional, and internal (direct) levies (which the Stamp Act duties were), viewed as unconstitutional.

He proposed that Parliament enact, as it did, the Townshend Duties, which levied an import tax on glass, paint, paper, lead, and tea. The Townshend Acts also reaffirmed the right of justices to issue writs of assistance (general search warrants), establish new vice-admiralty courts, and create an American Board of Customs. The duties were designed to raise 40,000 pounds sterling annually; the money raised was specifically designated to defray the costs of a British military presence and British civil government in the colonies. These acts were specifically designed to free British colonial governments from financial dependence on colonial assemblies and to bring about more efficient enforcement of British colonial regulatory and taxing policies. Colonial opposition to the Townshend Duties was widespread and eventually successful in bringing about repeal in 1770 of all of the duties except those on tea. Several colonial towns (including initially Providence and Newport, Rhode Island, New York City, and later Boston) adopted new nonimportation agreements primarily on luxury goods and drew up plans to encourage domestic industries.

The most widely read and therefore the most influential pamphlets written in opposition to the Townshend Duties were John Dickinson's *Letters from a Farmer in Pennsylvania to the Inhabitants of the British Colonies.* In these twelve finely crafted essays, Dickinson seemed to capture and reflect the mood of most colonists. Conceding Parliament's right to regulate trade, the author denied its right to tax Americans for revenue. These letters gained Dickinson a deserved reputation as a political essayist of great force and persuasion, and an undeserved one as a radical leader. If read carefully, these letters certainly did not even hint of political separation from Great Britain or even of drastic modification of the imperial system. Rather, they urged reform within the existing British colonial system and by implication a return to the status quo antebellum in imperial relations. At the time of their publication (November 1767–January 1768), Dickinson's *Letters* represented the conservative views of most colonists regarding imperial relations.

As a colony, Massachusetts took the lead in opposing the Townshend Acts. In February 1768, the Bay Colony's House of Representatives approved Samuel Adams' draft of a Circular Letter to be sent to the other twelve mainland colonial assemblies in which the Townshend Acts were denounced as being unconstitutional because the colonists claimed Parliament did not have the authority to pass American revenue acts. Furthermore, the Circular Letter attacked the crown for attempting to make British colonial officials independent of any control by the colonial assemblies. The Letter also requested proposals from sister colonies for united colonial action in the face of alleged British tyranny. Massachusetts Governor Francis Bernard branded the Letter seditious, dissolved the General Court, and ordered the legislature to rescind it. The House of Representatives refused by a vote of 92 to 17 to rescind the Circular Letter or to expunge the resolution of approval from its journal.

By the summer of 1768 Massachusetts was clearly on a collision course with the mother country. Open defiance, in Boston in particular, of imperial regulations and of the governor's orders, and the intimidation, by the increasingly unruly Sons of Liberty, of customs collectors when they attempted to discharge their duties prompted the customs commissioners to request that Britain send troops to Boston to protect them. The June 10th seizure of John Hancock's sloop *Liberty* by customs officials for landing Madeira wine without the payment of appropriate taxes only incited further excitement and violence. An angry mob assaulted the customs commissioners involved in the seizure. The now thoroughly frightened officials fled to Castle William in Boston harbor. In response to the harried request by the customs commissioners for protection, Britain sent two infantry regiments to Boston. Their arrival in early October of 1768 marked a turning point in imperial relations. Never before in times of peace had Great Britain stationed troops in any of the coastal towns. The few British soldiers who were stationed in the colonies were posted at frontier forts to protect the westward-moving colonists from the frequent forays of Native Americans and from the threat of incursions by the Spanish along the southern frontier and by the French in the Ohio River valley and along the ill-defined boundary between French Canada and the New England colonies and New York. Now Boston was to be a garrison town occupied by soldiers who were there, seemingly, to enforce unpopular (and, to many, unconstitutional) trade regulations and to stifle the growing anti-British protest movement. The presence of "lobster-backs" (so called because of the bright red wool uniforms worn by most British troops) in Boston during a time of relative peace, more than any other single act, convinced many Bostonians that the Grenville/Townshend program was designed solely to deprive them of their hard-earned and long enjoyed rights as British subjects.

In May 1769 Virginia joined Massachusetts in open defiance of British policies. In the House of Burgesses George Washington introduced a series of resolutions, actually written by George Mason, that affirmed that only Virginians could tax Virginians, and that declared by implication that the Parliamentary proposal that rebellious colonists should be sent to Britain for trial was unconstitutional. When Royal Governor Norborne Berkeley, the Baron de Botetourt (1718–1770), dissolved the assembly because of this unseemly, disloyal behavior, the Burgesses reassembled informally the next day in Williamsburg's Raleigh Tavern and adopted the Virginia Association. This Association was a nonimportation agreement that prohibited the importation of most British goods. This nonimportation movement soon spread to the other mainland colonies. The result was a drastic reduction in colonial imports from Britain. As with the embargo instituted in the aftermath of the Stamp Act of 1765, these trade restrictions damaged British merchants who petitioned the ministry for the repeal or at the least modification of the Townshend Duties. With Massachusetts and Virginia taking the lead, the thirteen colonies were slowly coming together in their opposition to British attempts to tax and to affirm and tighten control over her increasingly obstreperous colonies.

By 1770 the pace along the Road to Revolution had quickened. Some of the obstructions that had previously slowed progress had been either removed or surmounted. Some few colonists (this number would grow every year) were beginning to see that the journey's end held the potential for armed conflict and even revolution.

The year 1770 opened with the newly appointed ministry of Lord Frederick North (1732–1792) urging repeal of all of the Townshend Duties except those on tea and promising to levy no new taxes on the colonists. North believed that retaining the tax on tea would reaffirm Parliament's right to tax the colonists, but would not be so burdensome as to provoke violent or even vehement colonial opposition. The partial repeal of the Townshend Duties did in fact result in the almost total collapse of the nonimportation movement. For the second time, colonial resistance had resulted in at least partial repeal of unwanted taxes. Colonial nonimportation agreements had helped earlier to bring about the repeal of the universally hated Stamp Act. In 1769 and 1770 the nonimportation provisions by the various Associations prompted British merchants to petition successfully for partial repeal of the Townshend Duties. The colonists thought that they had learned that economic boycotts would force Great Britain to back down in her attempts to tighten control over the colonies and to tax them for the purpose of raising revenue.

The years 1770–1773 were a period of relative tranquility in Anglo-American relations. Growing prosperity caused in part by a resumption of trade certainly helped to temper the antagonisms of the late 1760s, as did the repeal of the most onerous of the Townshend Duties. There were, however, two major as well as numerous minor instances of defiance and violence that marred this otherwise peaceful interlude.

The first involved a clash between British soldiers and citizens (primarily young unemployed or underemployed laborers and artisans) of Boston. Violence was perhaps inevitable given that most Bostonians objected strenuously to the stationing of two British infantry regiments in their midst. There were numerous, indeed almost daily, minor clashes between individual soldiers and young town laborers. The first major confrontation occurred in early March of 1770 when a British trooper sought part-time employment as a laborer at Grey's ropewalk. A fight ensued when the soldier was told in patronizing terms that the only job suitable for him was that of cleaning out the privy. By the evening of March 5th, quarrelsome bands of civilians and soldiers roamed the streets of Boston seemingly yearning for a fight. This ensued when an angry mob assaulted a lone sentry in King Street with snowballs and verbal abuse. The frightened soldier called for help, whereupon Captain Thomas Preston came to his aid with eight troopers. The scene was set for bloodshed. Nine British soldiers confronting a boisterous, unruly mob perhaps made unavoidable the ensuing clash of arms. The provoked, thoroughly frightened and intimidated soldiers fired shots; three rioters were killed outright and two were mortally wounded. Samuel Adams and other Boston radicals quickly exaggerated the extent and severity of this unfortunate confrontation into the famous, but misnamed "Boston Massacre." The radicals printed and distributed numerous broadsides, which depicted this incident as yet another example of the unjust and bloody exercise of British military power over a peaceful civilian population. However, if examined objectively, both sides were to blame for this regrettable, but perhaps inevitable bloody encounter.

For their part, the British felt justified in stationing troops in Boston to maintain law and order in the face of growing mob rule. Furthermore, the soldiers were provoked on March 5th by an angry, rowdy, ungovernable crowd. The radicals, on the other hand, questioned the need for these soldiers and claimed that they had been sent solely to intimidate and stifle what they considered to be appropriate and constitutional opposition to

British policies. The British used the incident to prove colonial intransigence, while the radicals depicted it as another illustration of blatant, unjust British despotism.

The anti-British protest movement in the 1760s and early 1770s was both revolutionary and conservative. It was conservative in that Lt. Governor Hutchinson agreed, immediately after the "Massacre," to the radical demand to remove the British troops from the city to Castle William in Boston harbor. Also it could be considered conservative in that a full-blown riot was averted when the nine British soldiers involved in the Boston Massacre were indicted for murder and actually stood trial in a civilian colonial court. Defended by prominent Boston attorneys John Adams, Robert Auchmuty, and Josiah Quincy, Jr., the soldiers were given as fair a trial as was possible under the volatile and unsettled conditions of mid-1765. The lengthy fall trials (there were actually two trials: one for the eight troopers and one for Captain Preston) resulted in two of the soldiers being found guilty of manslaughter, but significantly not of murder. They both pleaded benefit of clergy and were branded on the hand and set free. The other seven, including Captain Thomas Preston, were judged not guilty and released.

This resort to the civilian courts to resolve the explosive issues inherent in the British military occupation of Boston is a further indication that at this juncture the colonial protest movement was relatively conservative and that the goal of most colonists was a redress of grievances within the existing imperial structure, and not independence. The revolutionary component of the colonial protest movement involved the destruction of property, the intimidation of British officials, and the violence and coercion involved in the enforcement of the various nonconsumption, nonimportation, and nonexportation agreements.

The "Boston Massacre" was a turning point on the Road to Revolution. In many ways, it galvanized colonial opposition to what were perceived to be harsh (even bloody), and unconstitutional British policies. The master propagandist Samuel Adams and other prominent Boston radicals quickly seized upon the "Massacre" as an example of British brutality that would justify their working for colonial autonomy within the Empire, or even separation or independence. Many colonists were beginning to question the benevolence of a monarch who would sanction the stationing of troops in colonial towns and the need for a Parliament that continued to pass laws depriving them of long-cherished rights as British subjects.

The second occurrence, which marred the otherwise peaceful 1770–1773 interlude, was the burning of the British revenue cutter *Gaspee* near Providence, Rhode Island. On June 9, 1772, the armed schooner ran aground while chasing a ship suspected of smuggling. After nightfall, some sixty men, organized by prominent merchant John Brown, attacked the ship. In the ensuing fracas, the vessel's captain was wounded and the crew set ashore. The attackers then set fire to the ship, burning it to the waterline. Because of the overwhelming hostility of Rhode Islanders who were unwilling to testify before the Commissioners of Inquiry appointed to discover and punish the culprits, the attackers went undiscovered and therefore unpunished.

During 1772 there was yet another incident that quickened the gait along what was becoming ever more evident as the roadway to armed conflict and independence. Benjamin Franklin (leading colonial agent in London) obtained, under mysterious circumstances, original copies of six letters written in the period 1767–1769 by Thomas Hutchinson (then Chief Justice) and four by Andrew Oliver (provincial secretary) in which the two Massachusetts officials urged the ministry in London to adopt a tougher policy for the governance of her colonies, especially Massachusetts. Specifically, Hutchinson and Oliver insinuated that the tougher policy they both advocated might well involve a curtailment of colonial liberties and rights. After a careful reading of these letters, Franklin concluded that they were partially responsible for the ministry and Parliament's objectionable acts because these actions by the British government were based on the erroneous and prejudicial advice given by these two crown-appointed Massachusetts officials. Franklin sent the purloined letters to the Speaker of the Massachusetts House of Representatives, Thomas Cushing, with the admonition that they be read only by certain select colonial leaders and that they not be published or made public. Somehow Samuel Adams got hold of the letters, had them read before a secret session of the House of Representatives, and thereafter had them copied and published. In June 1773 the Massachusetts House petitioned the king to remove Hutchinson and Oliver from office. When this petition and news of the publication of the letters reached London, it precipitated a scandal that involved a relatively harmless duel between the brother of the original recipient and a prominent politician accused of stealing the letters. However, the threat of a second duel prompted Benjamin Franklin to step forward and admit publicly that he alone was responsible for their being sent to Boston.

The British government quickly disciplined Franklin. As the London agent of the Massachusetts House of Representatives, Franklin had, in early January 1774, presented the petition demanding the removal of Hutchinson and Oliver. The Privy Council began considering the petition of removal on January 29, by which time news of the December 16, 1773, Boston Tea Party had reached London. The Privy Council overwhelmingly rejected the petition and then the Solicitor General Alexander Wedderburn verbally attacked Franklin as a thief (he had apparently stolen the letters) and a man without honor (gentlemen do not have published or even read other gentlemen's letters).

Franklin was summarily dismissed as Deputy Postmaster General for America, a sinecure he had held since 1753. Throughout the Solicitor General's public diatribe against him, Franklin refused to respond, but remained somber and calm. It is true that his disenchantment with British rule had begun during the Stamp Act crisis of 1765, but this public humiliation before the Privy Council might well have been the deciding issue in transforming Franklin from a staunch supporter of the British empire to the revolutionary that he became by late 1775.

The peaceful interlude between 1770 and 1773 came to an abrupt halt in May 1773 when Parliament passed the Tea Act. Enacted to save the mismanaged venerable East India Company from bankruptcy, this act authorized the company to sell some seventeen million pounds of tea stored in British warehouses directly to the colonists without the payment of heavy taxes previously collected. Colonial merchants viewed the act as a blatant attempt to bypass them and to establish a trade monopoly in tea for the East India Company. A monopoly initially in the tea trade could, many colonists believed, lead to other monopolies equally detrimental to colonial interests.

The shipment of tea to America prompted a series of Tea Parties. Colonial merchants now often allied with local Sons of Liberty forced most of the tea consignees to resign. However, in at least four ports, tea shipments were either destroyed or confiscated. In Charleston, South Carolina, the tea consignment was stored in government warehouses for nonpayment of duties and remained there until July 1776, when it was sold by the revolutionary provincial government. In New York City, the Sons of Liberty were responsible for the throwing of at least one tea shipment into the harbor. In the case of Annapolis, Maryland, local rowdies were able to convince the owner of the tea ship *Peggy Stewart* to burn his own ship.

However, the Boston Tea Party, the most celebrated of the tea parties, precipitated a series of events that greatly quickened the pace along the Road to Revolution. The Boston radicals were able to prevent the unloading of the three tea ships, but could not convince Governor Thomas Hutchinson to issue permits allowing the vessels to leave. Radicals, led by Samuel Adams, were determined to prevent the unloading of the ships. They were prompted to action because the twenty-day waiting period before the ships could be legally confiscated for nonpayment of the import taxes was due to expire on December 17th. In the early evening of December 16th, Bostonians, some 8,000 of whom were gathered near the Old South Church, learned of the governor's final refusal to issue departure permits. Thereafter a group of thinly disguised "Mohawk Indians," upon a signal from Samuel Adams, proceeded to Griffin's Wharf, boarded the tea ships, and dumped 342 chests of tea into the harbor. Once again, it was hoped that concerted opposition to British policies would result in repeal or significant modification of an unpopular act. Twice before, united opposition had accomplished the repeal of unpopular acts: the first being the repeal of the Stamp Act in 1766 and the second the repeal of most of the Townshend Duties in 1770. What would be the consequences of this latest example of colonial intransigence?

Word of the Boston Tea Party reached London in late January 1774. Both the king and the North ministry now viewed the situation as a constitutional issue. They contended that Parliament was, and should be, the supreme authority in the empire and that this authority included the right to legislate in all cases whatsoever. Thus this authority included the right to regulate trade and levy taxes (both external and internal). While many colonists were slowly moving toward the idea that the colonies should be autonomous, but autonomous within the framework of the British empire, the monarch and the ministry in London had other ideas. Tired of repeatedly backing down in the face of concerted, increasingly destructive and even violent colonial opposition, Lord North introduced in Parliament a series of five measures known collectively as the Coercive Acts (1774). Designed to convince the colonists (especially in Massachusetts) of their proper subservient position within the empire and to punish the city of Boston for its riotous behavior, these five acts (dubbed the "intolerable acts" by the colonists) were overwhelmingly passed. One act essentially closed the port of Boston to all trade, another virtually revoked the Massachusetts Charter of 1691 by giving the crown the sole right to appoint the Massachusetts Council and prohibiting town meetings (aimed at the increasingly radical Boston town meeting), and a third permitted British officials indicted for a capital offense to be tried in Great Britain away from potentially hostile colonial juries and judges. Also passed at this time was a new Quartering Act (1774) that authorized the stationing of British troops in quarters other than barracks. Many colonists considered this revision of the 1765 Quartering Act an opening to permit the quartering of British troops in private homes. The fifth law, the Quebec Act, although not intended as a punitive measure, aroused widespread resentment because in granting religious freedom and tax support to Roman Catholics, it revived long-held colonial hostility to Catholicism and enlarged the province of Quebec southward to the Ohio River, thus nullifying or at least calling into question Virginia's claim to the rich Ohio River valley. While most of the Coercive Acts were aimed at punishing Massachusetts, the Quebec Act was designed to thwart the expansionist aspirations of many prominent Virginians. The Quebec Act, more than any other single parliamentary enactment—with the possible exception of the Stamp Act—galvanized opposition to British policies in Virginia. For example, opposition to the Quebec Act explains why many prominent Virginians (such as George Washington, Richard Henry Lee, George Mason, and Peyton Randolph) joined the growing number of New England radicals, especially from Massachusetts, who openly defied British policies. The Coercive Acts prompted calls for united action and the calling of an intercolonial congress, specifically from Rhode Island, Pennsylvania, and New York. Because most of the Coercive Acts were punitive measures aimed against Massachusetts, it is not surprising that it issued the formal invitations to the other twelve colonies to send delegates to what became the First Continental Congress. Understandably, Massachusetts did not want to defy Great Britain alone. The issue had now become more than the right of Parliament to tax the colonists; it had become one of ultimate authority. Delegates from twelve colonies (Georgia declined to send delegates to what appeared to the many loyalist Georgians to be a disloyal group of ungrateful, discontented colonists) met in Carpenter's Hall in Philadelphia on September 5, 1774. The importance of this gathering cannot be overemphasized. For many, this was their first trip outside of their own colony. This was an exceedingly important step in discarding the long-standing provincialism of most of the delegates. Local provincial leaders were becoming Americans.

Like the Stamp Act Congress of 1765, the First Continental Congress brought together many of the future revolutionary leaders. Of the two distinct factions that quickly emerged, the conservative group was in a slight majority. Led by James Duane and John Jay of New York, George Read of Delaware, and Joseph Galloway and John Dickinson of Pennsylvania, these men sought a status quo ante 1763, a return to the days of "salutary neglect." Dubbed reconciliationists, they sought, through petitions to the crown and to Parliament and as a last resort through economic boycotts, to persuade the King and Parliament to repeal some thirteen parliamentary laws passed since 1763 that they regarded as unconstitutional. These delegates advocated colonial autonomy within the existing British imperial structure.

The opposing minority radical faction was, by the fall of 1774, beginning to consider seriously the idea of colonial independence. Led by Samuel and John Adams of Massachusetts, Christopher Gadsden of South Carolina, and Richard Henry Lee and Patrick Henry of Virginia, these men, however, had to move slowly and sometimes somewhat clandestinely in the face of a solid group of middle colony delegates who rejected any suggestion of political separation from Great Britain. Most actions taken by the First Continental Congress represented compromises between these two opposing factions.

The election of Peyton Randolph of Virginia as president of Congress was recognition of the absolute necessity of involving Virginians in the growing anti-British movement. It is not mere coincidence that many revolutionary leaders, both civil and military, were Virginians. Their election or appointment to leadership roles would ensure that the largest, most populous, most influential colony would join and even lead the colonial revolt against the mother country. Elected secretary, nondelegate Charles Thomson of Pennsylvania would occupy that influential position throughout the fifteen-year life of the Continental Congress.

The first significant order of business was to determine the voting procedures. Large colonies (particularly Virginia) wanted proportional voting based on population whereas the small colonies insisted on each colony having one vote. After spirited debate, it was decided to give each delegation one vote. The one-colony/state-one-vote decision made in September 1774 would pertain throughout the life of the Continental Congress (1774–1789) and be opposed particularly by Virginia, Massachusetts, and Pennsylvania and supported by the smaller colonies/states.

The radicals succeeded in having the controversial Suffolk Resolves (1774) adopted. Drafted by Massachusetts radical Dr. Joseph Warren (1741–1775), these nineteen resolutions (1) declared the Coercive Acts unconstitutional and therefore not to be obeyed, (2) advised the people of Massachusetts to form their own colonial government to collect taxes, but to withhold these monies from the royal government of the province until such time as the Coercive Acts were repealed, (3) urged the people to arm themselves in preparation for the possibility of armed conflict, and (4) recommended harsh economic sanctions against Great Britain. Led by Joseph Galloway, the conservatives countered the approval of the radical Suffolk Resolves with a plan of union, which they hoped would help solve the problem of sovereignty. This so-called "Galloway's Plan of Union" would grant the colonies something approaching dominion status within the British empire. This proposal called for the royal appointment of a president-general who would serve at the pleasure of the crown and have veto power over acts of a grand council whose members were to be selected by the assemblies of each colony. The president-general and the grand council together would form an American branch of the British Parliament that would have veto power over all measures dealing with colonial affairs. By a vote of 6 to 5, this plan was defeated. The victorious radicals then had the plan with attendant discussion expunged from the journal. The endorsement of the Suffolk Resolves and the defeat of Galloway's Plan of Union reflected the early dominance of the radicals in the First Continental Congress. However, the conservatives (primarily delegates from the middle colonies of New York, New Jersey, Pennsylvania, and Delaware) were able to slow down the movement towards colonial autonomy and possible independence. They defeated a motion that sanctioned an independent government for Massachusetts and voted down a Virginia motion to demand the removal of British troops from Boston.

Adopted late in the congressional session and therefore reflective of growing conservative influence, The Declaration of Rights and Resolves (1774) set forth the prevailing colonial view. In it Congress denounced the Coercive Acts, the Quebec Act, the various revenue acts passed since 1763, the widespread use of vice-admiralty courts, and the stationing of British troops in colonial towns. The delegates supported economic sanctions against Britain until these onerous acts were repealed. Just a few days before adjournment, Congress adopted the Continental Association (1774). With its passage, the conservatives thwarted the more radical proposals for stringent nonconsumption, nonimportation, and nonexportation agreements. Instead the agreements adopted provided for numerous loopholes, postponed effective dates, and stipulated relatively lenient punishments for violators. Citizens in every locality (i.e., towns, villages, counties) were urged to elect committees that would in essence enforce these economic sanctions. These local committees, often working with the active assistance of the Sons of Liberty and other largely working-class mobs, were to encourage austerity and American agriculture and industry and to discourage extravagance and wastefulness. In many colonies, prominent local politicians and indeed many future revolutionary leaders got their first experiences in revolutionary politics as members of these mostly democratically-elected committees. These committees became, at the local level, the engines that drove the independence movement towards the July 2, 1776, decision for independence.

The First Continental Congress ended its deliberations by endorsing four addresses to the king and to the people of Great Britain, the British colonies, and Quebec. Carefully worded, they represented the views of the conservative majority. In them the colonists reaffirmed their allegiance to the crown, acknowledged the right of Parliament to levy external regulatory taxes upon the colonists, denied Parliament's right to impose internal taxes for the purpose of raising revenue, and insinuated that the present difficulties were not caused by King George III, but by evil ministers and scheming counselors. Congress adjourned on October 26, 1774, after passing a motion that it would meet again, in May of 1775, if Britain failed to repeal the Intolerable Acts in particular but also the other acts it regarded as obnoxious and/or unconstitutional. In other words, the colonists hoped and indeed expected another British retreat in the face of united colonial opposition.

The First Continental Congress accomplished more than it realized. The gathering of fifty-six delegates from twelve colonies was an important milestone along the Road to Revolution. This convention nurtured the seed of American nationalism. As delegate Patrick Henry had proclaimed, he was no longer a provincial Virginian but an American. Moreover, when the relatively conservative approach of the First Continental Congress did not lead to the desired redress of grievances, the radicals were able to gain control of the Second Continental Congress and steadily push their program of eventual independence from the mother country.

In the interim period between the adjournment of the First Continental Congress in late October 1774 and the first meeting of the Second Continental Congress in mid-May of 1775, the British government received and acted on the colonial petitions and declarations drawn up by the first Congress. The ensuing spirited debate within the British government of just how to respond to what was quickly becoming a crisis in imperial relations showed that there was opposition in Britain as well as in the colonies to the coercive policies of the king and Lord North. For example, Lord Chatham's (William Pitt the Elder) motion to remove troops from Boston received considerable support in the House of Lords, although it was defeated. In early February, the same Lord Chatham introduced his conciliation plan, which called for official British recognition of the Continental Congress, a promise of passing no revenue acts without the consent of colonial assemblies, colonial recognition that Parliament was the supreme authority in imperial matters, and the inauguration of a program under which the Continental Congress would pass revenue measures for the crown. The king and his parliamentary supporters were able to defeat this attempt at reconciliation. The Prime Minister, Lord North, then introduced his own plan for reconciliation. Although similar to Lord Chatham's proposal, this plan would allow Parliament to levy regulatory taxes on the colonies, but would require the colonial assemblies to tax themselves to provide for military and civil administration within each colony. If implemented, this plan would have enabled the British government to deal with each colony separately, thereby sidestepping any kind of official, or even tacit, recognition of the Continental Congress. This proposal was passed by both Houses of Parliament, but decisively rejected by the Continental Congress in July 1775.

In late March 1775 Parliament passed the New England Restraining Act, which amounted to an economic declaration of war against the increasingly obstreperous New England colonies (soon extended to most of the remaining thirteen mainland colonies). It provided that the colonies were allowed to trade only with Great Britain and the British West Indies. Clearly a crisis was brewing. Great Britain was apparently not going to back down this time to colonial demands as she had done previously. What would be the result? Would it be complete subjugation to British rule, would it be some sort of autonomous status for the colonies within the British empire, or would it be full independence from the mother country?

The meeting, on May 10, 1775, of the Second Continental Congress represented the failure, on both sides, at reconciliation. This Congress constituted officially the American government from May 1775 to March 1781 when the Articles of Confederation were promulgated, but actually to April 1789 when it was to be replaced by the government established under the Constitution of 1787. It is the Second Continental Congress that gave birth to the first American union, that created the Continental Army and Navy, that declared independence, that waged war, that made alliances with Britain's enemies abroad, that concluded a peace treaty, and finally that guided the newly created American republic through its difficult formative years under the Articles of Confederation. The May 10, 1775, meeting of the Second Continental Congress, in many ways, marked the beginning of what could be considered the "hot war" phase of the American Revolution replacing the "cold war" period of the preceding twelve years. The Road to Revolution had now merged into the Road to Independence.

CHAPTER 3

THE NECESSARY WAR

The American Revolution was, of course, much more than the War for American Independence. However, it is important to remember that the military actions of the Revolutionary War were an essential and even necessary part of the whole revolutionary epoch. But the Americans did not win the Revolutionary War militarily. The Americans clearly lost more battles than they won. General Washington spent much of his time as American commander in chief trying to avoid major engagements with his frequently more numerous, better equipped, better trained British/ German adversaries. Even after Lord Charles Cornwallis's (1738–1805) humiliating surrender at Yorktown, Virginia, in October 1781, the British still maintained a menacing military presence in America. Britain's decision, made soon after the defeat at Yorktown, to commence peace negotiations in Paris was based primarily on political, economic, and diplomatic considerations, although Britain's inability to annihilate or even defeat Washington's army certainly played a role in her seeking a diplomatic conclusion to the conflict.

Having stated that the Americans did not, in fact, win the war militarily does not mean or even imply that they lost the conflict. It was "the nature of the conflict" that made possible the American political, diplomatic, and what could be called psychological victory. To win the war, Britain would have had to destroy the Continental Army completely, to scatter and defeat the various state militias, and to occupy sizeable areas and the major cities. Britain was fighting "a people's war," a war against the majority of the colonial population. She was attempting to subdue an entire populace with a relatively small professional army. Although it appeared initially that the colonists were contending against seemingly overwhelming odds in their military struggle with Great Britain, it was, in fact, the mother country that had to confront overwhelming, impossible odds to achieve military victory. To win the conflict militarily, Britain had to subdue an entire country some three thousand miles from home. This she was unable to accomplish given the diplomatic situation in Europe and the Americas and the unstable political climate in Britain itself. Britain's role in the Revolutionary War can be compared to that of the United States in the Vietnam War. Both Britain and the United States were outside participants in what could be classified, at least in part, as civil wars. They were both endeavoring to quell, from afar, the indigenous people's aspirations for liberty, freedom, and political independence. Although the analogy is far from perfect, it is suggestive of the difficult task both faced when fighting in a war for independence far from home. The United States did not win or lose the Vietnam War militarily. The United States military remained the most powerful military force in the world even after the end of actual fighting. Likewise, Great Britain in the late eighteenth century remained militarily strong enough, even after acknowledging American independence, to play a major role in defeating Napoleonic France.

To win the war, Americans only had to survive militarily. As long as General Washington could maintain an army, even a small, ill-equipped, ill-trained one, in the field, he was not losing the contest. All the Americans had to do was maintain a feasible defensive posture until such time as Britain became convinced of the futility of trying to win militarily what was increasingly an expensive and frustrating conflict. Obviously, colonial victory did not require a successful invasion of Great Britain, nor even an offensive assault on neighboring Quebec (although this was attempted unsuccessfully in the winter of 1775–1776). To win their political independence from the mother country, the colonists were, however, obliged to fight a war. This war would eventually convince the stubborn British king, his largely inept ministers, and Parliament that military victory was not worth the cost financially and in fact could not be won given the European and American political and diplomatic climate of the late eighteenth century. Washington's great military achievement during the Revolutionary War was not in winning notable, decisive battles. It was rather his ability to maintain an American army in the field and avoid major engagements when there was little chance for victory. Washington's perseverance in the face of adversity and his survival instincts were his most remarkable contributions to the Revolutionary War effort. He was appointed Commander in Chief of the Continental Army in June of 1775. He resigned his commission as Commander in Chief after the conclusion of hostilities with his reputation as a military commander not only intact but enhanced. The Revolutionary War was "The Necessary War" because Britain had to be convinced that she could not wage a successful war, thousand of miles from home, against a majority of Americans who were fighting for their freedom, liberty, and political independence. To convince Great Britain of this, armed conflict became necessary and even inevitable.[1]

In 1775 the impending clash of arms appeared to resemble the biblical contest between David and Goliath. As the giant (Goliath), Great Britain had the advantage of a large navy; a well-trained, well-equipped, although not always well-led, army; the support, frequently active, of a large group of Americans who remained loyal to the mother country; the sympathetic support of hundreds, if not thousands, of Native Americans who resented the countless American incursions into Indians lands even more than the occasional British encroachment; and a sizeable war chest. These alleged advantages were more than offset, however, by several disadvantages that, in the long run, proved decisive in determining the war's outcome. Britain was fighting a war some three thousand miles from home. This meant sending all of the military equipment, the munitions, and most of the supplies needed to sustain a military presence across the Atlantic Ocean. This meant also trying to fight a European style war on unfamiliar terrain, a terrain that had few roads, few fords and even fewer bridges across the innumerable rivers, and vast stretches of uninhabited, forested wilderness.

The Americans (David) had advantages not readily apparent, especially to the British, at the beginning of hostilities. Fighting a defensive war on home ground proved a major advantage. The colonists also possessed a superiority in the number of men who could be readily called to service. Although there were large numbers of loyalists in each and every colony, a majority of Americans either favored the patriot cause or remained neutral. That meant that a majority of Americans who participated in the Revolutionary War did so on the patriot side. Fortunately too, the American patriots possessed superior military leaders. George Washington emerged at the end of the fighting as the most competent strategist and tactician on either side. There were, on both sides, generals and admirals with more experience, with more formal military training, and with more formal education. However, no leader, on either side, understood better than this former Virginian militia officer the kind of war that had to be fought to ensure that Great Britain would not win militarily and that America would win its political independence.

The first major military engagement of the American War for Independence not surprisingly took place in Massachusetts. Since its founding as an English colony in 1630, the Bay Colony had had religious, political, and economic differences with the mother country. Massachusetts led the prewar colonial opposition to Britain's attempts to reform and revamp her empire. This opposition often took a violent turn.

The Coercive Acts represented an economic declaration of war against Massachusetts. The most successful colonial opposition to these Intolerable Acts took the form of nonconsumption, nonimportation agreements. With the appointment of the Commander in Chief of the British army in America (General Thomas Gage) as governor of Massachusetts, Britain seemed on the verge of enforcing the punitive Coercive Acts and thereby smothering colonial opposition. For their part, patriot leaders Samuel Adams, John Hancock, and Dr. Joseph Warren were busy organizing and training the local Massachusetts militia companies and stockpiling munitions and supplies in preparation for what appeared increasingly to be an inevitable clash of arms between British troops and the colonial "Minute Men" (members of local militia companies who were designated to be ready to fight at a minute's notice).

General Thomas Gage's decision to seize the colonial arms and munitions known to be stored at Concord and capture, if possible, patriot leaders Samuel Adams and John Hancock precipitated armed conflict. On April 16, 1775, Dr. Joseph Warren sent Paul Revere to warn Hancock and Adams of Gage's planned foray. Two days later, General Gage ordered Lieutenant Colonel Francis Smith and Major John Pitcairn of the Marines to lead a force of 700 troops (mostly Light Infantrymen and Grenadiers) first to Lexington to capture the two rebel leaders, and then to proceed on to Concord to seize the militia supplies. Late in the evening of April 18th, the British troops embarked upon what became a bloody trip into hostile territory. Warned by Paul Revere, William Dawes, and Dr. Samuel Prescott that the British were indeed coming, hundreds of militiamen assembled on nearby village greens prepared to contest the British advance.

On Lexington Green, local militia commander Captain John Parker had assembled some 70 armed Minute Men. The British troops reached

Lexington in the early morning of April 19th. The stage was now set for the "shot heard around the world." Although it is not known who fired the first shot, there was an exchange of fire that resulted in eighteen colonial casualties (eight dead and ten wounded) and one British soldier being wounded. After this fifteen-minute delay on Lexington Green, Lt. Col. Smith marched the remaining five miles to Concord, where he was confronted by hundreds of armed American farmers. A skirmish at Concord's North Bridge resulted in over a dozen British casualties. Shortly after noon, the British started back to Boston. During the entire sixteen-mile return trip, the British soldiers were subjected to relentless assaults from all sides. Firing from behind trees and stone fences, the swarming militiamen inflicted heavy casualties on the panic-stricken British. What started out as an orderly return trip soon turned into a disorderly rout.

Luckily for the British, General Gage had sent a relief column, of some 1,400 men, to reinforce Smith's command. It met the retreating British troops at Lexington and escorted them back to Boston, thus saving Smith's command from possible total annihilation.

The Battle of Lexington and Concord was a significant American victory. The British sustained heavy casualties: 73 killed, 191 wounded, and 22 missing. Of the over 3,500 colonists who saw action on that fateful day, only 99 were listed as killed, wounded, captured, or missing.[2] Moreover, this battle demonstrated that ill-trained, ill-equipped New England farmers could stand up to British regulars. Also, this series of skirmishes aroused colonial opinion in favor of resisting what most New Englanders considered the brutal and unwanted British occupation of Boston. However, the thought of independence was not yet seriously considered or even mentioned publicly.

After the Battle of Lexington and Concord, Boston became a town under siege. In late April the Massachusetts Provincial Congress appointed Artemas Ward as commander of the militia and authorized the raising of some 13,000 men (a figure not reached). However, with the addition of sizeable contingents from Rhode Island, Connecticut, and New Hampshire, Ward, by late May, did command a militia army of over 9,000 men. This colonial siege of Boston lasted almost an entire year. During this time of relative inactivity on the part of the besieging militia, many militiamen wandered back to their villages (they did not consider their departure as desertion). Their place was then often taken by newcomers who answered the Provincial Congress's call for troops.

Soon after the Battle of Lexington and Concord, the Massachusetts Committee of Safety appointed Benedict Arnold (1741–1801) to lead a force of some 400 men to capture the strategic British Fort Ticonderoga on Lake Champlain. At the same time, Ethan Allen was assembling a force in Vermont to accomplish the same goal. Thus both Ethan Allen and Benedict Arnold were present on May 10, 1775, when the surprised British garrison of 42 men surrendered to the American force of 83. This minor engagement was followed by the American capture of Crown Point just north of Ticonderoga and St. John, which was situated just across the Canadian border. Britain was thus deprived at least for a while of these strategic outposts, which commanded the traditional invasion route between Quebec and New York. Of more immediate importance to the Americans was the capture of forty cannon, sixteen mortars, and a large quantity of powder at Fort Ticonderoga. In the winter of 1775–1776, Colonel Henry Knox (1750–1806) laboriously hauled these captured cannons over ice and snow to Cambridge, Massachusetts, where they were used to force the British evacuation of Boston.

In May of 1775, British generals Sir William Howe, Sir Henry Clinton, and John Burgoyne arrived in Boston with reinforcements, which brought the garrison up to some 6,500 effective combat troops. The besieging American force numbered around 10,000. Both sides were preparing for battle!

Meanwhile, the Continental Congress reconvened on May 10, 1775. News of the Battle of Lexington and Concord had reached Philadelphia, and this prompted Congress, under the urging of the Massachusetts delegates, to prepare for further military engagements. On June 10th, Congress designated the forces besieging Boston as the Continental Army. The struggle was therefore broadened from one between Massachusetts and Great Britain to one between the colonies, as represented in Congress, and Great Britain. On June 15th, at the urging of John Adams and his Massachusetts colleagues, Congress appointed Virginia delegate George Washington as Commander in Chief of the recently created Continental Army. Thus Washington was chosen commander not because he was necessarily the best qualified or most experienced military officer available; he was selected because he was from Virginia, the largest, most populous, and most influential colony. Congress also at this time appointed Artemas Ward, Charles Lee, Philip Schuyler, and Israel Putnam as major generals along with eighteen brigadier generals. Many of the appointees were prominent local politicians, and most were from New England and New York, thus offsetting the fact that the commander in chief was a Virginian. Washington's appointment would help, it was hoped, to secure Virginia's support (and southern help generally) whereas the northern appointments would cement New England and middle colony loyalty for the patriot side. Washington modestly accepted his commission and took command of the army around Boston just two weeks after the bloody encounter on Bunker Hill.

In terms of casualties, the Battle of Bunker Hill was the bloodiest engagement of the entire war. In mid-June, the Americans learned of General Gage's intention to fortify Dorchester Heights. As a countermove, the Americans fortified Breed's Hill and Bunker Hill, which were both situated on the Charlestown peninsula overlooking Boston harbor. American possession of these strategic hills would render the British position in Boston virtually untenable.

By June 17th, 1,600 men manned the American redoubt (temporary fortification) on Breed's Hill with a few hundred more working to complete the construction of the unfinished redoubt on nearby Bunker Hill. Under the direct command of Colonel William Prescott (1726–1795), the Americans on Breed's Hill had not yet fully completed construction of their defensive positions when British ships in the harbor started their bombardment. General Gage soon realized that the American redoubt on Breed's Hill threatened the British position in Boston and decided on a frontal attack against the entrenched Americans. Appointed to command the British attack, General William Howe (1729–1814) bravely led his 2,400 men on two unsuccessful assaults. The Americans were once again showing that they could withstand a concerted attack by seasoned troops. However, the acute shortage of gunpowder forced the Continentals to give way to the third British charge. Technically General Howe won the Battle of Bunker/Breed Hill. At the conclusion of fighting, he held the field. His victory, however, was a Pyrrhic one. British casualties numbered more than one thousand, of which a sizeable number were officers. American casualties, killed, and captured were about 400. Foremost among the American losses, the revolutionary leader Dr. Joseph Warren was killed during the disorderly American retreat.

The significance of the Battle of Bunker/Breed Hill cannot be overemphasized. New England farmers had stood up to the best the British could muster and gave ground only after running out of gunpowder. The battle boosted American morale while making the British more cautious. Although General Howe fought bravely and courageously in leading his troops up Breed's Hill, he never thereafter attempted a frontal assault against an entrenched enemy. The bloody encounter also dispelled, for most Americans, the hope of reconciliation.

Additionally, the battle highlighted British incompetence. Had Gage and Howe landed a force at the Charlestown Neck, they would have been in a position to surround and then destroy or capture the entire American force on the peninsula. Instead, they chose to intimidate and chastise the rebels for their audaciousness in openly defying British authority. Britain paid heavily for this imperiousness.

In the most audacious offensive American assault of the war, Congress authorized an invasion of Canada in the summer of 1775. Firmly convinced that the largely French-speaking population of Quebec was just waiting to be liberated from British rule, Congress authorized General Philip Schuyler of New York (1733–1804) to lead an invasion force of some 1,000 men. When forced to retire temporarily from active command because of ill health, Schuyler relinquished command of the invasion force to Brigadier General Richard Montgomery (1738–1775). As a former officer in the British army, Montgomery was one of the most experienced American field officers. He was to lead one prong of a two-prong pincer movement against Montreal and Quebec. In mid-September, Montgomery's force occupied Montreal. He then marched downriver towards Quebec City. Meanwhile, Benedict Arnold was given command of the second prong. Enduring unbelievable hardships, Arnold led his 1,000-man detachment through the wilderness of Maine seldom seen by white men. Arnold's harrowing trek ranks as one of the most daring, courageous exploits of the war. By the time he reached Point Lévis (directly across the St. Lawrence River from Quebec City), Arnold's force had been reduced by death and desertion to 650 men. In early December, Montgomery and Arnold joined forces to lay siege to Quebec. On the last day of December, when many of the American enlistments would expire, the two ill-fated commanders undertook a combined assault against the heavily fortified town. The twin attack ended in disaster. Montgomery was killed, Arnold was seriously wounded, over 100 Americans were killed or wounded, and over 300 (including the famous Virginian rifleman Daniel Morgan) were captured. Although failing to capture the city, Arnold doggedly persevered in his siege until early spring, when British relief ships were sighted on the St. Lawrence River rounding the Island of Orleans. Utterly depressed and defeated, the remnant of the American invasion force returned to New York to report the first major American defeat of the war.

Although New England and the middle colonies witnessed the heaviest fighting during the first few years of the conflict, there were sporadic skirmishes in the South, mainly between patriot militiamen and American loyalists. In late November 1775 the Royal Governor of Virginia, John Murray, Lord Dunmore, issued a proclamation in which he promised freedom to those slaves who deserted their masters. This proclamation convinced many wavering southern slave-owners to join the patriot cause. In December Dunmore was defeated by a rebel militia force near Norfolk, forcing him to evacuate that port city. However, he later was able to retake the town, which he then destroyed by fire.

In North Carolina, Royal Governor Josiah Martin (1737–1786) invited all loyalists to join him in establishing the King's authority throughout the colony. In mid-February 1776, Martin led his 1,600 loyalists to Moore's Bridge, some sixteen miles from Wilmington, where they were met by an approximately equal number of patriot militiamen led by Colonel Richard Caswell (1729–1789). In the ensuing confrontation, the loyalists lost 30 men killed or wounded and over 800 captured while the patriots had only 2 men wounded. The patriot victory at Moore's Bridge postponed a possible British invasion of North Carolina and convinced many planters to embrace the patriot cause.

In late January 1776 General Henry Knox reached Washington's headquarters at Cambridge with the cannon and mortars captured at Fort Ticonderoga. The Americans now possessed the means to bombard British ships in the harbor and Boston itself. The American ability to shell his besieged garrison along with the British inability to dislodge the Americans from the Charlestown peninsula convinced General William Howe (who succeeded Gage as British commander in October 1775) to evacuate Boston. By March 17th, all British troops plus a thousand loyalists had embarked for the safety of Halifax, Nova Scotia.

For a few months in the spring of 1776, the thirteen colonies were completely free of British troops. However, in early July, General Howe landed on Staten Island with 10,000 British soldiers. Joining his brother, Admiral Lord Richard Howe (British naval commander in America), who brought a strong fleet of over 150 ships, William Howe intended to make the more defensible New York City his headquarters. With the summer arrival of substantial reinforcements, General Howe commanded, by late August, a force of over 32,000 troops. When he learned in April of the Howe brothers' plan to occupy and fortify New York City, Washington moved his army southward to counter the British move.

By late August, General Howe was ready to begin his attack on New York. The ensuing Battle of Long Island (sometimes referred to as the Battle of Brooklyn Heights) showed Howe at his best and Washington at his worst. With numerical superiority and naval command of the waterways in and around the city, Howe outfought, outmaneuvered, and outflanked his inexperienced adversary. On August 27th, General Howe deployed two divisions (General James Grant with 5,000 men and General Leopold Philip von Heister with 6,000 Hessians) against the American right and center. A third contingent of some 10,000 troops, under the command of Generals Henry Clinton and Lord Cornwallis, was to turn the American left flank through Jamaica Pass, which Washington had left virtually un-guarded. This flanking movement was carried out brilliantly and resulted in a complete rout of the American army. Washington had been decisively defeated. Only Howe's unwillingness to press a final assault saved Washington's army from complete annihilation. In the Battle of Long Island, the Americans lost over 1,400 men; the British casualties were less than 500. The British would never again have such an easy opportunity to destroy completely Washington's army and thus possibly end the military phase of the American Revolution. Two days after what can be described as the nadir of his military career, Washington did recover suf-ficiently to execute a near-miraculous withdrawal of his thoroughly beaten army across the East River to Manhattan Island. This brilliant evacuation was made possible largely through the extraordinary efforts of John Glover's Marblehead militia unit, most of the members of which were in fact fisher-men. Washington was thus able to save his army to fight another day.

Howe then landed his army on Manhattan Island at Kip's Bay. On September 15th, he overran the city, then occupied the southern tip of Manhattan. There followed a series of skirmishes as the British slowly moved up the thirteen-mile-long island towards the northern tip around Harlem Heights. The Battle of Harlem Heights was militarily a draw, but it did reaffirm that the usually outnumbered Americans would fight. Fol-lowing the Battle of White Plains, in which the British were able to push the Americans out of their entrenchments on Chatterton's Hill, the battle for New York became one of maneuver. Throughout the battle for New

York City, Washington was gaining valuable battlefield experience. He became so adept at avoiding the various traps and envelopment moves of the British that they were soon referring to him as "The Sly Fox." However, with the surrender of the 2,800-man garrison at Fort Washington on the east bank of the Hudson River and the evacuation of Fort Lee directly across the river from Fort Washington in New Jersey in mid-November, Washington reluctantly left New York to the British and retreated with his bedraggled army across New Jersey to the relative safety of Pennsylvania. Up to this point in late 1776, Washington had not won a battle (he had, however, forced the British to evacuate Boston) and in fact had lost disastrously one major battle (Battle of Long Island) and a number of skirmishes that resulted in the British occupation of New York City.

After the successful repulse of the American invasion in the winter of 1775–1776, the British commander in Canada, Sir Guy Carleton (1724–1808) planned an invasion of New York down the Lake Champlain—Lake George—Hudson River waterway to New York City, where he would join his army to that of General Howe, thereby cutting off the New England colonies from the other mainland colonies. The British could then, it was hoped, retake Boston and bring the rebellious northern colonies back to their proper allegiance to the crown, thus ending the American rebellion. In pursuance of this grand plan, Carleton knew he had to gain control of both Lake Champlain and Lake George. In early October of 1776 Carleton led his 13,000-man army down to Lake Champlain. To counter this invasion, Washington sent General Benedict Arnold northward with orders to construct a small fleet on Lake Champlain that could thwart this waterway assault. On October 11th at Valcour Bay, Arnold's makeshift 83-gun flotilla, manned primarily by soldiers, encountered the British 87-gun flotilla under the command of naval Captain Thomas Pringle and manned by experienced sailors. In the ensuing seven-hour battle most of the American ships were badly crippled. A second engagement two days later resulted in the complete destruction of the American flotilla. Carleton then occupied the American fort at Crown Point. Because of the delay caused by the naval battle at Valcour Bay, Carleton decided to postpone his widely heralded invasion until the following year. He abandoned Crown Point and returned to Canada. Although clearly an American defeat (the entire American fleet was destroyed), the Battle of Valcour Bay may well have saved the American Revolutionary cause. By causing the British to delay their invasion for one year, it enabled the Americans to strengthen their forces to such an extent as to make possible the astonishing victory at Saratoga in October 1777. Although technically the losing commander at Valcour Bay, Benedict Arnold came out of the encounter with an enhanced reputation as Washington's most daring and resourceful field commander.

By mid-December 1776, General Washington had led his tattered army across New Jersey and over the Delaware River into eastern Pennsylvania. Up to that time, with the exception of the successful siege of Boston, Washington's forces had seemingly only lost battles and retreated. Determined to take the offensive, Washington planned an audacious midwinter assault on several of the British/Hessian garrisons Howe had left in New Jersey. During the night of December 25–December 26, Washington personally led a force of 2,400 men across the ice-choked Delaware River a few miles north of Trenton and attacked the garrison in the town (a Hessian force under the command of Colonel Johann Rall) in the early morning. Completely surprised, the Hessians could offer little resistance and after an hour of confused street fighting, surrendered. Hessian casualties numbered over 900 killed, wounded, or captured. The attacking American force suffered only minor casualties.

General Howe reacted quickly to the Trenton defeat by dispatching a large force under General Lord Cornwallis to the Trenton area. On January 2, 1777, Cornwallis's army encountered Washington's 5,200-man force and a major battle appeared imminent. However, Cornwallis chose to wait, for unknown reasons, until the following day to attack the American force. During the night, Washington quietly abandoned his position in front of Cornwallis and circled around and headed towards the college town of Princeton. In the brief Battle of Princeton, the attacking Americans showed great determination and skill in capturing the British garrison. In these two American victories, minor as they were in terms of numbers involved and casualties, Washington demonstrated a heretofore-unseen audaciousness and enterprise. Clearly, General Washington had learned a great deal since his poor showing earlier in the year at the Battle of Long Island. He emerged from these two minor battles a more self-confident, self-assured field commander. Furthermore, these victories boosted what had been sagging American morale. As Washington led his worn-out army into winter quarters at Morristown, New Jersey, he and his men were cautiously optimistic that the next fighting season would bring additional successful military encounters with the British and their Hessian mercenaries.

The winter's encampments endured at Morristown in 1777 and 1779 were in terms of suffering and hardship more dramatic than the more famous one at Valley Forge in 1778. In all three of these winter encampments, the Americans often lacked sufficient food, adequate shelter, warm clothing, and even minimal forage for horses. In addition, incessant boredom became a problem for the hungry, ill-clad, underutilized soldiers as they huddled in drafty wooden huts awaiting the arrival of spring. By early spring of 1777, Washington's army had dwindled to some 3,000 effectives. However, by June the American commander was able to build his effective army strength to over 6,000 men. With this largely newly recruited army, Washington prepared to defend Philadelphia against General Howe's expected thrust to the City of Brotherly Love from the headwaters of the Chesapeake Bay.

It was at this juncture that rivalries and jealousies among the British high command greatly helped the patriot cause. Especially devastating from the British point of view was the lack of communication and trust between the Secretary of State for the American Colonies George Sackville Germain, headquartered in London, and Generals John Burgoyne, Henry Clinton, and William Howe, stationed in America. General Burgoyne had received authorization from Lord Germain to mount an invasion from Canada along the Lake Champlain–Lake George–Hudson River waterway. He was to be aided by a small British force traveling east from Lake Ontario along the Mohawk River and yet another British contingent that would travel up the Hudson River from Henry Clinton's command in New York City. These three armies were to converge at or near Saratoga, New York, therefore cutting off and isolating New England.

This grandiose scheme for ending the war was really a modification of Carleton's plan of a year earlier that had been thwarted by Benedict Arnold's spirited delaying tactics at the Battle of Valcour Bay. Because of poor communications and/or rivalries among the British generals, General Howe, instead of leading a force up the Hudson River from New York City to join General Burgoyne, as both Germain and Burgoyne thought he would and should do, embarked upon an independent foray of his own against Philadelphia.

By late August 1777, after an exhausting sea voyage from New York City southward along the coast and up the Chesapeake Bay to its headwaters, Howe landed his 15,000-man army and headed northward toward

Philadelphia. When he learned of Howe's whereabouts, Washington moved his main army south from New York to Philadelphia.

In what became the opening engagement of the Battle for Philadelphia, advance units of Howe's army clashed with a large scouting party of New Jersey Continentals under the command of General William Maxwell. Referred to as the Battle of Cooch's Bridge, this lively skirmish confirmed that Howe was intent on confronting Washington's army in a major battle and capturing Philadelphia.

The major battle took place on September 11th when Howe attacked the entrenched American position along the eastern side of Brandywine Creek. Simultaneously attacking the American center and outflanking the American right, the British won a notable victory. American casualties numbered over 1,000 whereas British losses were just over 500. American General Nathanael Greene (1742–1786) led an orderly American retreat that possibly saved the Continental Army from complete destruction. The British victory at the Battle of Brandywine Creek and the successful early morning bayonet attack at Paoli (often referred to as the Paoli Massacre) on a force under the command of General (nicknamed "Mad Anthony" for his brash behavior in battle) Wayne (1745–1796) some ten days later opened the way for the British occupation of Philadelphia. The British occupied America's largest city for some nine and a half months, but were disappointed that the capture of the seat of government did not result in the end of hostilities or even greatly harm the patriot cause.

Even after the defeats at Brandywine Creek and Paoli and the loss of Philadelphia, Washington felt he had sufficient forces to confront Howe's army again on terms that at least held out the possibility of success. On the night of October 3rd, he maneuvered his 11,000-man army (approximately 8,000 Continentals and 3,000 militia) towards Howe's main encampment at Germantown five miles north of Philadelphia. Howe had divided his command in two, stationing Lord Cornwallis's contingent in Philadelphia proper and the remaining 9,000 men at Germantown. Washington attacked the British encampment at Germantown just before dawn on October 4th with some initial success. But the lack of coordination between the American attacking columns, a heavy fog which caused some American troops to fire on other Americans (referred to as friendly fire), and a delay in the overall assault at the Chew House where a British detachment held out against General William Maxwell's New Jersey Continentals for over a half hour spelled failure for the well-planned, but poorly-executed assault. General Nathanael Greene directed the orderly American retreat from Germantown, thus preventing a rout. American casualties numbered 700 killed and wounded and 400 captured against British losses of just over 500. Although considered a British victory in that the American attack was repulsed, the Battle of Germantown boosted American morale. Washington and his men thought the battle could have been won. They believed that only the heavy, seemingly impenetrable fog and the lack of communication between several of the attacking units prevented an American victory. On the whole, the Americans fought bravely. The courage and professionalism displayed by the American army, although its assault had been thwarted, in the Battle of Germantown (October 4, 1777) and General Burgoyne's surrender at Saratoga just thirteen days later (October 17, 1777) together might well have been decisive in convincing the French to enter into a military alliance with the now more confident Americans. However, on balance, the whole Philadelphia campaign was a series of British victories. Howe had badly beaten Washington at Brandywine Creek and General Anthony Wayne at Paoli, had repulsed the American assault at Germantown, had occupied Philadelphia, and had sent Lord Cornwallis to clear the lower Delaware River valley of American obstructions thus opening up for the British a water route to their garrison in Philadelphia. What was perhaps not so readily apparent to the British was the growing self-confidence of Washington's army that was caused in large part by its courageous performance at Germantown and by the welcomed news of Burgoyne's surrender at Saratoga. This optimism, of course, was to be sorely tested in the winter of 1777–1778 as Washington led his army into winter quarters at Valley Forge just two months after the bloody encounter at Germantown and the victory at Saratoga.

The pivotal, most significant battle (really a series of battles) of the War for Independence took place in the late summer and early fall of 1777 in upper state New York. Known collectively as the Battle of Saratoga, these victories, for victories they were, convinced both the French and the Americans that the colonists could indeed win their political independence. Upon learning of the British surrender at Saratoga, and also of the Continental Army's good showing, although defeated, in the Battle of Germantown, the French quickly concluded two treaties with America: a treaty of amity and commerce and, more importantly, a treaty of alliance.[3] Ever since her humiliating defeat at the hands of Great Britain in the Seven

Years' War (1756–1763), France had sought an opportunity to exact revenge upon her ancient enemy. The American army's dramatic victory at Saratoga provided that opportunity by convincing French Foreign Minister Charles Gravier, Comte de Vergennes (1717–1787) that the Americans could actually win their independence from Great Britain. France's entrance into the war in June of 1778 led to Spain's declaration of war against Britain in 1779. Spain entered the fray primarily to regain Gibraltar—lost to the British in the War of the Spanish Succession (1702–1714). The War for American Independence had become a worldwide conflict. With the now more confident America and the two Bourbon powers aligned against her, Britain was forced to change drastically her war aims and military strategy. Fear of a Franco-Spanish invasion across the English Channel and the need to defend her commercially valuable West Indian colonies against the French, the Spanish, and after 1780 the Dutch (Britain declared war against the United Provinces in December 1780) forced Britain to divert troops and ships from the North American theater to the Caribbean and to the homeland. The British decision to declare war against the Dutch was prompted by a desire to stop the Americans from obtaining contraband supplies through the Dutch West Indian colony of St. Eustatius, and to punish the Dutch for negotiating a commercial treaty with the American colonies—a treaty that the Dutch and Americans had in fact not negotiated at this time. Britain quickly captured this strategically situated island, thereby depriving the Americans of this valuable pipeline for supplies from Europe. From 1779 to the end of hostilities in 1781, Britain essentially conducted a holding action in America. The mother country was no longer able or even inclined to expend the necessary effort and money to subdue completely the rebellious colonies and destroy Washington's Continental Army. Britain's strategy, after the summer of 1778, was to capture several strategically and commercially important cities and gain control of some areas, particularly in the south and New York, where there was a significant number of loyalists to help the mother country maintain its control. Thus, in the peace negotiations ending the conflict, Great Britain would have to acknowledge and grant independence only to those colonial areas it could not subdue. The French Alliance that led to the changes in British war aims and military strategy was prompted in large part by the American victories at Bennington, Fort Stanwix, Freeman's Farm, and Bemis Heights that in turn all made possible the dramatic victory at

Saratoga over an entire British army. Thus the American victory at Saratoga was the final act of the most decisive battle of the entire war.

The Saratoga campaign got under way in mid-June of 1777 when British General John "Johnny" Burgoyne led a force of over 7,000 troops (British regulars, Canadian militiamen, Hessians, and Indians) southward along the traditional waterway invasion route into upper New York. Burgoyne had traveled back to London in winter of 1777 to secure royal approval of his overly ambitious plan (which he entitled "Thoughts for Conducting the War on the Side of Canada") for ending the conflict. Appointed to command the main invading army, Burgoyne was to meet two other British forces at or near Saratoga, New York, thereby cutting off and isolating the rebellious New England colonies. With the increasingly effective British naval blockade of the coast, New England would then be subdued, causing, it was hoped, the collapse of the patriot cause. Although Burgoyne's plan appeared feasible in theory, in practice almost everything that could go wrong for the British did go wrong.

The initial skirmishes of the campaign in fact went well for the invaders. On June 30th, Burgoyne's army had reached strategic Fort Ticonderoga on Lake Champlain. The American garrison there, under the command of General Arthur St. Clair (1737–1818), had neglected to fortify a nearby hill, therefore making the fort untenable when the British mounted cannon on the hill (Mt. Defiance) that could bombard Fort Ticonderoga into easy submission. St. Clair hastily abandoned the fort. By July 7th, Burgoyne had succeeded in taking Fort Anne south of Fort Ticonderoga. Thereupon the northern theater American commander General Philip Schuyler of New York adopted delaying tactics to slow the British advance. However, as a result of congressional dissatisfaction with his battlefield performance and in part because of his ill health, General Schuyler was replaced, on August 4th, by General Horatio Gates as commander of the defending American army.

In his now slow advance southward, General Burgoyne began to experience supply problems. In early August, he dispatched Lieutenant Colonel Friedrich Baum with a force of some 700 (approximately 300 Hessians and the rest a mixed force of loyalists, Canadians, and Indians) to capture the military stores that the Americans were said to have stored at Bennington near the New York/Vermont border. The loss of Fort Ticonderoga and news of the murder by pro-British Indians of Jane McCrea on July 27, 1777, finally provoked New England to action. The Americans used the senseless killing of the young white daughter of a Presbyterian clergyman as an example of British/Indian brutality to garner support for the American cause. General John Stark of New Hampshire was appointed commander of a 2,600-man militia force that met and decisively defeated Baum's smaller force in the Battle of Bennington. Baum was killed, the pro-British Indians ingloriously fled, and most of the British, German, and Loyalist troops were captured. A British relief force under Lieutenant Colonel Heinrich C. Breymann arrived too late to help the hapless Baum, and was in fact almost destroyed itself by Stark and a 400-man unit of Massachusetts Continentals under the command of Colonel Seth Warner. The British defeat at Bennington was devastating. Not only did the British not capture the much-needed American military supplies at Bennington, but also they lost almost 1,000 men (killed, wounded, or captured). Burgoyne could not well afford the loss of approximately 15 percent of his army. His attacking army was reduced to something just over 5,000 effective fighting men and that number was slowly being diminished by illness and desertion.

Meanwhile, the second prong of the three-prong British assault, under the command of Colonel Barry St. Leger, advanced eastward from Lake Ontario along the Mohawk River. By early August, St. Leger's mostly Loyalist and Indian 1800-man contingent reached and lay siege to Fort Stanwix. The Fort's 750-man garrison, under the command of Colonel Peter Gansevoort, put up a spirited, and what was eventually a successful, defense. Two small American forces were dispatched to relieve the besieged garrison. A loyalist and Indian force commanded by Chief Joseph Brant badly mauled the first relief column, commanded by General Nicholas Herkimer, in the Battle of Oriskany. The arrival of a second relief force, under the command of Benedict Arnold, however, prompted St. Leger to abandon the siege of Fort Stanwix. He retreated back to Lake Ontario, thereby effectively removing his army from what was supposed to be a three-part coordinated invasion of the Hudson River Highlands.

Under Burgoyne's original plan, troops from General Henry Clinton's New York City garrison were to advance northward along the Hudson River to converge with Colonel St. Clair's army from the west and with Burgoyne's main force from Canada at or near Saratoga, thus completing the encirclement of the New England colonies. After learning of the British repulse at Freeman's Farm on September 19th, General Clinton did, in early October, lead a small force up the Hudson, which captured Fort Clinton and Fort Montgomery. Hesitant to go further up the river for fear of leaving New York City vulnerable to an American attack and allegedly reluctant to miss the comforting embrace of his mistress, Mrs. Joshua (Betsy) Loring, General Clinton returned to New York City, thus effectively removing the second arm of the three-pronged assault envisioned by Burgoyne in his plan to bring the American war to an end. With the repulse of St. Leger's force at Fort Stanwix, Howe's decision to move his army southward to capture Philadelphia instead of joining the invading British army at Saratoga, and Clinton's refusal to send a large force north up the Hudson River, Burgoyne was left alone, with his depleted, ill-supplied army to face the growing American army being assembled under its new field commander Horatio Gates.

The Battle of Saratoga itself consisted of two separate major encounters. The first (sometimes referred to as the First Battle of Saratoga) took place on September 19th when Burgoyne attacked the well-entrenched American positions on Bemis Heights. He was met and finally repulsed at Freeman's Farm by an American force, which consisted primarily of riflemen under the combined command of General Daniel Morgan and Colonel Henry Dearborn. It was during the initial stages of this battle that Morgan's sharpshooting riflemen killed (some would call it assassinated, because the riflemen were ordered specifically to shoot the officers) a large percentage of the British and Hessian officer corps, thus leading to further confusion and chaos in the British ranks. Burgoyne sustained heavy losses at the Battle of Freeman's Farm; losses he could ill afford. The 600 British casualties (300 for the Americans) reduced further Burgoyne's effective fighting force and made more certain the eventual American victory.

The Battle of Bemis Heights (the Second Battle of Saratoga) occurred on October 7th when Burgoyne again attacked the American positions. Morgan and General Ebenezer Learned repulsed this second major British attack. Then General Benedict Arnold, although without a formal field command, led a determined counterattack on the British, forcing them back to Bemis Heights. This second phase of the Battle of Saratoga cost Burgoyne an additional 600 casualties (American casualties numbered around 150). During the early evening, Burgoyne disengaged, and the next day retreated northward to Saratoga. Burgoyne's position had become desperate. Soon his dwindling, ill-supplied army was surrounded by an

American force three times his own. On October 13, 1777, he asked for a cession of fighting. The American commander, General Horatio Gates, for reasons not fully understood today, signed the lenient "Convention of Saratoga" on October 17th. Under its terms, over 5,000 British and German troops laid down their arms, were to promise not to serve further in the present war, and then were to be marched to Boston and shipped back to Britain. Congress ended up repudiating a portion of the "Convention of Saratoga," and many of the captured soldiers spent the duration of the war as American prisoners. Many of the enlisted men were sent to American prisons where they endured unbelievable hardships. Most of the officers were sent to Virginia to experience a more endurable and even quasi-comfortable confinement.

The American victory at Saratoga was the turning point of the war. The surrender of an entire British army and the capture of a large stash of military supplies, arms, and munitions came just at the critical juncture, right after General Howe had completed the takeover of Philadelphia, to boost sagging American morale. The American army, still largely ill trained, although less so than previously, and ill supplied, had beaten decisively an army of British regulars and German mercenaries. Of more importance, the American victory influenced the French to enter into an alliance with America. Now massive French aid, in war materiel, financial aid, and troops and ships, would be forthcoming. The war to subdue thirteen rebellious colonies had become a world war with Great Britain standing alone, now aligned against not only the Bourbon powers of France and Spain, but also against the United Provinces and the thirteen North American colonies.

Rumors of a French army and fleet sailing to America convinced British General Henry Clinton to abandon Philadelphia and return to the more readily defensible New York City. On June 18, 1778, Clinton started his army across New Jersey. Washington's army, which had been in winter quarters just 20 miles north of Philadelphia at Valley Forge, now broke camp and followed Clinton's extended wagon columns. Washington now felt confident enough to confront the main British army in America. Although the Americans had certainly suffered with insufficient food and inadequate housing at Valley Forge, they had also undergone intensive military training under the watchful eye of Friedrich Wilhelm Augustus von Steuben. This Prussian drillmaster had spent hours drilling a select group of American soldiers during the weary months spent at Valley Forge,

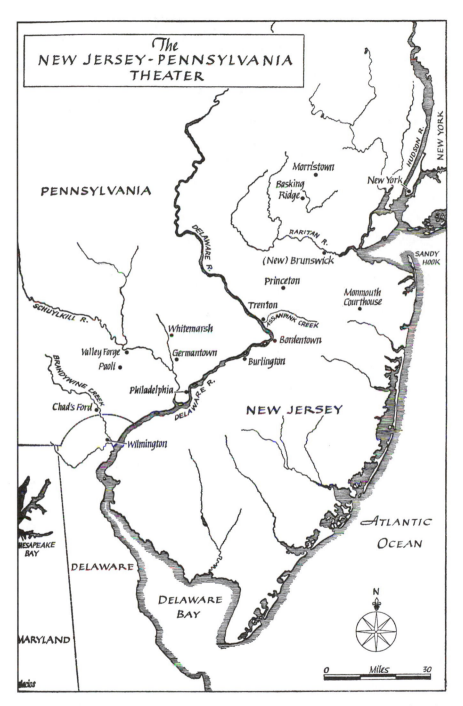

The
NEW JERSEY-PENNSYLVANIA
THEATER

PENNSYLVANIA

NEW YORK

Morristown

Basking
Ridge

New York

HUDSON R.

RARITAN R.

DELAWARE R.

SANDY
HOOK

(New) Brunswick

Princeton

SCHUYLKILL R.

Trenton

ASSANPINK CREEK

Monmouth
Courthouse

Whitemarsh

Bordentown

Valley Forge

Germantown

Paoli

Burlington

BRANDYWINE CREEK

Philadelphia

DELAWARE R.

Chad's Ford

NEW JERSEY

Wilmington

CHESAPEAKE
BAY

ATLANTIC
OCEAN

DELAWARE

N

MARYLAND

DELAWARE
BAY

0   Miles   30

Lacios

From *A History of the American Revolution* by John R. Alden, Copyright © 1969 by John
R. Alden. Used by permission of Alfred A. Knopf, a division of Random House, Inc.

who in turn trained others in the intricacies of military maneuvers and military discipline. The American army that Washington led in pursuit of Clinton's slow-moving, retreating army was relatively well trained and well supplied. Washington appointed General Charles Lee to command the 5,000-man American vanguard that was to harass continually the retreating British and offer battle if and when the opportunity for victory seemed feasible. On June 28th, Lee saw his opportunity and attacked Clinton's rear guard at Monmouth Court House. The Americans enjoyed the early advantage since the British had been caught somewhat by surprise, but confusing and even contradictory orders to field commanders Generals Lafayette and Anthony Wayne and Lee's hesitancy to press the attack prompted, when the British mounted a mini-counterattack, the American general to order his troops to pull back. When Washington arrived on the field, he chastised the timid General Charles Lee for ordering the retreat. The thoroughly angered Washington then rallied his troops to repulse the British counterattack. Despite Clinton's repeated attempts to dislodge Washington's troops, the Americans held their position. In the evening General Clinton resumed his retreat to New York. The Battle of Monmouth Courthouse was a draw. Both sides suffered approximately 350 casualties. Although Clinton's British army had been able to complete its return trip to New York City intact, it had been sorely tested in a major battle against an adversary that had evolved from a motley, ill-trained, ill-equipped collection of farmers and artisans into a reasonably well-trained, well-disciplined, well-led, although usually not well-equipped, citizen army. After the Battle of Monmouth Courthouse, General Washington was more willing to commit his army to a major confrontation. Relatively heavy casualties, highly contested in extremely hot weather, and the public verbal confrontation between Washington and Lee point to the Battle of Monmouth Courthouse as being one of the most important engagements of the war. This indecisive engagement was the last major European-style battle to be fought north of the Mason–Dixon Line. The remaining engagements in the north were typically guerrilla-like skirmishes with the Indians on the western frontier or in the Wyoming Valley, and vicinity, of Pennsylvania. The focus of attention, especially for the British, shifted southward after the summer of 1778.

The confrontation between Washington and his second-in-command Charles Lee was an interesting sideshow to the main battle. As commander of the American vanguard, General Lee had been ordered to press the attack against the rear guard of General Clinton's retreating army. When Clinton stopped and committed his main army to join what had been up to that point primarily a skirmish between the British rear guard and the American vanguard, Lee ordered an American retreat. As Washington's entourage approached the now retreating Americans, he confronted Lee in the presence of numerous witnesses and criticized him for his timidity just when victory seemed imminent. What precisely took place between the two generals will probably never be known. What is known is that Lee demanded and got a court-martial. Charged with misbehavior before the enemy, disobedience of orders, and disrespect for the Commander in Chief, Charles Lee was found guilty on all three counts and suspended from active service. In retrospect, Lee's removal from high command was a good thing for the Patriot cause. Up to the time of his court-martial, the mercurial Lee along with Horatio Gates (the victor at Saratoga) were the two generals that the anti-Washington forces, both in Congress and in the military, seemed to favor to replace Washington as commander in chief of the Continental Army. Now one of Washington's potential rivals was essentially eliminated. General Gates, however, was not to be rejected as a serious rival to Washington until after his defeat at the Battle of Camden (August 1780) and his disgraceful personal retreat immediately thereafter.

In the spring and summer of 1778, Virginia sponsored an expedition into the Illinois country to confront Colonel Henry Hamilton (British Lieutenant Governor at Detroit) and his Loyalist-Indian allies who were raiding American frontier settlements. With an army of some 175 frontier-hardened Virginian militiamen, Clark boldly attacked, and, with the help of the French inhabitants who were told that France was now an ally of America, occupied Kaskaskia on July 4th and then several other nearby French settlements including Vincennes. In mid-December, Hamilton retook Vincennes with a mixed force of British regulars and Indian allies. In February 1779, Clark led a force of some 150 veterans from Kaskaskia to Vincennes, where he convinced the Indians to desert Hamilton, therefore leaving the British little choice but to surrender to the determined Clark. Hamilton himself was seized and taken back to Williamsburg in chains. Virginia thereafter organized the Illinois territory into its westernmost county. Although the Clark expedition of 1778 and 1779 to the Illinois country compared favorably as to the hardships endured and the courage and bravery displayed with Benedict Arnold's difficult transit across Maine in the 1776 invasion of Canada, this American incursion into the Illinois country did not significantly affect either the outcome of the war or the treaty ending the conflict.

In late 1778 and 1779, there was likewise spirited skirmishing between American settlers and loyalists and Indians in both New York and Pennsylvania. In New York, loyalist-led Native Americans terrorized several outlying settlements in the Cherry Valley. In November 1778 the marauding Indians brutally killed a large group of American settlers who had surrendered. This Cherry Valley massacre and the widespread destruction of lives and property in the Wyoming Valley of Pennsylvania by John Butler's Loyalist Rangers and pro-British Indians prompted Washington to dispatch two sizeable forces under the command of Generals John Sullivan and James Clinton with orders to attack the Iroquois tribes involved and take numerous prisoners who could be held as hostages for future good behavior.

The Sullivan/Clinton expedition was eminently successful. Throughout the summer and fall of 1779, the two American contingents swept through the Iroquois settlements destroying everything in their path. Nothing was spared. Entire Indian villages, crops, and even orchards were completely destroyed. The joint expedition effectively eliminated the Iroquois as an effective fighting force. Never again were the Iroquois able to contest, as a confederacy, the inevitable American incursions into their homeland.

After the embarrassing surrender of Burgoyne's entire invading army in October 1777, the British turned their main military focus southward. Not only was this a significant shift geographically, it also resulted in a change strategically. Having failed to "bag the sly fox" (i.e., Washington and his main Continental Army), the British strategy became one of capturing militarily and commercially important southern ports (most notably Savannah, Georgia, and Charleston, South Carolina) and other areas where, it was hoped, a sizeable Loyalist population could help maintain British authority. Believing, erroneously as it turned out, that there were large numbers of loyalists in the four southern colonies (but especially in the two Carolinas) just waiting to be liberated from what would be, from their point of view, the arbitrary and traitorous rule of the local and state rebel governments, British commander General Henry Clinton shifted operations to the Deep South. In late November 1778, Clinton dispatched a small army of just over 3,000 men under the command of Lieutenant

From *A History of the American Revolution* by John R. Alden, Copyright © 1969 by John R. Alden. Used by permission of Alfred A. Knopf, a division of Random House, Inc.

Colonel Archibald Campbell to capture the important port of Savannah, Georgia. With the help of Commodore Hyde Parker, Campbell was able to transport his troops safety past Tybee Island at the mouth of the Savannah River to Girardeau's Plantation situated just a few miles seaward from the city. General Robert Howe, the American commander in the vicinity, attempted to defend Savannah with a small force of some 700 Continentals and 200 militiamen. Confronted by the superior British force, Howe ordered a retreat on December 29th across the Musgrove Swamp causeway. However, the British had arrived at the causeway before the retreating Americans and proceeded to kill, wound, or capture over half of Howe's fleeing army. With the fall of Savannah, the British were able to reassert their authority over most of the state of Georgia. Although American commander Robert Howe was blamed for the humiliating loss of Savannah, a formal court of inquiry exonerated him of any wrongdoing. However, his loss of Savannah effectively ended his military career.

During 1779, there were numerous minor battles, frequently between American partisans and American Loyalists, as the British attempted to widen their control over the two Carolinas and Georgia. By the end of January Campbell had followed his occupation of Savannah by capturing Augusta, thereby solidifying British control of the Savannah River. In mid-February an American militia force under guerrilla leader Colonel Andrew Pickens defeated a Loyalist brigade in the Battle of Kettle Creek, Georgia.

In the early fall the Americans, with massive French aid, made a concerted effort to recapture Savannah. French admiral Jean Baptiste d'Estaing sailed to the mouth of the Savannah River with a fleet of 35 ships and over 4,000 troops with the intention of laying siege to British General Augustine Prevost's 3,000-man garrison. Soon 1,500 Continentals, under the command of General Benjamin Lincoln, joined the French in besieging Savannah. The French admiral's stated intention to withdraw his troops and ships in mid-October to avoid the hurricane season prompted a premature Franco-American attack, which failed miserably. French-American losses exceeded 800 (almost 20 percent of the attacking force) while British losses were estimated to be fewer than 200. Among the allied casualties were d'Estaing (wounded) and the Polish nobleman Count Casimir Pulaski (killed). The Americans blamed this failure to recapture Savannah on d'Estaing's early departure before the siege could be formally and therefore successfully completed. D'Estaing had once again, as he had during the Franco-American siege of Newport, Rhode Island, in the summer of

1778, removed his ships and troops in the midst of the fighting, therefore dooming the attack to failure. D'Estaing's timidity (or was it his cautious prudence?) convinced many Americans of the inefficacy of French military and naval aid. After the repulse at Savannah, General Lincoln led the remaining American force northward to Charleston, South Carolina, where he took command of the American defense of the South's largest and most important city.

In late December 1779, leaving a sufficient force to defend New York City against Washington's main Patriot army, British Commander in Chief General Henry Clinton led an 8,000-man army southward to the South Carolina coast where it joined the troops already there to make a force of over 14,000 men. By late spring of 1780 the British had skillfully laid siege to Charleston. With naval superiority and a large, well-equipped army, Clinton captured Fort Moultrie in Charleston harbor on May 6th, which made inevitable the capitulation of the entire city six days later (May 12, 1780). Lincoln's entire garrison of over 5,000 troops surrendered in what would be the gravest, most humiliating American defeat of the war. British losses were minimal. Seemingly, the British were succeeding in their plan to capture and occupy the main southern ports, which would, it was thought, give them control of the entire colony. With the widely heralded capture of Charleston, Clinton returned to New York to confront Washington's army, leaving Lord Cornwallis with 8,000 soldiers to solidify British control of South Carolina.

Until the arrival of General Horatio Gates, with a detachment of Continentals from Washington's army, in the South in late July 1780, the British hold on South Carolina and Georgia seemed secure. Only the harassment of British supply lines and depots by the increasingly active American guerrilla bands led by Francis Marion ("the Swamp Fox"—so nicknamed because he seemed to appear suddenly out of the swamp to attack British patrols and supply trains), Andrew Pickens, and Thomas Sumter prevented the complete subjugation of the South Carolina hinterland. With a total force of some 4,000 (Continentals, militiamen, and "over mountain" frontiersmen), Gates, appointed American commander of the southern theater by Congress over the opposition of Washington, who would have preferred Nathanael Greene as his southern commander, undertook the task of integrating the various guerrilla bands of Marion, Pickens, and Sumter with his Continental units into a force strong enough to first challenge Cornwallis's marauding forces in the interior and then to recapture Charleston.

By August 1780, Gates had decided to move against the British supply depot at Camden, South Carolina. Cornwallis's force of some 2,400
men confronted Gates's attacking force just north of the city early on
August 16th. Sustaining heavy casualties, the Americans suffered defeat
in the ensuing largely European-style battle, which favored the disciplined
tactics of Cornwallis's professional army and which at the same time made
ineffectual the guerrilla tactics preferred by the American militiamen (especially the riflemen). The American defeat soon became a rout when
Colonel Banastre Tarleton's saber-wielding dragoons attacked the American rear. The Battle of Camden was a disastrous American defeat. Gates
had been clearly outmaneuvered and outfought. American losses exceeded
2,000 (approximately 1,000 killed or wounded and 1,000 captured);
British casualties were about 400. The most famous of the American casualties was the giant Baron Johann de Kalb, who died three days after
the battle from the eleven wounds received while leading his division of
Maryland and Delaware Continentals. During and after this devastating
setback, Gates not only demonstrated great incompetence, but he also
displayed apparent cowardice. He left his defeated army and hurriedly
traveled, in just three days, the 160 miles to Hillsboro, North Carolina.
Gates's ignominious defeat at Camden greatly tarnished what was up to
that time clearly an undeserved reputation as a brilliant field commander
because of his victory at the Battle of Saratoga. In mid-October, Nathanael
Greene replaced the discredited and possibly cowardly Gates as the American commander of the South. It would be the capable Greene who would,
without actually winning outright a single battle, drive Cornwallis out of
the Carolinas into Virginia and to eventual defeat at Yorktown.

Intermittently during 1780 and 1781, there were bloody skirmishes
between the British with their loyalist compatriots and the guerrilla units
of Marion, Pickens, and Sumter. These encounters often pitted relatives
against relatives and neighbors against neighbors and were therefore frequently among the bloodiest clashes of the entire war. Although usually
involving only a small number of combatants, these guerrilla attacks convinced the British to establish a series of frontier outposts that would en-
able them to maintain control over the interior. The Americans had mixed
success in attacking these outposts. Although defeated or repulsed at Fishing Creek, Hobkirk's Hill, Ninety-Six, and Eutaw Springs, the Americans
were able, primarily by attacking and capturing British supply columns,
to force the British back to the Charleston area.

After what he thought was a decisive victory at Camden over the main American army of the South, Cornwallis led his army northward for an invasion of North Carolina. A Loyalist unit of some 1,100 men under the command of British Major Patrick Ferguson who was protecting Cornwallis's left flank was confronted by a militia force led by Colonel Isaac Shelby, Colonel William Campbell, and the leader of the "over mountain men," Colonel John Sevier, at King's Mountain, South Carolina, which was just south of the North Carolina–South Carolina border. Ferguson had aroused frontier resentment against the British by issuing proclamations that claimed that the rebellion had been crushed in the interior regions of South Carolina, and then had demanded that the patriot population (especially the "over mountain men" who inhabited the area west of the mountain in what is today Tennessee) cease in their resistance to British arms and take oaths of allegiance to the British crown. If they continued to resist, Ferguson claimed that he would hang the rebellious leaders and lay waste their scattered western settlements.

Ferguson's threat prompted hundreds of "over mountain men" under the command of John Sevier (later to be elected the first governor of the state of Tennessee) to join the Piedmont militia groups under Shelby and Campbell. The ensuing Battle of King's Mountain (October 7, 1780) was to be one of the bloodiest encounters of the southern theater. For one thing, most of the combatants on both sides were Americans. For many participants, the fighting had as much to do with long-standing and/or existing feuds and rivalries between neighbors and even relatives as it did with the larger Anglo-American contest over the issue of American independence.

At every turn, the American rebel leaders and their rifle-toting frontier marksmen out-maneuvered and out-fought the Ferguson-led loyalist troops. Ferguson, who was interestingly the only non-American on either side, displayed an uncharacteristic incompetence in the Battle of King's Mountain. In this battle, he made the first mistake by allowing his force to be encircled on top of King's Mountain, which was a rocky, relatively flat ridge with heavily wooded approaches. Second, he ordered his men to counter the American assaults with bayonet counterattacks. The attacking American marksmen, first on one side and then all four sides, quickly decimated the poorly entrenched loyalist forces, killing a high percentage of the opposing officer corps and then forcing the survivors into surrendering after only an hour's fighting. While American casualties were light (approximately 25 killed and 60 wounded), the British lost their entire force (some 150 killed, 160 wounded, and over 600 captured). The dramatic American victory at the Battle of King's Mountain was the turning point in the southern phase of the War for American Independence. The relatively ill-trained Americans demonstrated the superiority of guerrilla tactics over European-style fighting in wooded, rocky areas like King's Mountain. Moreover, the Americans displayed a bravery and courageousness in battle that perhaps compensated for their lack of formal military training and battle experience. Most importantly, the patriot victory tilted the balance between loyalist and patriot in favor of the patriot. The loyalists in the south suffered irreparably as a result of their humiliating defeat at the hands of their fellow countrymen at the Battle of King's Mountain. This British defeat forced Cornwallis's army to abandon its planned invasion of North Carolina and retreat back, at least temporarily, into winter quarters in South Carolina.

As the new American commander in the southern theater, General Nathanael Greene, as yet not strong enough to attack Cornwallis's main army, resorted to guerrilla tactics in the areas between Cornwallis's main encampment at Winnsborough and Charleston to stop the flow of reinforcements and supplies. In mid-January Greene specifically ordered General Daniel Morgan and his riflemen and Colonel Henry Lee and his elite cavalry unit to intercept the wagon trains the British desperately needed to sustain their presence in the interior.

To counter Greene's moves, Lord Cornwallis ordered Banastre "No Quarter" (so nicknamed after troops under his command, in the spring of 1780, offered "no quarter" by slaughtering a group of American militiamen who had surrendered) Tarleton to lead his mounted dragoons against Morgan's riflemen and force them back into the main British army. With his army situated between the main American army under Greene and Morgan's raiders, Cornwallis believed he now had an excellent opportunity to annihilate Morgan's small force, thus eliminating the damaging assaults on his supply columns. Trapped as he would soon become and in anticipation of upcoming battle, Morgan assumed a defensive position at Hannah's Cowpens, South Carolina. Consisting of a mixture of experienced Continentals under the command of Colonel William Washington and Colonel John Eager Howard and frontier-hardened militia units led by Andrew Pickens, Morgan's troops were deployed with great care. He placed Georgian militiamen along the first line with orders to fire twice and then retreat to a predetermined place behind the second line manned by Pickens's guerrilla force. This second line was to fire twice, targeting primarily British officers, and retreat along the side and behind the third American line, which consisted of Howard's Continentals. Colonel Washington's light infantry and dragoons were held out as a reserve force with orders to mount a charge around the British left flank when the British had broken through the first two lines of apparently retreating and disorganized militiamen. Although there was great confusion on both sides during the one-hour battle, the American tactics of firing and then retreating to take up firing positions again baffled the British into thinking initially that they had won a spectacular victory when in reality they charged in disorderly fashion into the withering fire. The Battle of Cowpens, although a spectacular American victory, did not deter Cornwallis from accepting Greene's challenge of yet another battle, this time between the main British and American armies. British losses at Cowpens (over 300 killed and wounded and 600 captured) were irreplaceable. The American casualties were under 10 percent of the 800 engaged.

Even after Cowpens, Cornwallis was determined to destroy Greene's main southern army and then travel northward into Virginia, where he hoped to hook up with units from General Clinton's New York army and subdue Virginia, thereby crushing the rebellion. Greene also seemed eager to commit his army, now a reinforced force of some 4,400 men, to battle. Thus both commanders were ready to commit to a major encounter. Greene deployed his troops in defensive positions at Guilford Courthouse, North Carolina, seemingly daring Cornwallis to attack. Although outnumbered two-to-one, the confident British general led his 1,900 seasoned troopers in costly assaults against the American positions. During a crucial time in what became a hand-to-hand melee, Cornwallis ordered his cannoneers to fire into the midst of the battling troops, killing and wounding scores of soldiers from both sides. This cannonade helped to convince Greene that he should avoid further bloodshed, and he ordered an orderly retreat. The Battle of Guilford Courthouse (March 15, 1781) was technically a British victory in that Cornwallis won the field. However, Cornwallis suffered heavy, irreplaceable losses. One-fourth of the British combatants were casualties (almost 100 killed and over 400 wounded). American losses were approximately 75 killed and 180 wounded. Greene's strategy in fighting a war of attrition would eventually force Cornwallis out of the Carolinas and into Virginia, where he would face eventual defeat at the hands of the large Franco-American army at Yorktown.

In April 1781 Cornwallis marched his army northward to Virginia, where he hoped to join a sizeable force to be detached from General Clinton's New York garrison. Together this enlarged army would join forces with Virginia Loyalists to destroy the American forces there. This would be followed with the reassertion of British control in Virginia and then possibly would bring the rebellion to a successful conclusion. With his army now numbering something over 7,500 men, Cornwallis was ordered to establish a defensive fortified position either in the Norfolk area or at the tip of the peninsula between the York River and the James River abutting the Chesapeake Bay. With British naval superiority in the adjacent coastal areas and in the Chesapeake Bay, Cornwallis's choice of Yorktown seemed to be the proper one. He entrenched his army behind an elaborate system of redoubts and trenches and awaited the Franco-American siege.

Meanwhile, Washington was planning a joint Franco-American attack against Henry Clinton. In fact, Washington's main focus during much of the war was recapturing New York City. In a meeting with French Commander General Jean Baptiste Rochambeau at Wethersfield, Connecticut, in late May of 1781, Washington secured the reluctant approval of the French general for an attack against New York City. This coordinated attack was to be aided by the French West Indian fleet under the command of Comte Francois de Grasse. In his orders to de Grasse, however, Rochambeau gave the French admiral the choice of sailing to New York or to the Virginia Capes. De Grasse sent word to Rochambeau that he would lead his fleet, with 3,000 French soldiers, to the Chesapeake Bay in late August 1781 and would remain there until late October. Washington and Rochambeau thereupon scrapped their plans to attack New York City and moved their respective armies south through Philadelphia, across the Potomac River, and into Virginia. Their goal was to besiege and then destroy or capture Cornwallis's entire army. Washington left a sufficient number of troops around New York City to fool General Clinton into thinking Washington's entire army was still there.

With the arrival of Rochambeau's army and de Grasse's fleet with its 3,000 soldiers, the French contingent in the siege of Yorktown numbered something over 8,000 troops. When Washington added his army to the forces under Lafayette, von Steuben, and Wayne already in the Virginia tidewater, the American force numbered over 11,000. Thus the combined Franco-American army greatly outnumbered Cornwallis's entrenched army of something over 7,000 men by over a two-to-one margin.

Although greatly outnumbered, Cornwallis could, however, hold out as long as the British controlled the sea approaches to Yorktown. The British did enjoy naval superiority in American waters for most of the war. However, for a brief time in early September 1781, French admiral Comte de Grasse's fleet gained control of the mouth of the Chesapeake Bay. In the little-known but highly significant Battle of the Chesapeake Bay Capes of September 5th, de Grasse's French fleet bloodied, but did not destroy the British fleet under Admiral Thomas Graves in what can be considered in naval terms an indecisive encounter. However, when French Admiral Barras arrived from Newport, Rhode Island, with his small flotilla three days later, the combined French fleet gave the French a numerical advantage over Graves's badly damaged squadron. Thereupon, the overly cautious Graves, for reasons not fully understood even today, sailed for New York for repairs, leaving the French fleet in control of the Chesapeake Bay. Graves's departure, of course, doomed Cornwallis's command. Surrounded by a French fleet on the waterside and a large Franco-American army on land, Cornwallis's only hope for survival was for General Henry Clinton to send a relief army southward from New York City. Belatedly, Clinton did send a 7,000-man force to Cornwallis's aid. Unfortunately for Cornwallis, this relief expedition arrived at the entrance to the Chesapeake Bay on October 24th; exactly five days after his mortifying surrender at Yorktown on October 19th.

The successful Franco-American siege at Yorktown was the result of cooperation and coordination rarely achieved among the French navy, the French army, and Washington's American army. The French admirals de Grasse and Barras, French general Rochambeau, and of course George Washington planned and executed with rare unanimity the combined military and naval campaign, which resulted in Cornwallis's surrender, thus effectively ending the military phase of the American War for Independence.

The siege of Yorktown formally began in early October, 1781. Without British control of the sea approaches to his beleaguered army, Cornwallis's only two hopes for survival were either to break out across the half-mile-wide York River to Gloucester and then make his way northward up the Delmarva Peninsula to join General Clinton in New York, or to hold out until Clinton's relief expedition arrived. Flight northward was attempted on the night of October 16th, but a sudden storm and high winds made the water passage across the York River to Gloucester impossible or at least extremely hazardous. To the end, however, Cornwallis clung to the hope that a relief force from Clinton, which he had heard was enroute from New York, would arrive in time to break the Franco-American siege.

Initially Cornwallis had constructed an outer and an inner line of defensive fortifications. On September 30th, he somewhat inexplicably abandoned the outer fortification line, thus allowing the allies to bring up siege cannons capable of bombarding his entire encampment. His explanation for this abandonment, written later, was that because he was expecting help from Clinton, he wanted to make sure the numerically superior Allied army would not be able to encircle and/or demolish the thinned British ranks manning the outer defenses. By constricting his defensive entrenchments, Cornwallis hoped to consolidate his outnumbered force and thus save it from annihilation while awaiting the arrival of desperately hoped-for reinforcements. Cornwallis's plight became critical when, on the night of October 14th, a French force attacked and captured Redoubt Number Nine, with heavy losses for the attackers, and an American assault unit, under the command of Lt. Colonel Alexander Hamilton, overran Redoubt Number Ten. With the loss of these two defensive bastions, Cornwallis became convinced of the futility of continued bloodshed. In mid-morning of October 17th, a drummer appeared and then a British officer carrying a white flag. The officer carried a message from Cornwallis to Washington proposing a twenty-four-hour truce to work out the precise terms of surrender. Washington replied that he would only agree to a two-hour cession of hostilities for the British proposal of surrender. Around 4:00 P.M. the British proposal arrived at Washington's headquarters. The next morning, commissioners from both armies met at the Moore House to work out the final details of the British surrender. In the early afternoon of October 19th, the British troops marched out and laid down their arms. They were later sent off to prison camps in Virginia, Maryland, and Pennsylvania.

An interesting, almost comical matter of military etiquette occurred when Lord Cornwallis, pleading illness, sent his second-in-command General Charles O'Hara to offer his sword (the official final act of surrendering) to the French Commander Comte de Rochambeau. With great savoir faire, the French general directed O'Hara in French to surrender his sword to the Allied Commander General George Washington. After hearing his halting apology for this apparent breach of surrender etiquette, Washington ordered Cornwallis's second-in-command General Charles

O'Hara to surrender to Washington's second-in-command General Benjamin Lincoln. This must have been sweet retribution for Lincoln, who carried the onus of being the American commander who surrendered Charleston to the British back in May of 1780.

The Battle of Yorktown was the crowning American military achievement of the war. With minimum battle casualties (under 200 Americans killed and wounded and a slightly higher figure for the French), the Allied army, under the command of the former Virginia militia officer, had not only defeated but also captured an entire British professional army. Throughout the siege, the British casualties numbered about 600 killed and wounded. When the British crown learned, on November 25th, of the humiliating surrender at Yorktown, King George III finally became convinced of the futility of pursuing what had clearly become an unwinnable war. He dismissed his long-suffering Prime Minister Lord North with hardly a word of thanks for his twelve years of faithful and loyal service in carrying out the King's prewar policies of intimidation and coercion and in directing the war effort to subdue the colonial revolt. Although General Washington did not realize it at the time, the Battle of Yorktown was the last major military confrontation of the war. The British still, however, maintained strong garrisons in Charleston, Savannah, and Wilmington, North Carolina, in the south and New York City in the north. The Yorktown defeat led directly to diplomatic overtures that eventually led to the highly favorable Treaty of Paris of 1783 in which Britain recognized American independence.

Although unable to destroy the Continental Army and thereby quell the American rebellion on land, the British did, however, enjoy naval supremacy throughout the period 1775–1783. In fact, it was this naval predominance that enabled the British to wage and sustain a large-scale land war thousands of miles from home for over seven long years. At the beginning of hostilities in 1775, the British navy consisted of some 270 ships (of which approximately 130 were ships of the line). By the conclusion of the war, the navy had grown to over 460 ships (of which 100 saw service in American waters). These figures indicate that Britain had numerical superiority over any single adversary. However, by 1780 when the United Provinces, Spain, and France had joined in the war on the American side, Great Britain was forced to retain a large fleet in European waters to thwart a possible Franco-Spanish invasion of the homeland, and to maintain a sizeable naval presence in the Caribbean to protect her valuable sugar colonies. Despite these heavy demands on her maritime resources, Britain was able, with her naval superiority, to keep her size-able military force in America well supplied by sea, to bottle up several French fleets sent to aid the colonies, and to capture and occupy most of the more strategic American seaports along the east coast of North America. Thus, at one time or another, Britain occupied Newport, Rhode Island; Philadelphia, Pennsylvania; Norfolk, Virginia; Wilmington, North Carolina; Charleston, South Carolina; and Savannah, Georgia. Moreover, from 1776 on, she occupied New York City, making that well situated port her army headquarters in America. However, Britain never effectively uti-lized what was clearly her naval superiority to full advantage.

The small American navy created by the Continental Congress in 1775, the several state navies (most notably that of Massachusetts), and the hundreds of American privateers all were unable to challenge openly British control of American waters. However, American ships, especially the privateers, destroyed or captured over 700 British vessels of varying tonnages, thus forcing up insurance premiums at an alarming rate. By the end of the conflict, British merchants, especially those who had been hit the hardest by these American assaults on their overseas commerce, were in the vanguard of those advocating a cessation of hostilities.

Privateers were a blessing and a curse to the American cause—a blessing because they did at times impede British trade, particularly be-tween the mother country and her Caribbean colonies, although never to the point of serious disruption. Authorized by letters of Marque and Re-prisal from Congress and from state governments to prey on enemy ship-ping, privateers were, at times, a curse because thousands of able-bodied American young men chose to serve as privateers and were not, therefore, available for service in Washington's Army or the Continental Navy. Motivated primarily by personal greed (privateer seamen shared in the prize money obtained from captured ships), privateers were nothing more than an irritant to the British.

Although the small Continental Navy could never challenge the British control of the seas, it could and did challenge British seamanship. In several famous single-ship encounters, American crews proved to be the equal of or superior to their British counterparts in matters of gun-nery, general seamanship, navigation, and courage and bravery.

The two most celebrated American naval exploits of the entire war both involved the seafaring Scotsman John Paul Jones. Of the many naval heroes, he stands out as the most famous and indeed the most successful

American ship captain. Born to relative obscurity, he ran off to sea at the age of twelve. First as a cabin boy on a trans-Atlantic merchant vessel and then later as an able-bodied seaman and chief mate of a Jamaica-owned slave ship, John Paul Jones learned quickly and thoroughly the basics of seamanship. In 1768, at the age of twenty-one, his skill and boldness as a seaman were duly recognized when he was appointed captain of a brigantine that made numerous trans-Atlantic trips between England and the British West Indies in the years just preceding the outbreak of the American War for Independence.

In 1775 John Paul Jones was appointed a senior lieutenant, and then in August 1776 a captain in the newly created Continental Navy. His first notable exploit was as captain of the newly built *Ranger*. In 1778 he fearlessly sailed into the Irish Sea between Ireland and Scotland and audaciously went ashore at Whitehaven near his Scottish birthplace with the intention of seizing the local lord as a hostage. Although Lord Selkirk was absent and thus was able to avoid capture, this daring raid demonstrated the inability of the British navy to protect its homeland from such bothersome hit-and-run raids. During this spectacular expedition, Jones also commandeered a number of prizes and in a hotly contested encounter, defeated a British warship. Upon his return to the French port of Brest, Jones and his crew were honored as heroes. The French then asked him to lead yet another small naval flotilla into British waters. With his flagship the *Bon Homme Richard* (an old French East India merchant vessel) and several smaller ships, Jones set out in mid-August of 1779 and sailed completely around the British Isles, taking dozens of British prizes and causing near panic in British ports now, for the first time, deemed vulnerable to attack.

It was during this raid that John Paul Jones fought one of the most famous naval engagements in history. On September 23, 1779, just off of the east coast of Yorkshire, England, the *Bon Homme Richard* (forty-two guns) met and after a fierce three-and-a-half-hour battle finally defeated the British warship *Serapis* (fifty-four guns). It was a classic encounter pitting two capable, experienced sea captains against each other. Because the *Serapis* was larger and better armed than the American ship, Jones maneuvered his ship in close alongside of his opponent. After bitter hand-to-hand and gun-to-gun combat, the mast of the *Serapis* fell and the British captain surrendered. The *Bon Homme Richard* came out of this encounter so badly damaged (she sank two days after the battle) that Jones abandoned her and transferred his flag to the captured British ship. As a result of this daring victory over a British man-of-war in British waters, John Paul Jones was deservedly honored as America's master naval tactician. His boldness and success, at times against seemingly overwhelming odds, demonstrated the vulnerability of the vaunted British navy. However, as spectacular as some of these single-ship American victories were, they did not greatly affect the course of the naval war or interfere seriously with Britain's overwhelming naval supremacy during the Revolutionary War.

In reviewing the military and naval aspects of the American Revolution, it remains obvious that the waging of a war was essential in finally convincing the British to acquiesce in the heretofore-unthinkable idea of granting the rebellious American colonies their political independence from the mother country. For thousands of Americans, the wartime experience of fighting against a common enemy for freedom, liberty, and equality was a necessary and unifying step along the road to stable and lasting political independence and unification—goals that were finally achieved in 1789 with the promulgation of the Constitution drawn up in 1787. The young American Republic was, in essence, conceived and nurtured, in part at least, on the many, blood-soaked battlefields of the Revolutionary War.

Notes

1. There are eminent scholars who disagree completely with my interpretation that the colonists did not win, nor lose, the Revolutionary War militarily. In a recent informative survey of the more significant revolutionary battles, the author's main contention, which pervades the entire generally well-researched book, was that the Americans did more than just outlast the British. He states that the Americans won the military contest with superior strategy and tactics. William J. Wood, *Battles of the Revolutionary War, 1775–1781*. New York: DaCapo Press, 1995.

2. Stated battle casualty figures are always suspect. For the most reliable estimates of battlefield casualties, see Howard H. Peckham, editor, *The Toll of Independence: Engagements & Battle Casualties of the American Revolution*. Chicago: The University of Chicago Press, 1974, 3.

3. The text of this treaty of alliance can be conveniently found in Henry Steele Commager and Milton Cantor, editors, *Documents of American History*. Englewood Cliffs, N.J.: Prentice Hall, 1988, Tenth Edition, I, 105–107.

The Bloody Massacre, engraving by Paul Revere (1770). Library of Congress.

John Dickinson, portrait by C. W. Peale (1770). Library of Congress.

Declaration of Independence, painting by John Trumbull (1786). Library of Congress.

General Washington Firing the First Gun, engraving by Henry Alexander Ogden (between 1910 and 1930). Library of Congress.

Death of General Montgomery at Quebec, painting by John Trumbull (1778). Library of Congress.

The Signing of the Treaty of Amity and Commerce and of Alliance, painting by Charles E. Mills. Library of Congress.

Surrender of Lord Cornwallis, painting by John Trumbull (1824). Library of Congress.

CHAPTER 4

THE HOME FRONT

The American Revolution brought about many significant changes in the lives of most Americans. The most notable and obvious changes were, of course, the gaining of political independence from Great Britain and the creation of new American republics (national and state). However, less dramatically, the Revolution brought about or witnessed other changes—some noticeable and noteworthy, some not readily apparent.

On the home front, the Revolution altered the role of women. Women, at all levels of society, assumed additional domestic duties and responsibilities. With thousands of men leaving home to serve in the military or on ships, women took over completely the running of households, the raising and education of children, and the running of businesses. In competing successfully in what was, in point of law and practice, a highly patriarchal society, women contributed significantly to the war effort and to the transformation of American society. Often enduring great economic hardship, inconveniences, and even physical violence, women demonstrated convincingly that they were the equal of men in terms of abilities and innate talents. Although women did not, during the Revolutionary Period, attain political or legal equality with men, the small gains achieved were perhaps a necessary first step towards reaching the long sought-after, and unfortunately still not fully achieved, goal of gender equality.

The Revolution greatly affected other segments of the American population. Native Americans suffered grievously during the Revolutionary Era. They were mistrusted and exploited by both the British and the Americans. Most Indians probably hoped that the armed conflict between whites would lead to a mutual decimation, or at least a weakening of both sides to such an extent that they would be able to reclaim or reoccupy lands lost during the colonial period or at least to slow down the western advance of land-hungry Whites. Given the improbability of mutual White destruction, most Indians sought neutrality in the war or sided with the British. Almost constant warfare between Native Americans and colonists in the colonial period had convinced the Indians that all Whites were a threat to their way of life. However, the Cherokee War in the Carolinas (1759–1761), Pontiac's War in the Middle West north of the Ohio River (1763–1764), and the Treaty of Fort Stanwix (1768) in which the Indians relinquished most claims to lands immediately south and west of the Ohio River persuaded most Indians that the American frontiersmen posed the greater threat.

Most of the Iroquois tribes (Mohawk, Onondaga, Cayuga, and Seneca) sided with the British. Influenced by the legacy of Sir William Johnson, who befriended the Iroquois (especially the Mohawks) during his tenure as Indian Agent (1755–1774) and guided by his successor, nephew Guy Johnson, over 1,500 Iroquois warriors fought on the side of the British. However, two Iroquois tribes (Oneida and Tuscarora) chose neutrality during the conflict, although a few of them did fight on the side of the rebellious colonists. Encouraged by Indian Agent Guy Johnson and Mohawk chief Joseph Brant and led by Tory Sir John Butler, the pro-British Iroquois and their Loyalist allies swept through Pennsylvania's Wyoming Valley and New York's Cherry Valley in the period 1778–1779, destroying one thousand farms and capturing one thousand head of cattle. The Wyoming and Cherry Valley "Massacres" prompted General Washington to dispatch the Sullivan-Clinton Expedition in 1778 that almost completely destroyed the Iroquois Confederacy as a viable fighting force.

In the South, the Indians were divided in their loyalty. The Catawbas and the Cherokees remained neutral or sided with the Americans, whereas the Lower Creeks were steadfastly neutral, and the Upper Creeks were mostly pro-British. In the Ohio country, profitable trade with the British and the British policy of generous present-giving (some would consider this bribery) prompted most Indians to side with the British. Also, the British allegedly intimated that they would, at the end of hostilities, reserve a large area west of the Allegheny Mountains for the Indians who supported them during the war. Although it is not known if such a promise or even such an intimation was ever actually made, the British did not, at the conclusion of fighting, establish a western Indian buffer state. As a result of the Revolution, many Indian tribes were decimated. In addition, with the coming of peace in 1783, Americans, by the thousands, moved west onto traditional Indian lands west of the mountains, causing the destruction of hundreds of Indian villages and the death of thousands of Indians. Regardless of their allegiance during the war, Native Americans suffered tragically in a conflict they did not start and in which many were pressured into a halfhearted participation.

The Revolution affected greatly the lives of most African Americans. Hundreds of Black slaves gained their freedom by serving either in the British army or in various state militias and the Continental Army or Navy. Although a sizeable number of Black slaves in Virginia responded to Lord Dunmore's Proclamation of November 1775 in which freedom was promised for those slaves who deserted their American masters, few actually gained their freedom. Many soon died of mistreatment and neglect or were sold into slavery in the Caribbean. Most Blacks were slaves, and they did not benefit immediately or directly as a result of the American Revolution. However, approximately five thousand Blacks served in the American military, and hundreds of these were slaves who were manumitted as a reward for their service.

The proclamation in the Declaration of Independence "that all men are created equal" is the most obvious manifestation of an incipient abolitionist movement during the Revolutionary Era. A growing number of white Americans saw the incongruity of fighting against alleged British denial of fundamental rights while at the same time systematically denying fundamental rights to enslaved Blacks. Other indications of antislavery sentiment included the establishment of two antislavery societies: the first by Quakers in Philadelphia in 1775 and the second in New York City in the mid-1780s. Several prominent New York revolutionaries (including Gouverneur Morris, Alexander Hamilton, and John Jay) assumed leadership roles as members of the New York Society for Promoting Manumission. Moreover, in his initial draft of the Declaration of Independence, slave owner Thomas Jefferson indicted British King George III, in an article that the Continental Congress eventually deleted at the insistence of the South Carolina and Georgia delegations, for promoting and encouraging the slave trade.

In addition, several state constitutions contained provisions for gradual emancipation of slaves. In Massachusetts, slaves were freed by a judicial interpretation of the state Constitution of 1780 that proclaimed that all men were born free. Although enacted after the conclusion of hostilities, the Northwest Ordinance of 1787 reflected growing antislavery sentiment by prohibiting slavery in the newly created Northwest Territory (present states of Michigan, Ohio, Indiana, Illinois, and Wisconsin). Although the American Revolution did not bring an end to the "peculiar institution" of Black slavery, it did plant the seeds of what would blossom into the full-fledged abolition movement of the 1830s and to the ratification of the Thirteenth Amendment to the Constitution in December of 1865.

As with all wars, the civilian population, both Black and White, experienced undue hardships, inconveniences, and occasionally outright brutality. Some of the bloodiest armed clashes involved Americans fighting Americans. Especially in areas near the contending armies, there was frequent fighting and plundering on both sides. Of necessity, both the British and the Americans had to forage for hay for the horses and for food to feed the armies. These foraging expeditions were often nothing more than plundering expeditions that resulted in the illegal seizure of civilian farm produce and livestock. The British usually, but not always, paid in pound sterling for the food and supplies they seized whereas the Americans commonly had to resort to giving almost worthless promissory notes or depreciated currency to the embattled farmers from whom they commandeered much-needed provisions. This "friendly" foraging, actually a form of taxation, enabled Washington's army to survive, especially during the difficult winter encampments of 1777 and 1779 at Morristown, New Jersey, and of 1778 at Valley Forge, Pennsylvania. The looting and foraging in the South, especially late in the war, were sometimes only a continuation of prewar antagonisms and feuds. Whether the result of immediate military necessity or of previous animosities, the policy pursued by both the Americans and the British of living off the land by plundering and foraging brought economic hardship and in some cases even physical harm to many American civilians, both patriot and loyalist, unfortunate enough to live near the battle areas.

With the publication of the Declaration of Independence in July of 1776, Americans were finally forced to take sides. However, starting as early as 1774 when the colonies adopted economic sanctions against the mother country, local patriot committees of safety were established to enforce the nonimportation, nonconsumption, and nonexportation agreements enacted by the First and Second Continental Congresses, by state legislatures, and by counties and villages at the local level and to discover those Americans who supported, with word and deed, the British side and were therefore deemed enemies to their country. Despite initial public ridicule and even ostracism and later loss of political rights, confiscation of private property, and in a few cases imprisonment and loss of life, many Americans remained steadfastly loyal to Great Britain and to the British crown. These loyalists were often from the upper levels of American society. Although it is risky to generalize in the absence of precise information about individual loyalists, most royal officials and many wealthier merchants and large landowners remained loyal to Britain; that is, many who had wealth, power, and status favored the British side because the mother country would be expected to preserve the status quo, whereas the rebellious Americans might well bring about changes that could threaten their economic, social, and political dominance. The overwhelming majority of loyalists, however, supported Britain either out of a belief that the colonies could not possibly win their independence from mighty Great Britain or out of a fear that independence would bring unwanted anarchy, lawlessness, and unbridled political and social unrest. After July 1776, all thirteen states passed laws, which required oaths of allegiance and renouncement: allegiance to the state and a renouncement of any fealty to the British monarch. These state laws requiring oaths of allegiance effectively forced most Americans into one of three broad categories: loyalists, patriots, and neutrals. The traditional view has been that one-third of the population was loyalist, one-third patriot, and one-third neutral. Recent estimates, however, have changed the formula to read less than one-third loyalist, more than one-third patriot, and one-third neutral.[1]

Most loyalists (derisively known as Tories) suffered economically, socially, and politically for their fidelity to Great Britain. The legal punishments imposed upon avowed loyalists ranged from verbal reprimand to execution. All states forbade nonjurors (i.e., persons who refused to take the oath of allegiance) to hold public office, to serve on juries, or to sue for debts. Eight states enacted laws that provided for the banishment of loyalists, five states disfranchised Tories, and in most states, at one time or another, loyalists were assessed double and even treble taxes. All the states passed laws that called for the confiscation of loyalist properties, especially of those who fled abroad or were banished. The confiscation of loyalist lands, especially in New York and the Tidewater areas of Virginia and the Carolinas, resulted in the breakup of a few large estates. However, taken altogether these confiscatory state laws did not result in a drastic redistribution of land. Frequently confiscated property reverted to the same class of people as its former owners. Moreover, it is not known with any degree of precision how much land was eventually confiscated.

Altogether over eighty thousand American loyalists left their native land, making their exit one of the biggest migrations in early American history. Nearly half of the exiled loyalist refugees went to England, Scotland, and the British West Indies (Jamaica, Bahamas, and Bermuda). Especially in the mother country, these displaced persons frequently suffered social, political, and economic ostracism. Towards the end of hostilities, the exiled Loyalists in Britain sought compensation for losses incurred as a result of their adherence to the British side. In 1783, Parliament established a Commission of Enquiry into the Losses and Services of the American Loyalists. After a thorough investigation, this commission, having received over four thousand applications for recompense, awarded a little over three million pounds sterling to some 2,200 claimants. Many loyalist refugees, however, found it feasible to migrate to nearby Canada or to the Maritime Provinces of Nova Scotia and Prince Edward Island rather than to the British Isles. They were no doubt attracted, at least in part, by the prospect of obtaining land and being able to maintain, unhampered, their allegiance to the British crown and nation. By 1784, these transplanted Americans were so numerous as to constitute a majority of the population in many parts of Nova Scotia and Prince Edward Island. Moreover, the founding of the Province of New Brunswick and its seaport, St. John, on the Bay of Fundy, in 1784, was largely the work of these displaced American loyalists.

Hundreds of the more recalcitrant loyalists suffered greatly from imprisonment, often under conditions of extreme deprivation and hardship. Imprisonment was often a death warrant because a high percentage of prisoners, on both sides, died as a result of neglect, lack of food, sickness, extremely crowded and unsanitary conditions, and sometimes even deliberate mistreatment. There were relatively few executions for loyalism per se. Most of the three score or more executions of known loyalists were for actual crimes committed and not for their fealty to Great Britain.

The extralegal or illegal forms of punishment for those who openly and defiantly declared their allegiance to Britain varied all the way from abusive verbal intimidation to the extreme of a vigilante execution. In many cases Sons of Liberty, committees of safety, or local gangs subjected loyalists to such physically and psychologically painful punishments as tarring and feathering, being dunked in a creek or river, or being ridden out of town on a wooden horse. However, most who refused to proclaim public support for the American cause were most often just ridiculed in public and forced to sign oaths of allegiance.

A large number of American loyalists escaped punishment and even public notice by keeping their views to themselves. Especially in areas away from the fighting, pro-British colonists could live unmolested. A sizeable group of colonists were able to maintain a neutral stance, especially if they did not serve in the military on either side, or if they were willing to sign, but not necessarily adhere to, an oath of allegiance when required, or if they were willing to give or sell produce to both sides, or if they appeared, by word and outward show, to be loyalists when the British army was nearby and patriots when the American army was in their vicinity. Many Americans did not want to become involved in, or did not understand, the ideological, economic, social, religious, or political disputes that precipitated the conflict; they just wanted to be left alone to live their lives without interference from either side.

The single most significant political achievement of the American Revolution was the creation of the American Republic. The official severing of political ties with Great Britain, in July of 1776, made necessary the establishment of some form of government in America to replace the repudiated imperial one in London. Actually, there were fourteen American governments established: thirteen state governments and one national. All thirteen state constitutions adopted in the Revolutionary Period, although different in detail, were based on the single underlying principle of the sovereignty of the people.

In early May 1776 Congress passed resolutions calling upon the states to establish republican governments that would replace the British provincial governments still in existence or the American revolutionary governments that had been temporarily established. Actually, four states had written and adopted constitutions even before July 4, 1776: New Hampshire (January 5, 1776), South Carolina (March 26, 1776), Virginia (June 29, 1776), and New Jersey (July 2, 1776). Altogether, between 1776 and 1788, thirteen states adopted state constitutions: one each for eleven states and two each for South Carolina (1776 and 1778) and New Hampshire (1776 and 1784). Connecticut and Rhode Island used their royal charters of 1662 and 1663, slightly amended, as their state constitutions.

All the state constitutions established republican governments. Philosophically, this meant the establishment of state governments by the consent of the governed. The basic assumption was that the people as a whole were virtuous. They would therefore choose or elect virtuous people, making tyranny impossible or at least improbable. The republicanism inherent in the state constitutions also denoted the creation of governments of limited powers. Having successfully asserted their political independence from perceived British tyranny, the revolutionaries established governments under the premise of the less government the better. Governments, it was thought, were inherently power-hungry and therefore potentially tyrannical. To protect the people's basic rights of freedom, liberty, and equality, constitutions should be written so as to delineate specifically the few limited powers governments could legally and constitutionally exercise.

In general, all state constitutions were similar. They all adhered to the principle of a separation of powers between the three branches of government (i.e., executive, legislative, and judicial). This separation resulted in a system of checks and balances in which no single branch of government could wield dominant power. Thus the rights of the people would be protected from the arbitrary exercise of governmental power, by either the executive or legislature, with constitutional restraints.

In creating governments of limited, delineated powers, the state constitutions, especially those promulgated before and immediately after July 1776, reflected, in the main, the radical political philosophy of the Declaration of Independence. Likewise, the country's first national constitution (The Articles of Confederation) reflected the prevalent distrust of unbridled governmental power so elegantly stated in the July 4th Charter of Liberty.

In the crafting of new state constitutions, the framers drew heavily upon the British model of government and on their colonial experience. The bicameral legislatures established (only Pennsylvania retained, in its exceedingly democratic constitution of 1776, the unicameral assembly first instituted by William Penn early in the seventeenth century) were similar, in structure and powers to be exercised, to the two-house assemblies of the colonial period and to the British Parliament. Fearful of unbridled democracy, the state framers established, in every state, systems of checks and balances. The lower house of assembly, representing the people and therefore the democratic element of the legislature, would check the upper house that, in most states, represented the "better sort" (i.e., the wealthy merchant class and landed gentry). In most states, the legislature was the most powerful branch of government. In eight states, the legislature actually elected the governor. Moreover, in nine states, only the lower house of assembly could originate money bills. With only a few exceptions (most notably New York and Massachusetts), the executive (designated governor in every state except Pennsylvania, which had an executive council) was weak and in nine states shared appointive power with the legislature. In nine states, the governor was elected for a term of one year. In seven, eligibility for reelection was variously limited. Significantly, the governors in nine states did not possess veto power over legislation thus ensuring executive subservience to the legislature. The fear of strong executive power, seen in most of the state constitutions, reflected the revolutionaries' view that the War for Independence was in large part a struggle against unbridled British executive (monarchical and parliamentary) power.

A democratic feature shared by ten states in their constitutions was the annual (in the case of Rhode Island and Connecticut, semiannual) election of assemblymen to the lower houses. Frequent elections and therefore continual rotation in office would, it was hoped, prevent the entrenchment of political power by an elite as had been experienced in most colonies during the colonial period under British rule.

Most states retained the property qualifications for office holding and for voting. It was thought that the ownership of land, especially in an agricultural society, gave the property owner "a stake in society" and thus ensured responsible citizenship. Another common feature of the state constitutions was the creation of an appointive, usually independent judiciary. In New Hampshire, judges were appointed for seven years, in Connecticut and Rhode Island for five years, and in eight states for one year. In most states, judges served their appointed terms with tenure for good behavior, thus ensuring at least a modicum of judicial independence.

Twelve state constitutions (Connecticut's amended colonial charter did not originally have a specific list of rights) contained, in some form or another, bills of rights. The Virginia declaration of rights, drafted by George Mason and adopted June 13, 1776, served as a model for state bills of rights and later for the national bill of rights formally adopted in 1791. The rights usually enumerated included protections against self-incrimination, unlawful arrest, excessive fines and bail, cruel and unusual punishment, and general search warrants (Writs of Assistance). In addition, most state bills of rights guaranteed the right to vote for those who met the various property, gender, and religious (rarely enforced) qualifications, to trial by jury, to freedom of speech, to freedom of the press, and to freedom of religion and conscience.

The drafting and promulgation of written state constitutions was well under way before the adoption of the country's first national constitution. Thus when Congress adopted the Articles of Confederation in November 1777, the constitutional framers had completed the creation of the first or at least one of the first viable federal systems of government in which political power was formally divided between the states at the local level and a central government at the national level. However, the pre–American Revolution Iroquois Confederacy could be considered an early version of a practical federal system and thus claim the honor of being the first to implement such a governmental arrangement. A workable federal system of government, first inaugurated either by the Iroquois or by the American Revolutionaries, has become one of America's major contributions to the science of government.

The country's first national constitution, the Articles of Confederation and Perpetual Union, reflected, in constitutional form, the democratic, radical spirit inherent in the Declaration of Independence. The fear of a strong, arbitrary central government (which most revolutionaries considered the British government to be) prompted the framers (most notably John Dickinson) to create a governmental system under which political power was defused and finite. All governments, it was felt, were potentially oppressive. However, the limited powers to be given should go primarily to the states, since they were more responsive to the will of the people than a faraway national government would be.

A third part of Richard Henry Lee's famous June 7, 1776, motion urging independence called for the drafting of a plan of confederation. Pursuant to that motion, Congress, on June 12, 1776, established a committee of thirteen to draft the country's first national constitution. As chairman of that committee, John Dickinson, the leader of those in Congress who favored union before independence, wrote an initial draft. However, the radicals (primarily the Adams-Lee faction) successfully pushed through Congress the July 2nd motion calling for independence and the July 4th motion that adopted the Declaration of Independence before serious congressional consideration of Dickinson's draft of a plan of confederation could be undertaken. After resolving the independence issue, Congress took up consideration of Dickinson's initial draft. After spirited debate, this draft was rejected because of the fear of many congressmen of establishing any national government with more than the power to debate. For the next sixteen months, there were desultory congressional debates on the issue of union. Finally on November 15, 1777, after learning of the American victory at Saratoga and after considering a number of amendments to earlier drafts, Congress accepted the Articles of Confederation. Ratification, however, required the approval of all thirteen states. The document was finally ratified when Maryland, upon learning that Virginia had agreed to surrender to Congress its land claims north and west of the Ohio River, accepted the Articles on March 1, 1781.

Symbolically, there were thirteen articles to the young American republic's first national constitution. In essence, the Articles ratified the form of government that had evolved during the early life of the Second Continental Congress and was therefore already in place. They established a weak, one branch (legislature) national government. This one branch (Congress) was given a long list of powers that included the power to make war and peace, to enter into treaties and alliances, to maintain an army and navy, to ask the states for money, to borrow money, to emit bills of credit, to settle boundary and land disputes between states, to establish a postal system, and to manage Indian affairs.

Significantly and purposefully, Congress was not given the power to tax or to regulate trade and commerce. Moreover, it was not given the power to enforce its laws. Experience soon showed that the failure to include these three significant powers plus the absence of a system of national courts rendered the national government incapable of dealing successfully with the manifold problems it faced at the conclusion of the War for Independence. The requirement that amendments to the Articles needed the approval of all thirteen states meant the document would rarely if ever be amended. This inflexibility was one of the reasons why the Articles were replaced, after only eight years, by the more flexible Constitution of 1787. Do its short life and its apparent weaknesses mean the government established by the Articles of Confederation was a failure?

Quite to the contrary, it can be argued that the government established by the Articles of Confederation was a necessary and maybe even inevitable step between colonial status under the British and independence as an enduring new world republic. The Confederation Period (1781–1789) was a time of constitutional experimentation. The concepts in the

Articles that were found to be unworkable or inappropriate, such as with-holding the power to tax and regulate trade and making it virtually im-possible to amend, were either discarded or ignored when the Founding Fathers wrote the country's second constitution in 1787. On the other hand, those ideas in the Articles that were found to be sensible and ser-viceable were retained, albeit sometimes in slightly altered form, in the Constitution of 1787. The Articles of Confederation, along with the Dec-laration of Independence, reflected the early radicalism of the American Revolution. The nation's first constitution was the practical implementa-tion of many of the democratic ideals of the better-known Declaration of Independence. Inherent in the Articles of Confederation were such con-cepts, initially articulated in the Declaration, as that government was a necessary evil and, if left unchecked, would be oppressive and arbitrary; governments should rule only by the consent of the governed; and gov-ernments should be given only clearly specified limited power.

The constitutions of the Revolutionary Era were, at least in part, the implementation of a philosophy that combined the best from the British and colonial past with several essentially new ideas (such as government by the consent of the governed and the right of revolution) to produce what is sometimes referred to as the American Revolutionary Philosophy. This revolutionary philosophy has become the most enduring legacy of the American Revolution.

Note

1. William H. Nelson, *The American Tory*. Boston: Beacon Press, 1960, pp. 91–92.

CHAPTER 5

REVOLUTIONARY DIPLOMACY

The winning of American independence was a diplomatic triumph of the first order. Against seemingly insurmountable obstacles, American diplomats were able to obtain badly needed military supplies and money from Great Britain's ancient Bourbon foes, France and Spain, and to negotiate two timely loans, in 1781 and 1782, with Dutch bankers. Of greater consequence, however, the inexperienced American diplomats were able to negotiate two treaties with France that greatly helped to ensure success in the War for American Independence and gave the almost bankrupt American Republic much-needed commercial and financial help. The February 1778 signing of a Treaty of Amity and Commerce and a Treaty of Alliance with France represented the crowning diplomatic achievement of the entire revolutionary period.

This triumph of American diplomacy convinced the British ministry to change drastically its war aims. When France, and later Spain and the United Provinces, entered the conflict against her, Great Britain saw the folly of an all-out war against America when her European enemies posed the more immediate and greater military and economic threat. After 1778, Britain focused increasingly on defeating the French, Dutch, and Spanish in the Caribbean and on defending the home island from a possible (although not probable) Franco-Spanish invasion.

Although the American colonists would have achieved their independence from Great Britain even without French military and financial aid, these two treaties, but especially the Treaty of Alliance, by changing the war from a family squabble between mother country and colonies into a worldwide conflict between longtime enemies, hastened the process that led to the advantageous Treaty of Paris (1783).[1] For Great Britain the

American War for Independence became a sideshow to the larger conflict with France and Spain. What started out as a colonial independence movement became, after 1778, another episode in what could be considered "The Second Hundred Years' War, 1689–1763" (the First Hundred Years' War was a series of conflicts fought between 1337 and 1453, always with Britain and France as adversaries).

Initial American diplomatic efforts predated the Declaration of Independence. In late November 1775, Congress appointed a five-member committee (the most prominent member was the renowned Dr. Benjamin Franklin) with wide discretionary powers to contact possible friends abroad. It was well understood that the contacts to be made would be with France and Spain. In December, Congress appointed Arthur Lee, who had been serving as an agent for Massachusetts in London, as its first unofficial diplomatic representative abroad and appropriated $3,000 for his discretionary use. In March 1776, Congress sent Silas Deane of Connecticut as its first accredited overseas diplomat to Paris with instructions to work with Arthur Lee in purchasing much-needed supplies and a few months later added Benjamin Franklin as the third member of its overseas diplomatic team. As a result of the lobbying efforts of the Americans, most opportunely in early May, the French King, Louis XVI, ordered that one million livres' worth of munitions and military supplies be handed over to the Americans through a fictitious commercial firm, Roderique Hortalez and Company, a company headed by the French playwright and bon vivant Pierre de Beaumarchais. This timely French aid represented the first of many diplomatic achievements for the American diplomats.

With Franklin, who arrived in Paris in December 1776, came specific instructions for the soon-to-be-squabbling American diplomats. The commission was first to secure French recognition of American independence. Following formal French recognition, the Americans were to negotiate a favorable commercial treaty and a treaty of alliance with France. Finally, they were instructed to obtain additional French aid.

The congressional instructions were, however, so ambiguously worded as to leave in doubt the exact nature of the French aid being sought. Was this French aid to be a gift or a loan? Disagreement over this issue led to unseemly squabbling among the American commissioners and a serious split in Congress. The ensuing Silas Deane–Arthur Lee Affair brought credit to neither side, but did highlight the first significant split in the original American patriotic leadership.

Arthur Lee, a brother to Richard Henry Lee and therefore a supporter of the Adams-Lee faction in Congress, maintained that all French aid received before the signing of the Treaty of Alliance in February 1778 was a gift from France. Silas Deane, on the other hand, considered French assistance as a loan that must be repaid. The first discernible split over this issue occurred in the American diplomatic corps in Europe. Deane and his steadfast supporter Benjamin Franklin were aligned against Arthur Lee, his brother William Lee (commissioner to Vienna and Berlin), and Ralph Izard of South Carolina (commissioner to the Court of Tuscany). Soon, however, this quarrel spread across the Atlantic Ocean. Both commissioners had their supporters in Congress. The ensuing congressional split was noticed initially when the Adams-Lee faction, in late November 1776, rammed through Congress a motion to recall Silas Deane for allegedly misappropriating public funds and for granting scores of military commissions in the Continental Army to adventurous, and frequently incompetent and inexperienced, French soldiers of fortune. However, the main underlying cause of the animosity towards Deane was that because there was some validity to the charges of financial irregularities, he was the most vulnerable member of the anti-Adams-Lee faction.

Deane's congressional critics included two of Arthur Lee's brothers from Virginia (Francis Lightfoot Lee and Richard Henry Lee), James Lovell of Massachusetts, Roger Sherman of Connecticut, and Henry Laurens of South Carolina. Deane, however, had powerful support, both in Congress and without. John Hancock of Massachusetts, Robert Morris of Pennsylvania, and John Jay, Gouverneur Morris, and George Clinton of New York opposed the recall campaign of Deane's congressional detractors.

This sordid controversy tainted the reputations of everyone involved, but especially those of Deane's critics. Although Deane was never formally found guilty of the charges of dishonest financial dealing and incompetence, his career was ruined, especially after 1781 when he publicly advocated an accommodation with the mother country. He died enroute from Britain to Canada in 1789, disgraced, bankrupt, and broken in body and spirit. Interestingly, Congress eventually upheld Deane's contention that the military supplies and money received from France before February 1778 were loans, not gifts. As Deane's chief tormentor, Arthur Lee, for his part, emerged from this quarrel with a deserved reputation as a suspicious, cantankerous troublemaker. Along with his more famous brother Richard Henry Lee, Arthur opposed ratification of the Constitution of 1787. He

)2 on his Virginia estate "Lansdowne" in relative obscurity. The
eputations of some of the other anti-Deane principals (most
illiam Lee and Ralph Izard), while not ruined, were tarnished
by their involvement in the sordid attack against Silas Deane and his chief
supporter, the ever-popular Benjamin Franklin.

The treaty of alliance with France negotiated by Benjamin Franklin,
Arthur Lee, and Silas Deane demonstrated conclusively that "rustic" American provincials could operate successfully in the often murky, dangerous
waters of European diplomacy. Franklin, who had spent most of his adult
life after 1757 in Europe first as a colonial agent in London and after 1776
as a diplomat in Paris, was particularly well suited to lead the American
mission in Paris. After his much-heralded arrival in Paris in December
1776, Franklin, by dressing plainly, by appearing in public without a wig,
and by generally affecting the role of a simple, provincial American (which
he certainly was not), gained the adoration of Parisian high society and
of the French people generally. He was also greatly admired, on both sides
of the Atlantic Ocean, for his earlier celebrated experiments in electricity.

In the months following his arrival in France, Franklin skillfully
nurtured the French Foreign Minister's (Charles Gravier Comte de
Vergennes) fear of a rapprochement between Britain and America. He first
cleverly held not-so-secret conversations with Peter Wentworth, an American Loyalist who was sent to Paris by the British ministry to convince the
American diplomats to accept, for their country, dominion status within
the British Empire. The wily Franklin then intimated to Vergennes that the
Americans were considering (but in fact this was never seriously considered) reconciliation with the former mother country. Primarily the stun-
ning American military victory of October 17, 1777, at Saratoga, New
York, news of which reached Paris in December 1777, but also this threat
of a rapprochement finally convinced Vergennes that France should enter
into an alliance with the fledgling American Republic. France was eager
to avenge her defeat at the hands of Britain by striking at the source of
British power and prosperity—namely her vast colonial empire. In early
January 1778, Vergennes tried to induce Spain into a triple alliance with
France and the United States. Spain refused. Thereupon on January 8th,
Vergennes notified the three American diplomats that France was prepared
to enter into an alliance with the United States.

The ensuing negotiations were intense and spirited. On February 6,
1778, a Treaty of Amity and Commerce and a Treaty of Alliance were

signed amid great fanfare. In the Treaty of Amity and Commerce, both France and the United States were granted most-favored-nation status by the other. Significantly for the future, this treaty incorporated a few of the principles advocated by the Americans respecting the rights of neutrals in time of war. The Treaty of Alliance with France (the next such treaty of alliance would not be concluded until 1949 when the United States joined the North Atlantic Treaty Organization) would become effective if war should break out between Great Britain and France. The alliance became operative in the summer of 1778, when naval skirmishing in the English Channel ushered in a state of war between these two ancient enemies. In these two treaties, France recognized American independence. In the Treaty of Alliance, the United States was, in essence, given a free hand to conquer Canada and Bermuda. France, for her part, was given the right to acquire British possessions in the West Indies. Finally, each country agreed not to negotiate a separate peace with Britain.

Although the American diplomats failed to entice Spain into a formal alliance with the United States, Spain did render significant financial aid, especially after Arthur Lee's visit to Madrid in early 1777. Spain finally did declare war against Britain in June 1779 after negotiations between Spain and Great Britain involving the Spanish ultimatum that Britain must cede Gibraltar to Spain as the price of Spanish neutrality broke down. Late in the war, the Spanish were active militarily in Florida and the Caribbean. Spain's financial contribution to the rebelling colonies was substantial. Altogether Spain gave America over $600,000 in subsidies and loans. However, Spanish aid was not given openly because overt support of the rebelling British colonies would set a bad example for Spain's own colonies. Spain's entrance into the war added to Britain's diplomatic isolation. This isolation was made more apparent when Great Britain, in an effort to shut down the clandestine trade between the United States and the Dutch Island of St. Eustatius in the West Indies, declared war against The United Provinces in December 1780. The Dutch, although not allied formally with the United States, were helpful to the American Republic as bankers. Two sizeable Dutch loans (altogether Dutch bankers loaned America approximately $1.25 million) greatly helped the debt-ridden infant American Republic during the financially troubled years 1781 and 1782. The League of Armed Neutrality completed Britain's diplomatic isolation, and thus helped to convince the British to negotiate an end to the conflict and to grant American independence. Prompted by British violations of neutral rights on the high seas, Catherine II of Russia invited other European neutrals to join Russia in a loose association for the protection of neutral shipping. Sweden and Denmark joined Russia in the league in 1780, followed by Prussia, Portugal, and Austria in 1781 and the Kingdom of Naples in 1783. Although the League did not contribute militarily to the conflict against Great Britain, its advocacy of the principle of "free ships make free goods" helped define neutral maritime rights, in international law, in a time of war. Soon after the signing of the two treaties with France, King Louis XVI formally received Arthur Lee, Silas Deane, and Benjamin Franklin as duly accredited representatives of the United States of America and appointed Conrad Alexandra Gerard as the first French minister to the young American Republic. With this official French recognition, the United States of America gained legitimacy as a sovereign, independent nation.

Foreign aid, especially French, helped the United States greatly during the Revolutionary War. Altogether in subsidies and loans, Dutch bankers contributed $1.25 million, the Spanish government $600,000, and the French government approximately $8 million. Although most of these gifts and loans were spent in France for military equipment, ships, and advances to American sailors, the foreign aid received enabled Congress to supply (although often inadequately) and maintain an army in the field. Moreover, the thousands of French soldiers and sailors stationed in America after 1778 spent the equivalent of several million dollars, which greatly benefited the slumping American economy.

In an effort to forestall U.S. ratification of the two French treaties, British Prime Minister Lord North introduced, in mid-February 1778, into the House of Commons a series of bills for bringing about reconciliation with her colonies. A peace commission (composed of Lord Frederick Howard Carlisle, William Eden, George Johnstone, General William Howe, and Admiral Lord Richard Howe) was established with instructions to offer the Americans the following terms: 1. Parliament would repeal the Tea Act and Coercive Acts, 2. Parliament would not pass any new revenue acts on her American subjects, and 3. Parliament would appoint a commission with powers to negotiate with the Continental Congress regarding a possible suspension of all Parliamentary revenue acts passed since 1763. The so-called Carlisle Commission reached Philadelphia in early June 1778 and received a chilly reception. Congress declared that negotiations could begin only after all British troops and naval forces were withdrawn and after

Great Britain formally recognized the independence of the United States of America. Because the Carlisle Commission was not authorized to negotiate a military withdrawal or the issue of independence, this attempt at reconciliation was a failure from the start. Even before the Commission's arrival, Congress had formally declared that any person or group who seriously negotiated with the Carlisle Commission would be branded an enemy of the United States. In a futile effort to jump-start even unofficial talks, British negotiator George Johnstone (former British governor of West Florida) tried to bribe congressmen Joseph Reed and Robert Morris. Both Pennsylvania congressmen rejected Johnstone's offer of money and preferment, whereupon the British commissioner resigned from the commission in disgrace. On October 3rd, the Earl of Carlisle and William Eden issued a Manifesto and Proclamation that threatened Americans with a war of increased destructiveness if they did not abandon their French allies and conclude peace with Great Britain. The total disregard of this Manifesto and Proclamation by the Americans only confirmed that the Carlisle Commission was sent too late and that it offered too little to the increasingly confident Americans. After the American victory at Saratoga and the signing of a military alliance with France, the United States felt strong enough to reject outright all British attempts to offer to her former colonies what amounted to dominion status within the British Empire. Had the Carlisle Commission been sent in 1776 with the same instructions it was given in 1778, it might well have been successful. Great Britain was not willing to offer dominion status in 1776; America was not willing to accept dominion status in 1778.

Actually, the Carlisle Commission was the second British attempt at reconciliation. The first took place in 1776 on what is now known as the infamous 11th day of September. Meeting on Staten Island, for the British, the Howe brothers (Admiral Lord Richard and General William) demanded a revocation of the Declaration of Independence as a necessary preliminary to any negotiations. The British demand left no ground for further meaningful negotiations. Therefore the American delegation (John Adams, Benjamin Franklin, and Edward Rutledge of South Carolina) rejected the British demand, and the meeting ended. Had Admiral and General Howe offered the terms in 1776 that the Carlisle Commission offered in 1778, the Continental Congress might have accepted, before Saratoga and the French Alliance, something less than complete independence as the price for peace.

The brilliant diplomatic triumph of the drawing up and signing of the French Alliance treaty made possible the highly favorable Treaty of Paris of 1783 in which Great Britain finally recognized American independence. With France, Spain, the United Provinces, the League of Armed Neutrality, and the United States aligned against her, Great Britain became almost totally isolated diplomatically. This isolation plus the obvious fact that Britain was not winning the American war militarily, especially after Lord Cornwallis's humiliating surrender at Yorktown, Virginia, in October 1781, convinced Lord North to consider making peace with the former colonies. A huge war debt and a growing realization that her true enemies were in Europe, not in America, prompted Britain to bring to an end what was fast becoming an ever more expensive, bloody, and unpopular war. There was also a feeling among British mercantile interests that Britain could continue to exploit an independent United States economically just as she had previously exploited the thirteen mainland colonies.

In preparation for the hoped-for peace conference, Congress, as early as September 1779, appointed John Adams as its sole negotiator and instructed him, in any negotiations with the British, to secure recognition of American independence first, then to obtain generous geographic boundaries for the new nation, to secure fishing rights for Americans near Nova Scotia and Newfoundland, to obtain the right of navigation on the Mississippi River, and to get immediate and complete evacuation of all British land and sea forces. In June 1781 Congress modified the 1779 peace instructions. Now only British recognition of American independence and American sovereignty were given as the essential, nonnegotiable provisions of any treaty. Other matters in dispute were to be handled by the commissioners at their discretion without definite binding instructions. At the same time, Congress enlarged the American peace delegation by adding the names of Benjamin Franklin, John Jay, Thomas Jefferson, and Henry Laurens to that of John Adams to make a five-member commission. However, only three members took part in the protracted negotiations that led to the 1783 treaty. Because of the illness and subsequent death of his wife Martha in September, 1782, Jefferson did not participate in the negotiations. Henry Laurens was captured by the British while traveling to Paris and was imprisoned, for fifteen months, in the Tower of London. Finally he was exchanged in late December 1781 for British general Lord Cornwallis, and he reached Paris in time to sign the Preliminary Treaty in November 1782.

The trio of Adams, Franklin, and Jay was responsible for negotiating the highly favorable treaty that confirmed American independence and gave birth to the American Republic. Each of these three diplomats made positive contributions to what finally became the Definitive Treaty of September 3, 1783. At the age of 77, Benjamin Franklin, with years of diplomatic experience, was the dean of the American delegation. Adams and Jay, for their part, mistrusted the French and persuaded the wily Philadelphian to go along with them in negotiating separately with the British, thus violating the Treaty of Alliance with France, which mandated joint negotiations with Britain. Franklin's main contribution to the proceedings was to act as a mediator between the sometimes-irascible John Adams, the mistrusting and dour John Jay, and the British negotiators Richard Osward and Henry Strachey. At the end of the negotiations, Franklin was given the unenviable task of convincing Vergennes that he should support the treaty even though France played no role in its drafting. This he was able to do mainly because he was able to convince Vergennes that it was in the best interests of France to end what had become for her an expensive war.

During October and November of 1782, the British and American diplomats worked assiduously to put the final touches to a treaty that both parties could ratify and honor. The issue of recognition of American independence was not in dispute inasmuch as Britain acknowledged, from the beginning of the negotiations, that she was negotiating with a sovereign nation—the United States. The issues to be worked out involved fishing rights around Nova Scotia and Newfoundland, control of the trans-Appalachian west, repayment of prewar debts, and restoration of loyalist properties and legal rights. In the drafting of the Preliminary Treaty, which was signed on November 30, 1782, both sides made concessions in the interest of arriving at a mutually acceptable treaty. However, because she was especially anxious to end what had become for her an exceedingly expensive, increasingly unpopular, unwinnable, unduly protracted, frustrating conflict, Great Britain acceded to most of the American demands while the United States held out until the last before agreeing to the insertion of two clauses, to which she formerly objected, concerning the vexing issues of Loyalist claims and prewar debts.

On September 3, 1783, the weary negotiators finally signed the Definitive Treaty of Paris. First and foremost, Great Britain formally recognized the independence of the United States of America. The other major terms of the treaty, with the exception of the clause stating that all debts

owed to citizens of both countries were to be honored and the stipula-
tion that Congress was pledged to "earnestly recommend" (a meaningless
phrase because, under the Articles of Confederation, Congress did not have
the authority to enforce its demands upon the states) to the legislatures
of the states a full restoration of the rights and properties of loyalists, were
favorable to the United States. To the newly created American republic,
the former mother country granted generous boundaries. The boundaries
were drawn along the St. Lawrence River and the 45th parallel to the
middle of the Great Lakes, then Lake Superior to the Lake of the Woods,
down the middle of the Mississippi River, and then the 31st parallel to
the Atlantic Ocean. Thus at its formal birth in 1783, the United States
emerged as one of the largest countries in the Atlantic World. In addition,
Americans were granted the "right" to fish in their accustomed areas off
of Newfoundland and Nova Scotia and the "liberty" to dry and cure their
fish on any uninhabited shore on Labrador, the Magdalen Islands, and
Nova Scotia. Finally, the Treaty specified that hostilities were to cease, and
that all British land and sea forces were to be evacuated "with all convenient speed."

The Treaty of Paris (1783) and the French Alliance of 1778, with its
companion Treaty of Amity and Commerce, represented only the highly
favorable results of a lengthy diplomatic campaign in which American
commissioners (as they were officially designated) learned and then played
the European diplomatic game with skill, understanding, and determination. The Americans (especially Benjamin Franklin and, in his own often
forthright way, John Adams) understood the geopolitics of late eighteenth
century Europe and cleverly played upon the fears and aspirations of the
dominant European powers to achieve their notable diplomatic triumphs.
Importantly, the United States had become involved, on the winning side,
in the long-standing rivalry for maritime and colonial supremacy between
the Bourbon Powers (France and Spain) and Great Britain. In uniting its
goal of political independence from the mother country with France and
Spain's design to exact retribution for their humiliating defeat in the Seven
Years' War (1756–1763) and for Britain's maritime arrogance and colonial
dominance, the United States was able to help build and maintain a
coalition that helped make possible the successful conclusion of the eight-
year war against the mother country. Although American independence
would have eventually been achieved even without the financial and
military aid of France, Spain, and the United Provinces and the moral

support of the League of Armed Neutrality, it is obvious that the French Alliance made possible, and perhaps even inevitable, an accelerated pace towards the drafting of the Treaty of Paris (1783) with its confirmation of American independence. That the United States was able to achieve these diplomatic victories was due in no small part to the ways the intelligent, talented American envoys (particularly Franklin, Adams, and Jay) took full advantage of the volatile diplomatic and political climate of late eighteenth century Europe to advance their country's diplomatic agenda. American diplomatic success during the American Revolution was an early example of the United States benefiting from Europe's distress.

Note

1. Henry Steele Commager and Milton Cantor, editors, *Documents of American History*. Tenth Edition. Englewood Cliffs, N.J.: Prentice Hall, Inc., 1988, I, 117–119.

CHAPTER 6

CONCLUDING INTERPRETIVE ESSAY: THE GLORIOUS CAUSE

The American Revolution (1763–1783) was the Glorious Cause.[1] Many of the most cherished hopes of people everywhere came out of the American Revolutionary Epoch. Even today, in the early years of the third millennium of the Christian Era, people still yearn for the freedom, the liberty, and the equality proclaimed over two hundred years ago in what is now venerated as America's most precious Charter of Liberty, the Declaration of Independence. The radical, revolutionary philosophy of the Declaration has remained the beacon of hope that the world's oppressed and exploited aspire to implement.

Specifically, America's commitment to, although not always adherence to, the high ideals of freedom, liberty, equality ("that all men are created equal"), constitutionalism, the sovereignty of the people, and what could be referred to as classical republicanism make the American Revolution truly revolutionary. However, the American Revolution was not of the classical variety (such as were, for example, the French Revolution of the late eighteenth century and the Russian Revolution of 1917) that brought about the almost complete overthrow of the existing political, social, economic, and religious order. Rather, the American Revolution was largely philosophical in its impact. At least originally, the Revolution was a struggle on the part of the colonists to regain rights previously enjoyed or confidently hoped for. This has led many historians to characterize the Revolution as being conservative or evolutionary. However, these consensus or conservative historians neglect to consider the revolutionary nature of the consequences of the revolutionary struggle. What had started out as a family squabble within the British Empire soon became a crusade, on the part of Americans, to overthrow the existing order of monarchy, corruption, and luxury and establish in its place a society based upon the philosophical republican ideals that came out of Great Britain in the seventeenth century.

What makes the American Revolution revolutionary is that it gave birth to and nurtured an optimistic view of what the world could be. The founding patriots of the American Republic felt and indeed acted on the premise that they, almost uniquely, had been given the opportunity to remake society. Fundamental to their idealistic vision for the future was the concept that ordinary people were virtuous and were consequently capable of establishing and maintaining governments of virtue and high-mindedness. Because the founders considered governments at all levels to be, at least potentially, oppressive and corrupt, they advocated giving to government only specific, limited powers. It was further believed that the powers to be given must be clearly delineated in written constitutions.

This questioning of governmental authority led inevitably to a questioning of authority generally. Traditional ways and institutions were examined closely and, if found to be destructive of the people's well-being (often defined as life, liberty, property, and pursuit of happiness), they were eliminated or overthrown. In their place, the revolutionary leaders either created new institutions or changed existing ones, which would more perfectly conform to the basic principle of the sovereignty of a virtuous people. The philosophical transformation of American society from a monarchical one given over to luxury, corruption, and greed to a republican one based upon virtue constituted the real American Revolution. The War for American Independence only provided the ideal opportunity for American patriots to bring about what is today referred to as the American Revolution.

It is especially important for Americans, in these unsettling times, to learn their country's history; particularly the history of its conception, birth, and infancy. The political, social, and economic principles brought forth during and largely, but sometimes imperfectly, implemented during or soon after the American Revolutionary Era are still, in the twenty-first century, under attack from an ill-defined enemy. Knowledge of the exciting history of these early years will inevitably lead to increased appreciation of these principles Americans still hold most dear. This appreciation will in turn lead to a willingness on the part of Americans today to be ever vigilant in the defense of these principles against a determined and often unrecognized adversary.

The Glorious Cause (the American Revolution) was the proclaiming and implementation of the revolutionary premise that ordinary people were capable of self-government. From this basic concept of the sovereignty of the people came most of the other revolutionary principles we associate with the Revolution. The establishment of governments, at all levels, which were, certainly for that day and age, more responsive to the will of the majority than the ones they replaced constituted an unprecedented democratic revolution. During the tumultuous decade before the outbreak of hostilities in 1775, ordinary colonists became involved politically as never before.

In New England, for example, craftsmen, artisans, laborers, and small farmers joined, many for the first time, their social "betters" in gaining appointment or election to local governing bodies, both official and extralegal. In many communities, committees of correspondence or committees of safety were established to replace the increasingly unpopular British-controlled provincial governments, and their membership often included a large number of heretofore-disenfranchised elements of society. Various secret organizations, usually designated as Sons of Liberty, appeared first in 1765 to protest the Stamp Act. Largely composed of lower-class elements of colonial society, these groups, in the name of liberty, were responsible for mob action and violence against British officials and Loyalists. In Massachusetts, the Sons of Liberty were so successful in intimidating British officials and flouting the trade and navigation laws that the governor felt compelled to request, in 1768, the sending of British troops to Boston to restore effective British rule. Although the former colonial elites frequently retained the leadership roles in these emerging revolutionary groups, many rank-and-file members gained, for the first time, a sense of political empowerment. Political power once achieved is not easily or often relinquished.

In the middle colonies, urban laboring groups, often manipulated by such popular leaders as Alexander McDougall and John Lamb of New York City, contended with or even took over political control from the duly constituted public officials, thus politically empowering large numbers of ordinary citizens. In fact, the newly created democratic element in Pennsylvania became strong enough to draft and promulgate the most democratic of all state constitutions in 1776. In the South, although the planter and/or mercantile elite retained control of the anti-British movement, thousands of ordinary men participated, many for the first time, in the political process as members of local Sons of Liberty groups or various revolutionary committees of safety and correspondence. Wider participation in the political system, even at the lowest level, was an important first revolutionary step in the democratization of American society.

Belief in the sovereignty of the people led to a broadening of the suffrage in a few states. Although most states retained property and tax qualifications for office holding and voting, a few lowered the requirements, thus enlarging the total number who could vote (Pennsylvania, for example, gave the vote to all tax-paying adult white males). The breakup of large Loyalist estates into smaller parcels, which in turn were sold or given to ordinary folks who could now meet the property qualifications for voting still retained by most states, further expanded the voter rolls. Finally, land grants given to soldiers enabled many more to exercise the right to vote. The broadening of the suffrage was revolutionary in its impact. The franchise was, of course, the primary vehicle by which the sovereignty of the people was exercised.

The right of revolution, American constitutionalism, and American republicanism are also derivatives of the basic principle that ultimate political power and authority comes from the people. The right of the people to overthrow government if it becomes destructive of certain inalienable rights is not only an exceedingly revolutionary idea, but is also a natural appendage to the fundamental premise that people are the source of governmental authority. If the people possess the right to establish a government, it is presumed that they have an equal right to disestablish or abolish it.

American constitutionalism can be defined as the belief that governments should be given only limited powers and that these powers should be clearly specified in a written document. Basic to this belief, because all governments are, at least potentially, oppressive and tyrannical, is the premise that the less government the better. Thus the written constitutions of the revolutionary period were the means both to grant certain powers to government and, perhaps more importantly, to withhold or prohibit others.

American republicanism was a radical doctrine that called for the overthrow of the monarchy and the establishment of an elective republican form of government. In this process, the corruption, the oppression, the political favoritism, and the hedonistic dissipation usually associated with monarchical rule would be eliminated. In the place of what was viewed as the corrupt British monarchical system, the Americans established republics (actually fourteen: thirteen state and one national) that were based, at least in theory, on the classical republican principles of patriotism, optimism, honesty, moral integrity, and, most importantly, virtue. The idealistic American version of republicanism was utopian in the extreme and therefore rarely, if ever, implemented. It was likewise revolutionary! It was particularly utopian (and revolutionary) to think that people were virtuous, patriotic, hardworking, honest, and moral and that they could establish and then democratically maintain republics in the hostile monarchical world of the late eighteenth century. However, the American revolutionaries accomplished what seemingly was an eighteenth century version of mission impossible. They established numerous republics, which have endured to the present, that were based philosophically on the twin premises that the people were innately virtuous and that they were capable of creating and governing for themselves their republican governments. American republicanism, first set in motion during the American Revolution, has set the philosophical standard to which people still aspire.

The basic premise that ultimate political authority rests with the people led to a belief in equality (originally equality for all white adult males). Equality did not mean equal talents or equal merit. As used by the American revolutionaries, equality inferred, for all peoples, equal opportunities and equal unalienable rights. Although the revolutionaries' eighteenth-century definition of equality differs greatly from any reasonable twenty-first-century definition, the belief of equality for even a portion of the population represented a significant break with the past. However, it is obvious, more than two hundred years after the introduction of the idea of equality, that all Americans do not yet enjoy complete, meaningful equality. The notion of equality for women, for Native Americans, for African Americans, and indeed for the underclasses of all races and creeds, although not implemented during the revolutionary era, was inserted by the founders into the lexicon of American revolutionary philosophy. This insertion into the American consciousness was, however, a necessary first, and certainly revolutionary, step towards the achievement of true equality for all Americans.

The abolition of many of the more obvious symbols of aristocratic rule was another corollary to the concept of the sovereignty of the people. Entail and primogeniture were traditional legal devices by which large landowners could keep and even increase their property holdings, thus perpetuating a landowning gentry. Land ownership by a relative few, especially in the agrarian society of eighteenth-century America, brought with it political, social, and economic dominance. Largely through the efforts of Thomas Jefferson, Virginia abolished entails (defined as a legal scheme to make land unalienable) in 1776. Soon thereafter, the other states that allowed entails followed Virginia's lead in abolishing this symbol of aristocratic rule. Primogeniture (defined as the bequeathing of an entire estate, in the absence of a will, to the oldest son) was likewise abolished in the seven states where it had been legally practiced. Although entail and primogeniture were not often resorted to in colonial America, their abolition, during the American Revolution, represented a significant, albeit mostly symbolic, step towards the democratization of land ownership.

President Abraham Lincoln, in the midst of the tragic American Civil War, proclaimed, for the ages, the revolutionary ideals of the Glorious Cause in his memorable Gettysburg Address with his opening sentence that "Four score and seven years ago our fathers brought forth on this continent, a new nation, conceived in Liberty, and dedicated to the proposition that all men are created equal" followed by the oft-quoted closing phrase that the government of the United States was "of the people, by the people, for the people." He could very well have added that the republic was also conceived in freedom. With these eloquent statements, Lincoln was only reaffirming the basic revolutionary principles of the American Revolution. The American Revolution not only produced a new nation conceived in freedom, liberty, and equality, it also gave birth to a revolutionary philosophy under which that new republic has flourished ever since.

In these troubled, uncertain times, it is particularly imperative for Americans to become well acquainted with their revolutionary beginnings. If knowledge is power, knowledge of their glorious revolutionary past will help give Americans the power and the will to meet, with confidence, the challenges and opportunities of the new millennium.

Note

1. The precise origin of the phrase "The Glorious Cause" to describe the American Revolution is unknown to this author. However, I suspect the phrase was uttered frequently by contemporary Americans to describe their long struggle

with Great Britain. Historian Robert Middlekauff, in his highly readable and masterful survey of the entire revolutionary period, agrees with me that the Revolution was The Glorious Cause. Robert Middlekauff. *The Glorious Cause: The American Revolution, 1763–1789.* New York: Oxford University Press, 1982, vii.

BIOGRAPHIES

Abigail Adams (1744–1818)

Abigail Adams spent a lifetime working to overcome the political, social, and educational disadvantages endured by women of her day. Primarily by example but also through her numerous letters, Abigail espoused a philosophy that refused to accept female inferiority. She viewed women and men as partners, each having equal but separate spheres. She believed each had unique duties and responsibilities. A woman's place was in the home, where she had the duty to raise the children to lead godly and useful lives, and to be an ever-present partner to her husband, whose domain was outside the home.

As the second child of the Reverend William Smith and Elizabeth Quincy, Abigail had deep roots in colonial Massachusetts. From her father (a Harvard graduate and Congregational pastor), she inherited Puritan respectability and a love of learning. From her mother, Abigail inherited an almost aristocratic status, because the Quincys, for five generations, had occupied positions of great political and social prominence and enjoyed enviable wealth. Abigail Smith took full advantage of the opportunities that her inheritance and comfortable life provided to live a life that demonstrated convincingly that an intelligent, widely traveled, and widely read woman could live a productive, influential, and rewarding life even in the male-dominated society that was eighteenth-century New England.

After her marriage in October 1764, Abigail's name would be inextricably linked with that of her husband, John Adams. Although she was willing to assume the traditional subordinate role assigned to married women outside the home, she would only accept this time-honored role in the context of a partnership with the husband—a true partnership where each spouse was given, within the home, a separate but equal sphere. John brought middle-class respectability to this union, and Abigail a socially and politically superior family name and a handsome dowry.

During the first years of marriage, Abigail was kept busy caring for her four children (Abigail—"Nabby," born 1765; John Quincy, born 1767; Charles, born 1770; and Thomas Boylston, born 1772) and managing the homestead during her husband's frequent absences. Abigail's efficient management of the farm and her raising of the children permitted her ambitious husband to pursue his legal and political careers uninterrupted by domestic concerns. By 1776, John Adams had become, in the Second Continental Congress, "Mr. Congressman," serving on some ninety committees and chairing over twenty. "Mrs. Delegate," as Abigail was sometimes called, was understandably proud of her hardworking spouse. Moreover, she found satisfaction in knowing that most of her husband's views on public policy and political theory were hers as well. Abigail and John Adams were true partners intellectually.

In the spring of 1776 when Congress was debating the issue of independence, Abigail admonished her husband, probably only half facetiously, to ". . . Remember the Ladies, and be more generous and favourable to them than your ancestors. . . . If perticuliar care and attention is not paid to the Laidies we are determined to foment a Rebelion, and will not hold ourselves bound by any Laws in which we have no voice, or Representation."[1] Thomas Jefferson, John Adams, and their congressional colleagues did not "Remember the Ladies" as they crafted the Declaration of Independence. The final document makes no mention of women.

During the War for Independence, Abigail managed the farm and family during her husband's frequent absences to the Continental Congress (1774–1777) and during his stay as a diplomat in Europe (1778–1784). In 1784 Abigail finally consented to John's pleas to join him in Paris. Although describing the French capital as the "very dirtiest place" she had ever seen, she did enjoy her brief stay there. When in 1785 John Adams was appointed the first U.S. minister to Great Britain, the family moved to London.

Abigail's four-year stay in London fulfilled a girlhood dream to visit the mother country. While in Great Britain, Abigail visited many of the cultural, artistic, and historical attractions in and around London. Despite her Puritan upbringing, she shamelessly enjoyed going to the theater. She particularly admired the celebrated Mrs. Sarah Siddons, who was able to combine happily and successfully a professional career with that of a homemaker.

In 1788 Abigail and family returned home to the recently purchased Braintree, Massachusetts, "mansion"—ever after called "Peacefield." With husband John's election as the first vice president, Abigail once again sacrificed the relative tranquility of rural New England for New York City and Philadelphia. With John's election as the second president, Abigail performed her official duties as First Lady with the same efficiency displayed earlier in managing the family farm in Massachusetts and the American embassy in London. As ever, she was her husband's "Dearest Friend" and closest and most influential advisor.

With Thomas Jefferson's defeat of John Adams in the presidential election of 1800, Abigail and John returned to Braintree, where she became the "matriarch" of the Adams family. Always sickly, Abigail suffered, during the retirement years, numerous bouts with "melancholy," malaria attacks, arthritis, and rheumatism. She always endured these "medical adventures" with accustomed fortitude.

In 1818, Abigail contracted typhus fever. After a two-week bout with this deadly disease, she died on October 28th—just two weeks before her 74th birthday.

During her long and productive life, Abigail Adams demonstrated that a woman, if given equal opportunities, could be the equal of a man. Her legacies were positive achievements as wife, mother, and businesswoman and the raising and educating of four children, one of whom (John Quincy Adams) became the sixth president of the United States.

John Adams (1735–1826)

Born to middle-class Puritan respectability, this oldest son of John Adams and Susanna Boylston Adams rose from relative obscurity to become, in Thomas Jefferson's words, "the colossus of independence." John's father sent him to Harvard College to study theology and become a Congregational minister, but the studious young man soon became disenchanted with "frigid John Calvin" and took a teaching position upon his graduation in 1755. Two years of teaching to "indifferent scholars" convinced the ambitious John that the way to respectability and even fame and fortune could be better achieved through the study of the law.

Admitted to the Massachusetts bar in 1759 after a rigorous legal apprenticeship with the eminent barrister Jeremiah Gridley, the hardworking
young lawyer soon became one of the busiest attorneys in Boston. Thus
John Adams entered young adulthood at an auspicious time for a talented
attorney. In the 1760s and early 1770s, Boston was the center of opposition to British taxing policies. It was therefore perhaps inevitable that John
became involved, along with his distant cousin Samuel Adams, in the increasingly violent opposition first of the Stamp Act (1765) and later the
Townshend Duties (1767), the Tea Act (1773), and Coercive Acts (1773).

His marriage in 1764 to the talented middle daughter of the well-
respected Reverend Mr. William Smith only solidified John's position as a
young lawyer and politician who could reasonably look forward to the
fame and affluence he long ardently sought. Abigail Smith brought to her
marriage with John a finely cultivated mind that when blended with that
of the equally brilliant John, produced a lifelong, enviable intellectual
partnership. In addition, Abigail brought an even temperament to the
union, which often served as a needed antidote to the sometimes impetuous, but always honest husband. Their marriage was one of an intellectual partnership. They were a loving couple.

Passage by Parliament of the Stamp Act in 1765 prompted John Adams
to oppose openly British taxing policies. His opposition to this universally-
hated tax coupled with his growing hostility to the Hutchinson-Oliver pro-
British political faction led Adams to a leadership role, along with his political
mentor James Otis, Jr., John Hancock, Dr. Joseph Warren, and most notably Samuel Adams, in the radical faction in Massachusetts. His largely successful legal defense of the eight British soldiers involved in the so-called
"Boston Massacre" of March 5, 1770, confirmed his essential political conservatism and his belief in the rule of law. However, it did not deter him
from being increasingly active and vocal in his opposition to the British
policies that eventually led to open armed conflict in 1775.

Election to the Massachusetts General Court (legislature) in 1770,
to the First Continental Congress in 1774, and most importantly to the
Second Continental Congress in 1775 thrust John Adams onto the center stage of colonial revolutionary activity. With the initial clash of arms
in April 1775, John became convinced that political separation from
Great Britain and the establishment of an American republic were necessary to ensure Americans their inalienable rights. In the fifteen months

between the bloodshed at Lexington and Concord (April 1775) and the Declaration of Independence (July 1776), John Adams, along with Samuel Adams and the Lee brothers from Virginia, led the fight for American independence. By June of 1776 this Adams-Lee faction in the Continental Congress, with the help of Thomas Paine's persuasive pamphlet *Common Sense*, had gained enough support to secure passage of Richard Henry Lee's famous motion calling for American independence. Not surprisingly given his leadership in promoting the idea of independence, John Adams was appointed to the five-member committee that drafted the Declaration of Independence. At Adams's insistence, Thomas Jefferson was given the task of producing the initial draft of what would become the American Revolution's most famous document. However, the final document, approved by Congress on July 4, 1776, contained the essential political philosophy of John Adams as well as of that of a vast majority of the signers.

During the period 1774–1778, John Adams was "Mr. Congressman." He served on over ninety congressional committees, chaired over twenty of these committees, and was always diligent and conscientious in carrying out the duties of a congressional leader as the country prepared for and then conducted a war against seemingly overwhelming odds. Because of his legislative leadership in the critical years 1774–1778, John Adams can rightly be considered America's most productive and influential revolutionary legislator.

In 1778 Adams was appointed to his first diplomatic post as commissioner to France (replacing Silas Deane). With a brief interlude back in Massachusetts where he became the primary author of the Massachusetts state constitution of 1780, Adams resumed his diplomatic career first as commissioner to the United Provinces (where he secured a much-needed loan from Dutch bankers), then as one of the chief negotiators (along with Benjamin Franklin and John Jay) in drafting the Treaty of Paris (1783), which confirmed American independence and American nationhood, and finally as the first American minister to the Court of St. James in Britain. Because of his diplomatic successes, John Adams can rightly be considered, along with Benjamin Franklin, one of America's leading diplomats of the Revolutionary era.

Adams continued his distinguished political career upon his return from Britain in 1789. As the first vice president, he faithfully supported the Washington/Hamilton nationalistic program, which led to the establishment of the American republic on a firm foundation. As the heir apparent, John Adams was elected the second president of the United States.

While continuing the general policies of President Washington, he will be remembered primarily for his avoiding war against France. It is for this statesmanship in maintaining peace that John Adams is considered to be one of the better U.S. presidents—a president willing to sacrifice his own political career for the good of the country.

Bitter over his narrow defeat in his reelection bid in 1800 at the hands of Thomas Jefferson and Aaron Burr, Adams returned to his beloved "Peacefield" in Braintree, Massachusetts, where he became a farmer, a devoted father and grandfather, and a correspondent to a wide circle of friends and former colleagues. Of particular interest is his correspondence with Thomas Jefferson. Restarted in 1812, this epistolary exchange consists of the reminiscences of two of the most active and influential revolutionary figures. Incredibly, these two Revolutionary era giants died on the same day—July 4, 1826. Among the many eulogies given in honor of these two revered founders was the one delivered in Faneuil Hall in Boston by Daniel Webster. In this tribute to Adams and Jefferson, Webster made much of the fact that these two esteemed founders died on the 50th anniversary of the Declaration of Independence—a document and event in which they both played major roles. His legacy includes raising and helping to educate his oldest son, John Quincy Adams—elected the sixth president of the United States just two years before the father's death.

Samuel Adams (1722–1803)

Samuel Adams was the foremost political radical and propagandist of the entire Revolutionary era. More than any other founder, this Massachusetts Puritan kept alive the movement towards political independence from Great Britain in the immediate pre-war decade 1765–1775.

As the son of the locally prominent Boston politician Deacon Samuel Adams, young Sam had educational and economic opportunities not available to most Bostonians. His 1740 graduation from Harvard and the legacy from his father of political connections and a respected name all presaged a promising future. Moreover, by the early 1750s both of his parents had died and he inherited the family house on Purchase Street, Boston, and a thriving brewery. However, by 1760, through neglect, indifference, and mismanagement, Adams had managed to dissipate this ample inheritance. Elected Boston tax collector in 1756, by 1764 the somewhat careless but not dishonest Adams had accumulated a debt of some 8,000 pounds in uncollected taxes (a debt that was forgiven by a grateful town in 1772 in payment for his revolutionary leadership and obvious need). His popularity and hence his repeated reelection to the post of tax collector were made possible by his inattention to accurate accounting procedures and by a propensity to be too indulgent to his friends and neighbors in the collection of taxes.

It was the Stamp Act crisis that thrust Sam Adams into an active political career. As the son of the politically active Deacon Adams and as a member of several political clubs (most notably the Boston Caucus), Adams had become, even before 1765, a leader of the so-called "country party." The political division in Massachusetts was between the "country party" (consisting of a few wealthy merchants and craftsmen) and the "court party" (consisting of the more socially and economically prominent families and British-appointed public officials). This British or court party was headed by Lt. Governor Thomas Hutchinson and his Oliver family relatives. Samuel Adams's enmity towards the Hutchinson/Oliver clan dated back to 1741, when Hutchinson had been instrumental in destroying the Land Bank and thus almost ruining Deacon Adams financially. In 1764, the impending Stamp Act enabled the embittered Adams to oppose the "court party" on both philosophical and personal levels.

In the decade from 1764 to 1774 as the leader of the increasingly powerful Boston "country party," Sam Adams adroitly marshaled opposition to the "court party" and thus to British policies. By 1766, Sam Adams was the acknowledged leader of the radical, anti-Hutchinson group, which gained control of the Massachusetts House of Representatives. He served as a member of the House from 1765–1774. Throughout this exciting decade, Sam demonstrated the ability, time and time again, to garner effective, popular support for his anti-Hutchinson, anti-British policies. While he never condoned violence openly, Adams's influence, nevertheless, can be discerned behind the sometimes-violent intimidation of tax collectors, judges, and other British officials, the sacking of Hutchinson's Boston mansion (1765), the "Boston Massacre" (1770), and the destruction of private property in the so-called Boston Tea Party (1773).

Adams was also a master propagandist. With a ready and witty pen, Sam Adams based his opposition to British policies on Natural Law and on the unwritten British constitution. Essentially he claimed, in numerous broadsides and newspaper articles, that Britain was violating its own constitution in taxing the colonists without their consent. In supporting the colonial policies of George Grenville, Charles Townshend, and Lord North, Adams contended that King George III had forfeited his right to rule the colonies and therefore the mainland colonies should separate themselves from the mother country. In well-written, highly persuasive pamphlets, newspaper articles, and official public documents, Sam Adams converted many to his anti-British point of view and thus clearly established himself as the leader of the radical party in Massachusetts. As a proficient polemicist, Adams wrote the instructions for the Boston representatives in the legislature (1764), supported the activities of the increasingly violent Sons of Liberty, organized the effective opposition to the Townshend Duties (1767), helped organize the Massachusetts Non-Importation Association (1768), drafted the Circular Letter to the legislatures of the other mainland colonies (1768), set up a Boston committee of correspondence (1772), and led the opposition to the punitive Coercive Acts (Intolerable Acts). When Adams discovered that most of the other mainland colonies would not follow Massachusetts's lead in adopting non-intercourse measures, he was instrumental in setting up what became the First Continental Congress (1774). As a member from Massachusetts to this august gathering, Sam Adams (along with second cousin John Adams) became a leader of the minority radical faction. Although unable to gain support in congress for separation from Britain at this early date, the radical faction, under the leadership of a "Brace of Adamses," was able to push through a motion for congress to meet again on the second Monday of the next May if Britain did not revoke the hated Coercive Acts.

As a delegate to the Second Continental Congress (he served continuously in the Continental Congress from 1774 to 1781), Sam Adams became a leader of the so-called Adams-Lee faction, which worked diligently and eventually successfully to muster support for a Declaration of Independence. With his signature on this famous document, Sam Adams's influence began to wane. His major contribution to the revolutionary movement was in the destruction of British rule over the colonies. It would be left to others to construct a new American government, based, it must be remembered, however, in part on the philosophy he espoused in helping to destroy the old British imperial system.

With diminished influence, Sam Adams returned permanently to Massachusetts in 1781, serving among other state-level positions as a delegate to the state constitutional convention (1779), as a state senator, as Lieutenant Governor (1789–1793), and as Governor (1794–1797). His well-known opposition in 1786 to Shay's Rebellion (an uprising of debt-ridden frontiersmen against the conservative state government), his initial opposition, as a member of the Massachusetts Ratifying Convention, to the Constitution of 1787, and his growing political conservatism all marred his last years. His death in 1803 was widely reported and greatly lamented. Early during the Revolution Samuel Adams epitomized the "Spirit of 1776" with its emphasis on individual freedom and liberty, but by the 1780s his obvious provincialism alienated him from the "Spirit of 1787" with its emphasis on nationalism and government by the rich and the well born.

Benedict Arnold (1741–1801)

Benedict Arnold is one of the most fascinating and most controversial figures of the entire revolutionary period. Considered by many to have been General George Washington's boldest, most colorful, most successful field commander, his name, however, has become synonymous with traitor, turncoat, and Judas. He was, in fact, both a hero (for his daring military exploits as an American officer early in the war) and a traitor (for his later treasonous activities with British Major John André and subsequent service as a general in the British army). This duality (hero/traitor) plus a quarrelsome, arrogant, insolent, sometimes combative disposition have all made Benedict Arnold one of most enigmatic, interesting, daring, and unique figures in American history.

Born and educated in Norwich, Connecticut, Benedict Arnold served briefly as an apprentice to a druggist before running off to serve in a New York militia company during the latter years of the French and Indian War (1754–1763). Although available information is sketchy, he apparently deserted his militia company and returned home to complete his apprenticeship. Orphaned by the age of twenty-one, Benedict with his sister Hannah moved to New Haven, where he opened a drug/book shop. Success as a shopkeeper led to a mercantile career during which he sailed his own ships up and down the east coast and into the Caribbean. His marriage in 1767 to Margaret Mansfield (died 1775) produced three sons.

His Revolutionary War military career started in 1775, when as an elected captain in the Connecticut militia, he reached Cambridge, Massachusetts, with his company just ten days after the April 19th bloodshed at Lexington and Concord. Soon after his arrival in Cambridge, he was appointed a colonel in the militia and as such served with Ethan Allen of Vermont in the campaign that resulted in the British surrender of Fort Ticonderoga on May 10, 1775. Throughout this early campaign, Arnold displayed many of those traits that thereafter characterized his military career. He was often daring, bold, and quick-witted, but also frequently unduly sensitive, overly avaricious, disdainful of authority, and antagonistic to peers and superiors alike. Taken altogether these traits may well have contributed to his duality as a hero and a traitor.

Arnold's military career to 1778 was one of courageous battlefield leadership and controversial financial dealings. In one of the most heroic feats of endurance and courage in the entire war, Colonel Arnold led a small army through the Maine wilderness to join General Richard Montgomery in the 1775 invasion of Canada. However, the more numerous and well-entrenched British easily withstood the American assault on Quebec City. During the bitter late December fighting, General Montgomery was killed, hundreds of Americans (including Virginian Daniel Morgan) were taken prisoner, and Benedict Arnold was wounded. Throughout this ill-advised invasion of Canada, Arnold acquitted himself with great courage, determination, and boldness.

Promoted to Brigadier General for his exploits in Canada, Arnold next played a significant role in what culminated in the battle of Saratoga. After the American retreat from Canada in early 1777, the British commander in Canada, Sir Guy Carleton, undertook a counteroffensive southward along the Lake George–Lake Champlain–Hudson River corridor. Control of this waterway (especially Lake Champlain) was essential for British success. Although the Battle of Valcour Island (October 1776) is considered an American defeat in that Arnold's hastily built small fleet was almost completely destroyed, the delaying of the British advance prompted the British to postpone what would undoubtedly have been a successful military invasion of the Hudson River valley. Thus Arnold's actions at Valcour Island on Lake Champlain gained valuable time for the Americans. When the British resumed their invasion of New York the next year, the Americans were better prepared militarily to meet the invaders. This second invasion of New York ended disastrously for the British with Burgoyne's humiliating defeat at Saratoga.

The outcome of Arnold's exploits before and during the Battle of Saratoga is still a matter of controversy. In leading the military expedition to relieve besieged Fort Stanwix, Arnold contributed positively to the failure of British Colonel Barry St. Leger's attempt to join General Johnny Burgoyne in the Albany, New York, region. Turning back St. Leger's incursion along the Mohawk River deprived Burgoyne of much-needed men and supplies and thus helped to make possible the glorious American victory at Saratoga.

During the Battle of Saratoga, Arnold performed with his usual cool courage and audacity. At Freeman's Farm (September 19, 1777), Arnold, with boldness and determination, thwarted the British attempt to outflank the American army, thus preventing a possible American defeat. Later during the second phase of the Battle of Saratoga (usually referred to as the Battle of Bemis Heights—October 7, 1777), Arnold was seriously wounded while recklessly leading a frontal assault on a British redoubt.

There is still great controversy surrounding Arnold's actions during the Battle of Saratoga. Some say his decisiveness at Freeman's Farm and boldness at Bemis Heights helped to ensure the American victory. Others claim that his recklessness caused heavy casualties and that his insubordination actually imperiled the success of General Horatio Gates's more conservative battle plan. His unseemly quarrel with American commander Gates added to the controversy. In Gates's official battle report to Congress, Arnold was given no credit for his bold battlefield initiatives. This official slight may well have added to Arnold's conviction that his services were unappreciated and thus contributed to his later decision to desert to the British.

Arnold, of course, is most well known for being the arch-traitor who defected to the British seemingly for gold and glory. During his years as an American commander, Arnold was repeatedly accused (apparently with ample justification) of using his official position for personal financial gain. For example, in 1779 as military commander in Philadelphia, he was found guilty of questionable, if not downright dishonest, business practices and given a mild reprimand by General Washington. Anger that he had been found guilty of any impropriety whatever, belief that his services as an American officer had long been underappreciated and even overlooked, and his need for money to maintain an extravagant lifestyle, particularly after his marriage to 19-year-old Peggy Shipton (a daughter of prominent Philadelphia Tory Edward Shipton) prompted Arnold to enter into a treasonous correspondence with British Captain (later Major) John André, British Commander in Chief General Henry Clinton's chief of intelligence. Despite Washington's mild rebuke for his questionable financial dealings, Arnold retained the esteem of the American commander. He sought and eventually received appointment as commander at West Point.

Arnold entered into his secret correspondence with André in May 1779. The negotiations with the British took some fifteen months, during which Arnold offered to hand over the strategically important American fort at West Point to the British. For this obvious treason he was to receive a lifetime annuity of 500 pounds sterling, a commission as a general in the British army, and compensation for his property that would be confiscated when his defection became known. The accidental capture of the British intermediary between Arnold and British General Henry Clinton led to Arnold's narrow escape to the British lines and to the execution, as a spy, of the promising and dashing young British intelligence officer Major John André.

Now fighting on the side of the British, Arnold conducted a devastating raid into Virginia in late 1780 and early 1781. With 1200 troops, Arnold was able to wreak havoc in and around Richmond, burning tobacco crops and capturing numerous tobacco ships along the James River and at the mouth of the Chesapeake Bay.

Arnold's last twenty years were spent in unhappy exile first in St. John, New Brunswick, and later in Britain. Hated by most Americans and interestingly by most British for his traitorous activities, he was also scorned and despised on both sides of the Atlantic for his obvious avarice, arrogance, and unstable personality. He died in England in 1801 a broken man, unheralded and unlamented.

Daniel Boone (1734–1820)

Daniel Boone, like his famous contemporary George Washington, became a legendary hero in his own lifetime. He came to personify, to many Americans then and ever since, the pioneering, wandering, restless spirit often attributed to the revolutionary generation.

Boone spent his long and exciting life mostly hunting, fishing, trapping, scouting, surveying, exploring, and fighting. Early in life, he acquired a love of the outdoor life and, most importantly, the necessary skills and patience to cope and survive in what was frequently an unfriendly or even hostile outdoor frontier environment. Although often involved in dangerous and deadly combat, Boone claimed never to have killed except in self-defense. Born into a Quaker family, Boone always adhered to the essential pacifism associated with the Society of Friends.

As the sixth child (of eleven) of Squire and Sarah Boone, Daniel inherited the wanderlust of his grandfather George who, in the early eighteenth century, moved his family from Devonshire, England, to the relative wilds of Berks County, Pennsylvania. As a boy growing up in William Penn's new world Quaker haven, Daniel learned early and well the ways of the forest. He received his first rifle at the age of twelve, and by constant practice, he soon gained an enviable reputation as a marksman. He also mastered the complexities of cleaning and repairing his weapon and of loading it quickly. This mastery of the rifle, on more than one occasion, saved Daniel Boone's life. While his parents and siblings farmed the Boone homestead and operated a small blacksmith shop, young Daniel provided food obtained on frequent and often lengthy hunting trips. When Daniel's older brother Israel "married out" (i.e., he married a non-Quaker or "worldling"), the entire Boone family was disowned by the local Friends' Meeting. This and a wanderlust spirit prompted Squire Boone to move his family first to the beautiful Shenandoah Valley of western Virginia and then "up the valley" to Buffalo Lick in the Yadkin River Valley of western North Carolina.

During the French and Indian War (1754–1763), young Daniel Boone got his first taste of frontier combat. As a teamster and blacksmith in British General Edward Braddock's ill-fated attack (July 1755) against Fort Duquesne, Daniel witnessed firsthand this disastrous defeat of British arms and the death of the brave, but foolishly stubborn British commander. It was during this campaign that Daniel Boone, the future legendary frontier hero, first met the Virginia militia officer George Washington, the future legendary revolutionary general and political leader.

Upon his return to North Carolina, he helped his father work the hardscrabble farm, hunted, and fell in love. The simple wedding in 1756 of the twenty-one-year-old Daniel Boone and the sixteen-year-old Rebecca Bryan was performed by Daniel's father in his capacity as a justice of the peace. During their fifty-six years of marriage, Rebecca proved to be a loving and caring wife to her frequently absent and wandering husband. Altogether she had ten children by Daniel, and one by Daniel's brother Edward or "Ned." The baby daughter born out of wedlock was conceived and born during one of Daniel's lengthy absences during the Cherokee War of 1759–1760. When asked how this could have happened, Rebecca replied that she thought her husband Daniel had been killed, she was lonely, brother "Ned" looked like Daniel and reminded her of him, and finally "Ned" had comforted her in her hour of sorrow. Seemingly Daniel was not bothered by this illicit affair. The illegitimate child, named Jemima, soon became a favorite of both Rebecca and her forgiving husband.

In 1758, Daniel Boone again joined, as a wagonmaster, in the British attack on Fort Duquesne, strategically located at the confluence of the Allegheny and Monongahela Rivers. After its capture Daniel returned to his family and small cabin on Sugartree Creek on the North Carolina frontier. Soon the restless Daniel was off to fight the rampaging Cherokee Indians, having moved his family eastward to the relative safety of Culpeper County, Virginia. It was during this two-year absence from his family that Jemima was born and that Daniel Boone became a skilled Indian fighter. He learned the need to strike quickly and quietly and to always expect the unexpected.

Daniel Boone's reputation as a famous explorer and Indian fighter came primarily from his activities during the period just preceding and during the American War for Independence. In 1767 he led a small group through the Cumberland Gap on an extensive exploratory trip into what became Kentucky. In 1775 he returned to the "dark and bloody ground" at least twice with the first sizeable groups of American settlers to move to the lush, beautiful "Blue Grass" region west of Virginia. Although in the Boone myth—a myth largely created and nurtured by Lord Byron, who devoted seven stanzas in his 1823 publication *Don Juan* to an exaggeration of Boone's alleged heroic exploits and adventures, and by several early overly filiopietistic American historians—Daniel is credited with discovering the Cumberland Gap, then discovering Kentucky, and finally with being its first settler, actually Daniel Boone did none of the above.

However, his actual accomplishments were such that the real Daniel Boone is more interesting than the mythological one. He was among those who constructed the famous Wilderness Road over which thousands of settlers would travel in the great post–Revolutionary War westward migration. He helped build the first blockhouse fort at what became the site of

Boonesborough, Kentucky. In 1778 in what would become the most famous and most often recited tale of his exciting frontier exploits, he was captured by the Shawnee Indians (allies of the British) and inducted into that tribe as Chief Blackfish's adopted son. During the four months living as the adopted son of Chief Blackfish, Boone seemed to have readily accepted his new life (he had his hair plucked from his head except for a tuft on the crown) and even to have defected to the British side. Blackfish took his "son" to Detroit, where he was shown (like a trophy of war) to the British commander. However, when told of the upcoming joint British/ Shawnee attack on Boonesborough, Boone managed a dramatic escape. His 160-mile trip back to Boonesborough in less than four days was one of the most remarkable feats of bravery, courage, and resourcefulness of the entire revolutionary period. Against overwhelming odds, Boone traveled through hostile Indian-infested forests and actually swam across the mighty Ohio River to warn the Boonesborough settlers of the impending British/ Indian attack. It was due in large part to his warning, planning, and efforts that the beleaguered fort was able to withstand successfully the ten-day British/Shawnee siege. The reports of his successful defense of Boonesborough only enhanced his reputation as a heroic, larger-than-life frontier leader.

Interestingly, for his alleged loyalist sentiments and activities while living as a captive of Blackfish, Boone was court-martialed in 1778. The specific charges were that Captain Boone had willingly surrendered to the Shawnees and that he had lived contentedly under Shawnee and British protection. Although the military court found him not guilty of all charges, this court-martial experience embittered him and undoubtedly prompted his move away from Boonesborough.

He moved with his family in 1780 to build his own settlement at Boone's Station. Now a local folk hero, he was promoted to the rank of lieutenant colonel in the militia, appointed sheriff and deputy surveyor of Fayette County, and elected to the Virginia General Assembly. During his years as a state legislator, Boone seemed to have usually deferred to his more politically experienced, better-educated colleagues. It was during this short tenure as a Virginia assemblyman that the British again captured Boone. In his 1781 audacious attempt to capture Virginia Governor Thomas Jefferson and members of the assembly, the notorious British Colonel Banastre ("No Quarter") Tarleton raided Charlottesville and then made his way up the nearby mountain to Jefferson's beautiful mountaintop home, Monticello. Jefferson and most of the assemblymen were able to escape, but Boone and several others were captured. Dressed as he usually was in buckskin and moccasins (never, however, in a coonskin hat), Boone did not look like a periwigged aristocratic legislator. Convinced that he was merely a plain-looking, plainspoken farmer, the British released him unharmed.

In the postwar period, Boone remained as restless as ever. Frequently resettling, he moved to Limestone on the Ohio River, then to Point Pleasant in what is today West Virginia, and then to the northern region of Louisiana (present-day Missouri). During these latter years, he was given what he thought was valid title to thousands of acres of land primarily in Kentucky and also in what is today Missouri. Apparently he never legally entitled his land holdings. By 1799 he had lost, through legal action, or had given away, to pay off creditors, all of his land holdings.

Because of his lifelong aversion to living in crowded settled areas, Boone spent most of the last two decades of his life on the Missouri frontier hunting, fishing, trapping, and exploring. His wife of fifty-six years died in 1813, leaving the eighty-year-old frontiersman ever more depressed. Up to the end, however, Boone was active physically.

In 1815, he took two trips, one to Fort Osage, near the present city of Kansas City, and the second one further west to the area of present Yellowstone National Park. In 1817 he walked back to Kentucky, where he finally paid off all of his creditors. Thus he was able to spend his last three years entirely debt-free.

When he died in September 1820, Boone was living with his daughter Jemima (the illegitimate child of his wife Rebecca and his brother "Ned"). After eating a big meal at his son Nathan's house, Daniel Boone retired to a bedroom where he died quietly and uncomplainingly. With his death, yet another American Revolutionary hero passed from the scene. He was honored during his lifetime and has been remembered ever since as the quintessential American frontier folk hero: rugged, resourceful, patriotic, talented, ingenious, and unpretentious.

Joseph Brant (1742–1807)

As the chief of the Mohawks, Joseph Brant (Indian name: Thayendanegea) led four of the six Iroquois tribes (Mohawks, Onondagas, Cayugas, and Senecas) into an alliance with Great Britain during the

American Revolution. Commissioned in 1775 as a Captain in the British Army, this charismatic Indian leader fought so ferociously and successfully against the American incursions into traditional Iroquois lands that General Washington, in the midst of the War for American Independence (1778), was forced to detach a sizeable portion of his army to thwart Brant's continual assaults on American settlements in frontier New York and Pennsylvania. In battle, Brant demonstrated a coolness, bravery, and competence that often led to victory, sometimes against seemingly overwhelming odds.

Born in 1742 to a Mohawk father and Indian mother in what is today the state of Ohio, Thayendanegea joined Sir William Johnson (who was to be appointed the British Superintendent for Indian Affairs north of the Ohio River in 1756) in fighting against the French in the Battle of Lake George (1755) during the French and Indian War. At the tender and impressionable age of thirteen, he apparently fell under the influence and tutelage of the popular Sir William Johnson. Joseph Brant's sister Molly was to become Sir William Johnson's wife, and later Brant was appointed secretary to Sir William's successor and nephew Guy Johnson. Undoubtedly, the close filial relationship with the influential Johnson family greatly aided Brant's rise to prominence as the leading pro-British Indian leader. The Indian Superintendent sent the young Mohawk warrior to Moor's Charity School for Indians in Lebanon, Connecticut, where he learned English and became an Anglican convert. After two years of formal schooling (1761–1763), Brant became an interpreter for an Anglican missionary. During Pontiac's War (1763–1766) Brant again took up arms, joining the Iroquois tribes that supported the British against Pontiac and his Ottawa, Chippewa, and Huron allies. His loyalty to Britain was rewarded with a captain's commission in 1775 and a trip to the British court in London, where he was presented at court (as his father apparently had been back in 1710) and generally wined and dined.

Brant, along with the notorious loyalist leaders Walter Butler and his father John Butler, was present at the Cedars (a small American outpost some 30 miles west of Montreal) in May 1776 when a small American force, which had been sent to relieve the American garrison that had already surrendered, was ambushed and captured. The victorious Indians then reportedly were allowed to torture and kill a half dozen of the American prisoners. At the Cedars, the Butlers, especially the son Walter, gained a reputation for cruelty and savagery, although there is no certain proof that the reputation was deserved. There is not even a hint that Joseph Brant, who was present at the Cedars at the time of the savage, sadistic murders of the American prisoners, condoned or participated in the barbaric killings.

During the early part of the Revolutionary War, Brant led his Mohawk followers in several notable battles against the American patriots. As leader of the Mohawk contingent that accompanied Lieutenant Colonel Barry St. Leger's expedition eastward from Lake Ontario along the Mohawk River in 1777, Brant planned and then executed the successful Indian ambush of a New York militia unit under the command of General Nicholas Herkimer at the Battle of Oriskany. When St. Leger retreated after failing to capture Fort Stanwix, Brant and most of his Mohawk followers returned home to upper state New York. In late 1778 and into 1779, Brant, after a successful raid against the village of Cherry Valley, New York, ravaged the Mohawk River Valley and nearby New York and Pennsylvania frontier settlements. Brant's success in spreading fear and devastation among these frontier American villages and farms prompted General George Washington to order the Sullivan/Clinton expedition (May–November 1779), which almost completely destroyed the Iroquois tribes as serious military threats.

Brant's major contribution to the British war effort was to convince, with the aid of his political mentors, the Johnsons, most of the Iroquois tribes to remain loyal to Great Britain, even after the devastating military reversals of 1779. Even though he married the daughter of an Oneida chief, Brant was unable to convince her tribe or the Tuscaroras to join in the fight against the Americans.

After ratification of the Treaty of Paris (1783) ending the war, Brant urged his Mohawk followers and other western Indian tribes to end their depredations against western American settlements. In this he was only partially successful. His only real achievement in postwar Indian diplomacy was to help negotiate, on behalf of the American government, a peace treaty with the Miamis.

The British rewarded Brant for his military service and for his diplomatic successes in keeping most of the Iroquois tribes loyal with a sizeable land grant on the Grand River in Ontario. He moved his tribe to their new home, where he spent his remaining years in Christian missionary endeavors. In 1785, he again visited Great Britain to solicit money for the First Episcopal Church in Upper Canada. After his death in 1807 near

Brantford, Canada, friends and former foes alike honored Joseph Brant as a "noble savage" and compassionate Native American leader.

John Dickinson (1732–1808)

John Dickinson was one of the most highly respected and influential political figures of the revolutionary period. Born in 1732 to Quaker parents on Maryland's Eastern Shore, in 1740 he moved to Kent County, Delaware. In 1750 the now eighteen-year-old moved to Philadelphia to become an apprentice in the law office of the well-known John Moland. From 1753 to1757, John continued his study of the law in London at The Middle Temple, thus becoming one of the relatively few Americans to receive what was undoubtedly the best legal training in the English-speaking world. Returning to Philadelphia, he took up the practice of law and soon became one of the busiest and most eminent attorneys in Pennsylvania.

In 1760 he began his political career in the Delaware Assembly, and followed, in 1762, with his election to the Pennsylvania Assembly. Because he maintained residences in both Delaware and Pennsylvania, Dickinson was eligible to, and in fact did, hold public office in both colonies/states. As a staunch supporter of the proprietary government in colonial Pennsylvania, he gained the enmity of the eminent Dr. Benjamin Franklin, who was the leading opponent of the Penn family's proprietary government. In opposition to the Sugar Act (1764) and Stamp Act (1765), Dickinson published in 1765 "The Late Regulations Respecting the British Colonies . . . Considered." In this thoughtful and widely circulated pamphlet, he argued persuasively that the best way to get these almost universally despised acts repealed was to convince British merchants that their enforcement would damage their own financial interests. Therefore they would lobby Parliament for repeal. Chosen as a delegate to the Stamp Act Congress (1765), he drafted that body's declaration of rights and grievances. It is, however, for his twelve *Letters from a Farmer in Pennsylvania to the Inhabitants of the British Colonies* that John Dickinson is most well known and for which he gained the nom de plume "Penman of the Revolution." With the publication of these widely distributed, highly influential letters, John Dickinson became the leading spokesman for American rights and American liberty.

In 1774 as a delegate to the First Continental Congress, Dickinson wrote that body's "Declaration and Resolves," which was followed by his election to the Second Continental Congress. As a leader of the moderates in Congress, who wanted reform within the existing British imperial system but not drastic modification or political separation, he coauthored (with Thomas Jefferson) the "Declaration . . . Setting Forth the Causes and Necessity of Their Taking Up Arms" (1775).

However, it was Dickinson's refusal to sign the Declaration of Independence that tarnished his historical reputation and earned him the enmity of many of his contempories. John Adams, for example, characterized Dickinson as "a certain great Fortune and piddling genius, whose Fame has been trumpeted so loudly, has given a silly cast to our Whole doings."[2] Actually, he was not against declaring independence per se, but as the congressional leader of the reconciliationist faction, Dickinson wanted one last concerted effort at reconciliation to be made before the decision for separation from Great Britain was finally and perhaps irrevocably made. However, after independence was declared, he embraced "The Glorious Cause" enthusiastically and wholeheartedly. In 1777, he was the principal draftsman of the country's first constitution—the Articles of Confederation and Perpetual Union.

After serving briefly in the military and in Congress off and on until 1780, Dickinson was elected president (governor) of Delaware and a year later president of Pennsylvania. After three stormy years as president of Pennsylvania, he eagerly moved back to the relative peace and tranquility of Delaware, where citizens later sent him as a delegate to the Constitutional Convention. At the "Grand Convention," he was a leader of the small-state nationalistic faction, which helped fashion the "Great Compromise" between large and small states. During the ratification debate, Dickinson authored the widely read *Letters of Fabius* supporting ratification of the 1787 document. His death in 1808 was greatly lamented and widely reported.

Benjamin Franklin (1706–1790)

As a scientist, politician, and diplomat, Benjamin Franklin was a giant of the Revolutionary era. As the youngest son in a family of seventeen children, Benjamin did not inherit the wealth and status enjoyed by most of the Founding Fathers. Instead he was heir to lower-middle-class respectability and Calvinist piety.

Franklin's life and public career spanned the eighteenth century. Born in Boston in 1706, he was involved, frequently as a major player, in many of the most notable events of that eventful century. By the time of his death in 1790, he had been an important participant in the Great Awakening, the Enlightenment, the French and Indian War (1754–1763), the American Revolution (1763–1783), and the drafting of the Constitution (1787).

By 1763, Benjamin Franklin had become the most well-known American in both Europe and America. In Europe, for his electrical experiments (1745–1752), he had been awarded honorary doctorates by St. Andrews University (1759) and Oxford University (1762). From 1757 through 1775, except for a two-year hiatus in Philadelphia (1762–1764), Franklin lived in London as the colonial agent for the Pennsylvania Assembly. Appointed colonial agent for Georgia (1768), for New Jersey (1769), and for Massachusetts (1770), Franklin, by the early 1770s, had become the London-based "spokesman" for the thirteen English mainland colonies.

In America, Franklin had become well known as a printer and provincial politician. His publication of the highly respected *Pennsylvania Gazette* (purchased in 1729) and of *Poor Richard's Almanack,* in addition to several lucrative business ventures, such as the establishment of several colonial newspapers, enabled the entrepreneurial Franklin to amass a fortune and to retire from the business world in 1748—at the age of 42. The *Almanack* was his most profitable and long-enduring business success. Franklin sold over 10,000 copies of this popular publication annually between 1732 and 1757. Through the pithy aphorisms of Richard Saunders, the name of Benjamin Franklin became famous throughout the thirteen mainland colonies. These maxims, borrowed (often plagiarized) from a variety of sources, reflected Franklin's own personal formula for happiness and success. Sayings such as "God helps them that help themselves," "Eat to live, and not live to eat," "Haste makes Waste," and "Fish and Visitors stink after three days" constituted a practical philosophy well suited to British colonists living on the edge of civilization that was eighteenth-century America. After his retirement, Franklin would devote his considerable talents and abilities to scientific inquiry and public service, first as a politician and later as a diplomat.

As a provincial politician, Benjamin gained valuable political experience first as the clerk of the Pennsylvania Assembly (1736–1751) and later as an elected member of that colony's unicameral assembly, where he became a leader of the anti-proprietary party, which sought the overthrow of the Penn family proprietary government. In 1754 he was elected a delegate to the Albany Congress, where he presented a plan of union for the thirteen disunited British mainland colonies. Although not adopted, his plan contained many provisions later incorporated into the two national constitutions and into several of the state constitutions of the Revolutionary period.

Before 1765, Franklin was a staunch and enthusiastic supporter of British imperial policies and of the British Empire. However, with passage of the hated Stamp Act to which he initially urged compliance, he soon became disenchanted with British taxing policies and in fact became actively involved in the colonial protest movement. Dismissed from his sinecure as deputy postmaster general for North America because of his increased opposition to British policies and publicly humiliated before the Privy Council by the Solicitor General Alexander Wedderburn for his part in making public certain letters written by Massachusetts Governor Thomas Hutchinson urging curtailment of colonial rights, Franklin, by 1775, had become fully convinced that conciliation with Britain was a unrealistic hope.

Upon his return to Philadelphia in March 1775, he was immediately chosen as a Pennsylvania delegate to the Second Continental Congress. As a popular elder statesman, he quickly assumed a leadership role in Congress as it prepared for armed conflict and possible separation from the mother country. He actively served on the five-member committee appointed to draft a declaration of independence. Although primarily the work of Thomas Jefferson, the final draft approved by Congress on July 4, 1776, did include several changes suggested by Franklin and John Adams.

From 1776 to 1785, the now elderly Franklin served brilliantly as America's first minister to France. Beloved by the French people—men and women—for his wit and disarming charm and greatly respected by governmental officials, he was instrumental in negotiating two treaties with France—one a commercial treaty and the other a treaty creating an alliance with Britain's ancient foe. The 1778 alliance greatly helped the colonies to obtain their independence. As the most well-known member of the diplomatic team that drafted the favorable Treaty of Paris (1783), Franklin proved to be an adroit negotiator by appeasing the French, who resented the United States for concluding a separate treaty with Britain. Finally in 1785, Congress acquiesced in Franklin's oft-stated request to be relieved of his diplomatic post.

Upon his return to his beloved Philadelphia, he was elected President of the Pennsylvania Executive Council, serving in that position for three consecutive years. In early 1787 he was added to the Pennsylvania delegation to the Constitutional Convention. His election to and attendance at the "Grand Convention" gave the gathering legitimacy. His major role in this "assembly of demi-gods" was that of a conciliator.

In private life, Franklin was an indifferent husband (Benjamin did not have his wife Deborah join him during his lengthy stays in Europe), but loving and caring father and grandfather. In 1730, he "took to wife" Deborah Read, although this union was never formalized. To this common-law marriage, which lasted until Deborah's death in 1774, Franklin brought his illegitimate son William (born in 1729 or early 1730 to an unidentified mother). With long periods of separation, it was obvious that this union was one of convenience, not of love. Even so, Deborah and Benjamin had two children of their own: Francis Folger (born 1732), who tragically died in 1736 of smallpox, and Sarah (born 1743), who later married Richard Bache and was an enduring source of comfort to Franklin in his old age.

However, the illegitimate son William was a source of grave disappointment to Franklin. In the 1760s, Benjamin had helped to secure William's appointment as royal governor of New Jersey. However, father and son became estranged with the approach of the Revolution. The son remained loyal to Britain while the father embraced the patriot cause.

For the last few years of his life, Dr. Franklin was honored as the most revered senior statesman of the entire American Revolutionary era. After his death in April 1790, some 20,000 people followed his cortege to Philadelphia's Christ Church burial ground. This was surely a fitting final tribute to one of America's most famous citizens.

King George III (1738–1820)

George William Frederick (George III) was America's last king. As such, he has been somewhat undeservedly blamed (as in the Declaration of Independence) for pursuing policies that made the American War for Independence necessary and even inevitable.

During much of the nineteenth century after his death in 1820, George III was portrayed as the chief villain on the British side in the Anglo-American tempest of the 1760s, 1770s, and 1780s. On balance, however, this insecure, somewhat slow-witted, hardworking man turned out to be one of Great Britain's better monarchs. Although he is blamed for the breakup of the First British Empire during the American Revolution, he should be credited with successfully rallying his country to oppose Revolutionary France and then to defeat Napoleonic France. During George III's latter years as king, Britain started down the road to unchallenged nineteenth century industrial supremacy and to imperial greatness with the establishment of the Second British Empire.

As the first Hanoverian monarch to be born in Britain, George was, unlike his grandfather George II and great-grandfather George I, as much British as German, although he was, concurrently with his kingship of Great Britain, the elector (1760–1814) and then king (1814–1820) of the German state of Hanover. Unlike his two predecessors who were philosophically German who happened to occupy the British throne, George III gloried in being British.

George William Frederick had a troubled and probably therefore unhappy upbringing. He did not learn to read until the age of eleven. He fell under the influence of his strong-willed mother, who reportedly frequently admonished the seemingly apathetic youth to be a king (i.e., to act confidently and authoritatively). His boyhood Scottish tutor (John Stuart, third Earl of Bute) also greatly and perhaps unduly influenced the impressionable young boy.

At the age of twelve, the young, overly serious boy became heir-apparent to the British throne upon the death of his father Frederick. Soon thereafter, his grandfather, King George II, died and the twenty-two-year-old George ascended the British throne on October 25, 1760. He was almost totally ill prepared to guide Britain to victory in the then raging Seven Years' War (in America the French and Indian War) and to confront and then to solve the manifold postwar problems of debt, imperial authority, and crown/parliamentary relations facing the nation. Thus, at a crucial time in her history when statesmanship was desperately needed, Britain got a politically inexperienced, initially naïve, and intensely sensitive new king. The first ten years of George III's reign were ones of learning to be king. However, by 1770 with his appointment of Lord Frederick North as Prime Minister, George III became "the king" his mother had counseled him to be. Although George III and Lord North have become, for many on both sides of the Atlantic Ocean, the twin British villains of the American Revolution, these two leaders worked well together. Educated at Eton and

Oxford, Lord North was the perfect match as Prime Minister for a constitutional monarch who believed in Parliamentary supremacy in both domestic and imperial affairs. George III used the royal gifts of titles, honors, sinecures, and land grants to build up a political following (the King's Friends) headed by Lord North that carried out almost slavishly the king's policy of stubbornly attempting to subdue the rebellious colonies in America, even after it became apparent to many that it could not be successfully carried out.

Throughout his long reign (1760–1820), George III was the model constitutional monarch. He believed fervently in Parliamentary supremacy in the British government and usually worked within that framework to achieve what he thought was best for his beloved Great Britain. Thus the "buying" of support in both the House of Lords and the House of Commons with the granting of titles, gifts, sinecures, and land grants was not only appropriate but also even constitutional under the existing British system of parliamentary government.

If George III were to be blamed for anything regarding the American war, it would be his insistence in continuing the fight even after the entrance of the French, Spanish, and Dutch into the fray changed the conflict against thirteen rebellious colonies into a worldwide war that greatly diminished the prospects for a British victory. The king could also be legitimately criticized for appointing two incompetent ministers to oversee the waging of the conflict: John Montagu, fourth Earl of Sandwich as First Lord of the Admiralty and George Sackville Germain as Secretary of State for the American Colonies.

Unhappily, during the last thirty-six years of George III's reign, he was tormented intermittently with periods of apparent insanity. During these trying times (most notably 1784–1789 and 1811–1820) his son, the future King George IV, was appointed Regent. The exact nature of his affliction is not known for sure. The most plausible guess is that the unfortunate king inherited a condition known as porphyria, which is defined as a pathological state characterized by abnormalities of the metabolism. This condition often causes unaccounted-for pain, sensitivity to light, periods of disillusionment, and bouts of abnormal behavior. These are all attributes displayed by George III during the latter decades of his life.

During his last years, George III was much beloved by the British people. He had guided Great Britain through the turbulent times of the American Revolution, the French Revolution, and the Napoleonic Period.

He had recovered from at least one long bout of "madness." This devoted family man had become a symbol of conservative stability in an unstable world. Unfortunately for his historical reputation, he will always be remembered as the king who lost the American colonies.

Patrick Henry (1736–1799)

Born in Hanover County, Virginia, to John Henry and Sarah Winston, the future "Trumpet of the Revolution" inherited from his university-educated father an independence of mind and spirit and from his mother an abiding sense of self-worth. His formal early education was sporadic. However, in learning the basics of reading, writing, and mathematics, young Patrick had by his early twenties acquired the necessary skills to study the law and in 1760 to be admitted to the Virginia bar. With a keen intelligence, a quick wit, and an enviable gift for persuasive oratory, Patrick Henry embarked upon his legal and political careers at an auspicious time.

Indeed, the 1760s provided numerous opportunities for men of ability to display their talents for political leadership, for advancement in the legal profession, and, especially for Henry, for dynamic oratory. As a practicing lawyer and newly elected member of the House of Burgesses, Henry soon became a leader of the growing, radical, anti-British protest movement in Virginia.

On December 1, 1763, he entered public life with his impassioned speech in the so-called "Parson's Cause." This case involved the royal disallowance of a Virginia law, which in effect reduced the annual salary of Anglican clergymen. Arguing that the British king, in disallowing a law passed by the Virginia legislature, had forfeited the allegiance of his subjects, Patrick Henry became an instant hero to his embattled frontier neighbors and to the growing numbers of dissenting, anti-Anglican Virginians.

In 1765, during the Stamp Act crisis, Henry gave one of his most famous and oft-quoted speeches. In defending the resolutions he introduced to oppose the hated Stamp Act, Henry was reported to have said, "Caesar had his Brutus, Charles the First had his Cromwell, and George the Third—." Supposedly the Speaker of the House at this moment interrupted him with cries of "Treason! Treason!" He then allegedly completed his oration with ". . . may profit by their example! If this be treason, make the most of it."[3] As the recognized leader of the radical faction in the House of Burgesses, Henry was chosen as a delegate to the First Continental

Congress (1774), where he met many of the other revolutionary leaders such as John and Samuel Adams, John Dickinson, John Jay, and John Rutledge. His election in 1775 to the more radical Second Continental Congress completed his public service at the national level.

It was of course in Virginia, not in Philadelphia, that Patrick Henry was to achieve his reputation for effective leadership and persuasive oratory now associated with his name. In March 1775 Henry gave his most famous speech. Everyone who heard his spirited defense of his three motions proposed to prepare Virginia for what he thought would be the inevitable armed conflict with Great Britain, agreed that this was the most powerful and most compelling speech they had ever heard. Although there is no extant copy of this well-known speech, the most commonly accepted version is that of Henry's first serious biographer, William Wirt.

> Gentlemen may cry peace, peace—but there is no peace. The war is actually begun! The next gale that sweeps the north will bring to our ears the clash of resounding arms. Our brethren are already in the field! Why stand we here idle? What is it the gentlemen wish? What would they have? Is life so dear, or peace so sweet, as to be purchased at the price of chains and slavery? Forbid it, almighty God! I know not what course others may take; but as for me . . . give me liberty or give me death![4]

Chosen as a delegate to the convention, which drafted and adopted Virginia's first state constitution, Henry was, in 1776, also elected the state's first governor. During his three one-year terms as governor during the War for Independence, Henry vigorously supported the war effort by recruiting some 6,000 Virginians for service in the Continental Army and over 5,000 for the state militia. During his second term, he was instrumental in providing the encouragement and supplies for the famous and extremely successful George Rogers Clark expedition, which by capturing several strategic British outposts in the Illinois country greatly reduced British control in the upper Mississippi River Valley.

In the 1780s, Henry served once again as a member of the Virginia legislature (1780–1784) and then again as governor (1784–1786). When elected as a Virginia delegate to the Philadelphia Constitutional Convention, he refused to attend, allegedly stating—probably apocryphally—"he smelt a rat." As a strong advocate of states' rights, Henry considered the "rat" to be the obvious nationalism of most of the delegates.

In the Virginia ratifying convention, Henry led the anti-federalist faction, which opposed the document that created a strong national government. Although unable to prevent ratification, Henry, along with fellow anti-federalists George Mason and James Monroe, was able to secure assurances that a bill of rights would be added. Thus along with George Mason and James Madison, Patrick Henry can rightly be considered as the "father" of the U.S. Bill of Rights.

In the 1790s, Henry eschewed public office. As a private citizen, he vehemently opposed, in the early 1790s, the Hamiltonian fiscal program as being too nationalistic. However, by 1796, he had become an ardent Federalist supporting wholeheartedly the centralizing, pro-British policies of presidents George Washington and John Adams. During Washington's tenure as president, he offered Henry the positions of secretary of state, minister to Spain, and chief justice of the United States. In declining these offers, Henry cited ill health. Finally, in the year of both of their deaths, Washington was able to persuade the former governor to run for the Virginia legislature. During the election campaign, Patrick Henry gave his last memorable speech, in which he argued persuasively against a state's right to decide the constitutionality of a national law.

Henry died June 6, 1799, from what was probably stomach cancer. His death was greatly lamented and widely reported.

Thomas Hutchinson (1711–1780)

As the last civilian royal governor of colonial Massachusetts, Thomas Hutchinson was, for many colonists, the very embodiment of tyrannical British rule. Unfortunately this American-born royal official remained steadfastly loyal to the British crown even when he disagreed strongly with its policies of taxation and coercion. Thus, in the period 1765–1775, he became the most conspicuous scapegoat for many increasingly disgruntled colonists who opposed the British attempts to reform colonial administration and to assert more forcefully Parliamentary control over the thirteen mainland colonies. As a consequence of being on the losing side during the American War for Independence, he endured disgrace and exile during his lifetime. Moreover, his historical reputation has generally suffered because of his obvious and well-publicized loyalism. Honor and historical acclaim are usually reserved for winners. On the other hand, losers are habitually, and often unfairly, criticized and discredited. The patriot Revolutionary leaders (winners) are eulogized and revered, whereas the loyalists (losers)—often derisively referred to as Tories—are censured and maligned. As one of the more prominent colonial loyalists, Thomas Hutchinson has been vilified or neglected and even ignored.

The study of his public career as a longtime colonial and then royal office-holder makes obvious the salient fact that the American Revolution was first and perhaps foremost a civil war. Frequently the most acrimonious political battles before 1775 were between those Americans who remained loyal to Britain and those who favored and worked for independence. Likewise, some of the bloodiest military encounters during the war were those in which Americans were fighting and killing Americans.

As governor of one of the most rebellious colonies, Hutchinson found it impossible to serve two masters. As provincial interests increasingly deviated from imperial interests, this royally appointed governor could not satisfy his royal master and at the same time retain the support of his discontented Massachusetts constituents. Hutchinson's apparent avarice, his haughty lifestyle, and his rigid political conservatism did not cause the ever more evident political estrangement between the Samuel Adams–led radical faction in Massachusetts and the Hutchinson-Oliver clan, but they certainly exacerbated an already untenable situation. Unlike most of the patriot Revolutionary leaders who came to manhood and positions of power, wealth, and authority during, what were for them, auspicious times, Thomas Hutchinson finally reached his long-sought-after goal as governor during, what was for him, an inauspicious time for both his political/judicial career and his historical reputation.

A careful study of his long public career and of his well-ordered private life reveals a man of character, ability, vaulting ambition, and mild avarice. These are, of course, traits which Hutchinson shared with many, if not all of, the more famous and now venerated patriot Revolutionary leaders. Because he was the most conspicuous and most articulate spokesman for the loyalist perspective, a careful look at Hutchinson's life is exceedingly helpful to understand the multifaceted conflict between patriots and loyalists.

As a fifth-generation American, Thomas Hutchinson had ancestral roots that went deep in colonial Massachusetts. The great-great-grandson of the famous Anne Marbury Hutchinson, Thomas was born into wealth and privilege. After graduation from Harvard (B.A., 1727; M.A., 1730), he worked in his father's mercantile firm. Success as a merchant and his impeccable family connections made possible his entrance into politics in 1737 as an elected member of the Massachusetts House of Representatives.

During his twelve years in the House (served as Speaker 1746–1748), Hutchinson became a hard-money advocate (e.g., he opposed the Land Bank scheme of 1740–1741). Thus as early as the 1750s, Hutchinson had gained the everlasting enmity of several well-entrenched and politically powerful provincial families. In particular, Deacon Samuel Adams (father of Samuel Adams the Revolutionary) and James Otis, Sr. (father of the Revolutionary leader James Otis, Jr.) were outraged over Hutchinson's hard-money policies and over his accumulation of political and judicial offices often at the expense of the Adams and Otis families. This early estrangement helps to explain the political conflicts of the 1760s and 1770s between the coalition created by Hutchinson (usually referred to as the Hutchinson/Oliver court party) and the country party of Samuel Adams and James Otis, Jr. The political conflicts of the immediate prewar years in Massachusetts were obviously struggles between patriots and loyalists over British policies and actions. However, they were also, although less obviously, the result of long-seething antagonisms between two long-existing provincial political factions.

After 1749, Hutchinson's political advancement was rapid and note-worthy. As a member of the council (1749–1766), he attended the Albany Congress of 1754, where he supported Benjamin Franklin's famous, al-though never implemented, Plan of Union. Appointed lieutenant gover-nor of Massachusetts in 1758 and chief justice two years later, Hutchinson had, by 1760, achieved fame, fortune, and enviable political and judicial power and influence. His appointment as royal governor of Massachusetts (1770–1774) only capped a brilliant career as a royal placeman.

It was as lieutenant governor and later as chief justice that Thomas Hutchinson ran afoul of the Samuel Adams/James Otis, Jr. faction. In 1761 he issued several writs of assistance (general search warrants) that brought him into open opposition to James Otis, Jr. In opposing the writs of as-sistance issued by his longtime political rival Thomas Hutchinson, James Otis, Jr. revived the political conflict between his family and the Hutchinson/Oliver clan. Thus Otis's brilliant, but unsuccessful as it turns out, tirade against the use of writs of assistance was only in part a well-reasoned harangue against an illegal, oppressive British policy. It was also another battle in the already existing political war that had been raging since the early 1740s in colonial Massachusetts Bay.

Hutchinson's support of the Sugar Act (1764) and Stamp Act (1765) only further angered the growing radical faction led by Samuel Adams,

John Hancock, and James Otis, Jr. Although he personally opposed these two tax laws on the basis that they would greatly impede trade within the British empire, Hutchinson felt, as a highly placed royal official, that he was duty-bound to enforce them. His support of these hated taxes and his often publicly stated belief that Parliament had the right to tax the colonies made the name of Thomas Hutchinson anathema to most of his Massachusetts constituents. In the violence after passage of the Stamp Act, the Boston mob sacked the Hutchinson mansion. His subsequent enforcement of the Townshend Duties in the period 1767–1770 and his insistence that the Tea Act of 1773 be strictly executed only helped to intensify the anti-Hutchinson feeling. In adhering to the strict letter of the Tea Act, Hutchinson helped to precipitate the famous Boston Tea Party of December 16, 1773. Finally, the publication in 1773 of six letters he had written to imperial officials in London in which he advocated sterner measures in asserting the government's authority over the colonies convinced many in Massachusetts that Thomas Hutchinson was indeed an enemy to American freedom and liberty.

Despite the growing hostility to his policies and person, Hutchinson traveled to Britain, in 1774, to urge the Crown and Parliament to adopt a conciliatory policy towards his fellow colonists. The fighting that began in April 1775 at Lexington and Concord made impractical if not impossible his planned return to Massachusetts. He ended his days in Great Britain, a disillusioned, unheralded exile from his beloved Massachusetts homeland. His death in 1780 spared this loyal royal servant from having to witness the birth of the new American republic.

John Jay (1745–1829)

John Jay was respected as one of the most conscientious, intelligent, and experienced jurists, politicians, and diplomats of the Revolutionary Era. Born into the New York aristocracy, the always somber Jay had the family connections (he was related to the aristocratic Van Cortlandt family of New York through his mother and married into the patrician William Livingston family of New Jersey) and educational opportunities that were at least helpful, if not absolutely essential, prerequisites for legal, diplomatic, and political prominence in New York and in the emerging American republic.

Following graduation from King's College (now Columbia University) in 1764 and admittance to the New York bar in 1768, Jay embarked on a distinguished and busy legal career that eventually led to his appointment in 1777 as chief justice of New York, and in 1789 as the first chief justice of the United States under the Constitution of 1787. Like the other Founding Fathers, Jay came to manhood during auspicious times. With his patrician family connections, his excellent classical education, his legal training, and a growing and prosperous legal practice in New York City, it is perhaps inevitable that the young attorney became involved in the political unrest of the early 1770s. Public service as the secretary of the New York–New Jersey boundary commission in 1773 and thereafter as a member of the New York Committee of Correspondence launched Jay into a public career that spanned twenty-eight years, during which time he participated in many of the most noteworthy, significant events of the early American republic.

Jay's first foray into national politics came with his election in 1774 to the First Continental Congress. As one of the leaders of the conservative majority, John cautioned patience and restraint in opposition to the Coercive Acts. Even at this early date, John Jay's Anglophilia (caused in part by his Huguenot and therefore anti-French ancestry and by his admiration for the essential political conservatism of the British government) was evident. Up to July 1776, Jay was a reluctant revolutionary. Instead he favored reconciliation and a return to the pre-1763 policies of "salutary neglect" that allowed for semiautonomous colonial local control. However, by July 1776, as a member of the Second Continental Congress, Jay supported the growing movement towards independence. Although absent in New York during the congressional debate and vote on the Declaration of Independence, Jay championed ratification and would undoubtedly have signed it had he been present.

During the Revolutionary War, Jay was the chief architect of the New York state constitution of 1777, was an active member of the Congress (served as president 1778–1779), and was minister plenipotentiary to Spain. In all of these positions, Jay demonstrated a capacity for diligence and competence. However, his mission to Spain (1780–1782) must be considered a failure in that he was unable to negotiate a treaty of alliance with Spain, was not able to procure more than token military and financial aid, and failed to obtain even Spanish recognition of the American republic.

Jay's most notable achievement during the American War for Independence was as a member of the delegation that negotiated the highly favorable Treaty of Paris of 1783. Working with Benjamin Franklin and John Adams, Jay played a significant role in crafting the advantageous treaty, which not only confirmed American independence, but also gave the newly created republic generous boundaries. Jay's specific major contributions to the success of the Paris negotiations were first, his convincing both Franklin and Adams that America should negotiate unilaterally with Great Britain, and second, his withdrawing the demand that Britain cede Canada to the United States in order to get British approval of the Mississippi River as the western boundary of the United States. Of particular note was his insistence that the American delegation should negotiate unilaterally with the British. This was reflective of his mistrust of the French Foreign Minister Vergennes, of his even greater mistrust of Spanish motives, and finally of his inherent pro-British proclivities. The Treaty of Paris (1783) was a diplomatic success of the first order and John Jay was one of the chief architects of that diplomatic triumph.

Jay's post-revolutionary career was one of continued diplomatic, political, and legal achievements. In 1786 as the second Secretary for Foreign Affairs under the Articles of Confederation, Jay negotiated a treaty with Spain under which the right of navigation of the Mississippi River was restricted in return for Spanish trade concessions. Fortunately for the United States and for John Jay's historical reputation, the treaty failed to be ratified in Congress.

Although not elected as a delegate to the Constitutional Convention, Jay strongly supported the strong, centralized national government it created. Along with his close friend and fellow New Yorker Alexander Hamilton and Virginian James Madison, Jay authored the Federalist essays in support of ratification of the Constitution. His five essays (out of the eighty-five published) dealt mostly with foreign affairs in which he drew on his extensive experience as a diplomat.

In 1789 the newly elected President George Washington offered Jay his choice of any position in the incoming administration. After specifically declining the state department portfolio, Jay accepted appointment as the first Chief Justice of the United States. His most notable Supreme Court decision was *Chisholm v. Georgia*, which upheld the right of a citizen of one state to sue another state. In 1794 Washington appointed Chief Justice Jay special envoy to negotiate a treaty with Great Britain. The resultant Jay's Treaty was controversial. Although it might have prevented war with Great Britain, it did not deal meaningfully with the problems facing Anglo-American relations. Among other consequences, Jay's Treaty (narrowly ratified by the U.S. Senate) prompted the emergence of an opposition political faction, which evolved into the Republican party of Thomas Jefferson and James Madison.

Jay resigned from the Supreme Court in 1795 to be elected governor of New York. His six years (two three-year terms) as state chief executive were not noted for memorable accomplishments, but were rather marked by an honest, upright administration of state affairs. An unwillingness to suffer possible election defeat at the hands of an ever more popular Republican party prompted Jay to retire in 1801 to his 800-acre estate in Westchester County, New York. Upon his death in 1829, John Jay was eulogized as being one of the revered Founding Fathers who gave generously of his time and talents to the achievement of American independence and to the creation of the American republic.

Thomas Jefferson (1743–1826)

Political theorist, architect, writer, musician, educator, politician, horticulturist, bibliophile, diplomat, and linguist, Thomas Jefferson was indeed a Renaissance man. Moreover, he was the most elusive and complex of the renowned revolutionary leaders. He was during his long and distinguished public career both a states-righter and nationalist, a democrat and aristocrat, and a quasi-pacifist and imperialist. However, throughout his productive public life, Jefferson steadfastly remained the leading spokesman for the high ideals of the American Revolution.

Born the third child in a family of six sisters and four brothers, Thomas inherited from his father, Peter Jefferson, middle-class respectability and a love of learning, and from his mother, Jane Randolph, aristocratic status. As a member of the slave-owning, plantation-owning gentry of frontier Virginia, young Thomas was given opportunities denied most Virginians for formal education and genteel living. With his father's death in 1757, Thomas, age fourteen, became the patriarch of the Jefferson clan. In 1760 Thomas entered the College of William and Mary in Williamsburg, where he completed his classical education. Upon graduation, he studied law under the tutelage of the renowned legal scholar George Wythe and was admitted to the bar in 1767. By 1769 he had become one of the busiest lawyers in Virginia. His law practice led perhaps inevitably to a political career. Elected to the House of Burgesses, Jefferson, along with fellow

Virginians Patrick Henry, George Washington, George Mason, and Richard Henry Lee, became a quiet spokesman for those who opposed British taxing policies of the late 1760s and 1770s. With the writing in 1774 of *A Summary View of the Rights of British America,* Jefferson gained recognition as an effective and persuasive pamphleteer. This reputation as a writer would lead to his election to the Second Continental Congress in 1775 and to his appointment, along with John Dickinson, to draft the "Declaration of the Causes and Necessity for Taking Up Arms." In this manifesto, Jefferson and Dickinson wrote persuasively of the justification of Americans taking up arms starting in April 1775 against alleged British tyranny. Jefferson's deserved reputation for "felicity of expression" led to his appointment in June of 1776 to the five-member committee that wrote the Declaration of Independence. Urged by John Adams to write the initial draft of this famous document, Jefferson spent the last half of June writing what became the basis of the Declaration. The draft was presented to Congress on June 28th with minor changes suggested by Benjamin Franklin and John Adams; Congress debated and revised the draft, finally approving of the document on July 4, 1776.

It is for the Declaration of Independence that Thomas Jefferson is most honored. In it, he became the articulate spokesman for the high ideals of the American Revolution. Disclaiming originality, Jefferson drew on the writings of John Locke and other English Whigs to espouse in graceful language a philosophy that has become the beacon for downtrodden people ever since 1776. Government by the consent of the governed, "that all men are created equal" (certainly a controversial phrase), that all are endowed with certain "unalienable rights," and that among these rights are "life, liberty, and the pursuit of happiness" have become the central themes of American Revolutionary philosophy and the fervent hope of people everywhere right into the twenty-first century.

In 1776 Jefferson returned to the House of Burgesses, where he was instrumental in revising the Virginia legal code. In 1779 he was elected to the first of two terms as governor of the state of Virginia. His tenure as state chief executive was undistinguished primarily because he was unable to prevent a British invasion. In fact he barely avoided official censure for his alleged dereliction of duty.

During the early 1780s Jefferson was happy to return to his beloved Monticello, family, and books. He had designed and built his magnificent home near Charlottesville, Virginia, in stages. The first house, started in 1769, was altered and added to continuously. In 1796, he began a major remodeling program that led to the construction of the mansion essentially as it appears today. As he often remarked, his happiest days were spent on his Virginia mountaintop. Following his wife's greatly lamented death in the fall of 1782, Jefferson went into temporary political retirement at Monticello, from which he did not emerge until 1785 when he accepted appointment as the second American minister to France.

His post–American Revolution political career was one of continued distinguished service. His appointment in 1789 as the first Secretary of State was followed by his founding, along with close friend and Virginia neighbor James Madison, the Republican party, by his election as vice president in 1796, and finally by his contested election as president in 1800. His first inaugural address, containing many of the ideals of the Declaration of Independence, became a blueprint for his largely successful two terms as the third United States president.

In retirement, Jefferson happily returned to his "family, farm, and books." Always active, he was the founder of what has become the University of Virginia, he maintained a wide network of correspondence (most notably with John Adams), and he became an experimental horticulturist, introducing numerous new plants to America.

Since 1998 with the DNA disclosure that Jefferson probably fathered at least one child by his slave Sally Hemings, Jefferson has been under increased criticism for being a racist and a hypocrite regarding slavery. It is often asked how a man who wrote the immortal words "that all men are created equal" could live and seemingly prosper primarily from the labor of some two hundred slaves. The best answer is that Thomas Jefferson was a man of his time. He was born into and raised in a society that fostered and condoned slavery. Also, he was eminently a human being who shared with other humans the potential for behavior now (but not necessarily during his lifetime) considered immoral, unethical, or illegal. Although it is appropriate and understandable to condemn Jefferson's illicit, longtime sexual affair with Sally Hemings and his obvious racism, it need not detract from his manifold accomplishments as a legislator, a diplomat, an educator, a politician, and a statesman. He should be honored as the leading spokesman for the ideals of the American Revolution and perhaps forgiven for his alleged moral lapses.

His death on July 4, 1826, the 50th anniversary of the Declaration of Independence (John Adams died the same day), helped canonize the name of Thomas Jefferson as the apostle of American freedom.

John Paul Jones (1747–1792)

John Paul Jones has become a legendary American naval hero for his spectacular exploits during the American War for Independence. Born at Arbigland estate, county of Kirkcudbright, on Solway Firth, Scotland, John Paul (he added Jones to his name in 1773 probably to hide his true identity because he was then under suspicion of murder for killing one of his mutinous crew members) overcame humble, but respectable origins to become one of the most honored but at the same time the most maligned naval officers in the Contintental Navy. He is now and was during his lifetime rightly honored because of his heroic exploits during the Revolutionary War. He was maligned, sometimes unjustly, because he was considered by most of his fellow naval officers and associates to be a hypocrite, a social climber, and a womanizer who would do almost anything to advance his own career, even if at the expense of others.

As a young lad growing up on the Solway Firth, which forms the west coastal boundary between Scotland and England, John Paul spent many hours boating, fishing, and listening to the sea stories of sailors from nearby Whitehaven. Perhaps inevitably, he took to the sea.

In 1761, at the age of thirteen, he embarked upon his maritime career. With parental consent and encouragement, he entered into an apprenticeship as a cabin boy on the brig *Friendship*. It was during his three years as an apprentice seaman on the *Friendship* that John Paul made several trips across the Atlantic to Fredericksburg, Virginia, where he doubtless visited his older brother William. Also during this formative period, he learned the intricacies of navigation, rigging, and sailing.

For unknown reasons, in 1764 John Paul's master released him from his apprenticeship. For the next five years, John Paul served first as the third mate of the slave ship *King George* and then as chief mate of the slaver *Two Friends* out of Kingston, Jamaica. After years in what he later characterized as that loathsome traffic in human cargo (i.e., the slave trade), he accepted passage home to Scotland.

This trans-Atlantic trip was a turning point in John Paul's life. During the voyage home, both the captain and the first mate died of a fever, and the young, but now experienced John Paul assumed command of the vessel and brought it safely home to Kirkcudbright. The ship's owners then appointed the now twenty-one-year-old John Paul captain for the ship's next voyage to the West Indies.

The young captain made two round-trip voyages between Scotland and the West Indies as master of the brig *John.* During the second trip, John Paul ran afoul of the law. The ship's carpenter, Mungo Maxwell, became rebellious and was, on the captain's orders, flogged for disobedience. After docking at Tobago, the disgruntled Maxwell complained officially of what he considered the unduly harsh punishment at the hands of John Paul. After a brief hearing, the local vice-admiralty court dismissed Maxwell's complaint as unwarranted. Thereafter Maxwell took a ship to Britain, but died of a fever enroute. When Maxwell's father in Great Britain heard of his son's flogging and death, he brought formal murder charges against John Paul. Thus when he reached Kirkcudbright, John Paul was held over for trial on the charge of murder. Released on bail, John Paul quickly returned to Tobago, where he was able to obtain convincing evidence that when the unfortunate Maxwell left for Great Britain after the flogging he was in good health, if not entirely in good spirits. Thereupon John Paul was legally cleared of the murder charge.

Captain Paul then became part owner and captain of the *Betsy,* on which he sailed regularly between London and the British West Indies with occasional side trips to the Madeira Islands to pick up cargoes of wine. During his last trip as master of the *Betsy,* John Paul had his second and most serious quarrel with the law. In Tobago he needed what money he had to purchase the return cargo of sugar and rum. Therefore he refused to pay his crew advance wages, but instead planned to pay the sailors in Britain after the sale of the cargo. The crew members resented greatly this exception to the usual practice of paying advance wages. One unruly sailor threatened the captain, and in what he later termed self-defense, John Paul killed him with his sword. At this point, details become murky. John Paul did turn himself in to a local justice of the peace and was released. Apparently convinced that he would not receive a fair trial in Tobago for the death of a West Indian native, John Paul fled the island and added "Jones" to his name to hide his identity. The following two years were shrouded in mystery, although there is some evidence that he moved to Fredericksburg, Virginia, in 1773. He was at his brother William's bedside when he died in 1774 in Fredericksburg. Also during this mysterious period, Paul Jones, as he was henceforth always called, befriended two prominent congressmen and merchants. Both Joseph Hewes of North Carolina and Robert Morris of Pennsylvania were to play significant roles in Paul Jones's subsequent rise to prominence in the Continental Navy.

In late 1775, apparently with Hewes's help, the twenty-eight-year-old Paul Jones was commissioned a senior lieutenant in the new Continental Navy. With service as first lieutenant on the *Alfred* (the first ship purchased by the Continental Congress) and then as captain of the sloop *Providence,* Paul Jones gained valuable combat experience. During a six-week cruise in 1776, Jones captured eight British prizes and sank eight other ships. Upon his return to Rhode Island, he was greeted as a hero.

This highly successful excursion led to his appointment first as captain of the newly built *Ranger* and later, because of the lobbying efforts of the influential Philadelphia merchant and congressman Robert Morris, as master of the refitted old East Indiaman *Bon Homme Richard* (named by Jones in honor of Benjamin Franklin). It was as captain first of the *Ranger* and later of the *Bon Homme Richard* that Paul Jones achieved the fame he so long sought.

As captain of the *Ranger,* Paul Jones led an audacious raid on Whitehaven, England (the port from which he had sailed some seventeen years earlier as a cabin boy), in which he and his men spiked the cannon in two British forts. He then led his group to nearby St. Mary's Island with the intention of capturing the local nobleman Lord Selkirk for ransom. Fortunately for the lord, he was absent. Unfortunately for Lady Selkirk, she was at home, where she witnessed most of the family silver being taken by these uninvited guests. Interestingly, Jones later redeemed this stolen silver out of his own pocket and returned it to the Selkirks with profuse apologies. The importance of these two raids on British soil was not the prizes taken nor that two forts were rendered, at least temporarily, inoperable. It was that the American navy could sail into British waters virtually unchallenged, conduct two landings, and then depart unmolested.

In 1778, Paul Jones planned and then carried out a daring two-month expedition during which he, with his four-ship Franco-American squadron plus three privateers, captured a large number of prizes while circumnavigating the British Isles. Toward the end of this successful foray into British home waters, the *Bon Homme Richard* engaged and eventually captured the larger H.M.S. *Serapis* in what would become one of the most famous naval engagements in American history. This historic encounter occurred on September 23, 1779, off Flamborough Head on the east coast of Yorkshire, England. Because the *Serapis* was more heavily armed, Jones maneuvered the *Bon Homme Richard* in close alongside of his opponent. For three and a half hours, these two ships were so close that their rigging became entangled and the muzzles of their cannon almost touched. After bitter hand-to-hand and cannon-to-cannon combat, *Serapis*'s mast fell and Captain Richard Pearson surrendered to Jones. Earlier during the night engagement, Pearson had called out for the American captain to surrender and the impetuous Jones reportedly replied, "I have not yet begun to fight." Actually Jones apparently never did utter this apocryphal statement, but it has come down to us as an indication of his indomitable courage in the face of desperate circumstances and overwhelming odds. The *Bon Homme Richard* was so badly damaged that Jones had to abandon her and transfer his flag to the captured *Serapis*. Despite heroic efforts to keep her afloat, the *Bon Homme Richard* sank two days after the battle, and the victorious American captain returned to France to a hero's reception on a captured British man-of-war. It is for his daring capture of H.M.S. *Serapis* that John Paul Jones is best remembered and honored.

The last twelve years of Jones's life were ones of grave disappointments and even despair. He felt ignored and forgotten by his adopted country even though Congress did award him a gold medal in 1787. However, during his brief service as an admiral in the Russian navy, he again was able to display the tactical nautical skills so much in evidence during the American War for Independence by winning two notable sea battles against the Turks. Before he left Russia for the last time in 1789, Jones had a final altercation with the law when he was accused, falsely, of attempting to rape a ten-year-old Russian girl. For reasons now unknown, Jones was allowed to leave the Russian capital. He spent the remaining three years of his life in Paris waiting for the call, which never came, to resume his career as a Russian admiral. Death came to the forty-five-year-old John Paul Jones on July 18, 1792, after which he was buried in the St. Louis cemetery for Protestants outside the walls of Paris. In 1913, his remains were brought back to his adopted country, where they were permanently put to rest in the crypt of the chapel of the United States Naval Academy in Annapolis, Maryland.

Richard Henry Lee (1732–1794)

Born into one of colonial Virginia's most prominent families, Richard Henry Lee enjoyed all of the advantages that such an ancestry could bestow. A middle son of eight children born to Thomas Lee and Hannah Ludwell Lee (there were six boys, four of whom played significant roles during the American Revolution, and two girls), Richard Henry rose to political prominence during the tempestuous years just prior to the outbreak of hostilities in 1775 to become a leading radical spokesman for independence. As a young boy, he was sent to England, where he was graduated from the well-known Wakefield Academy in Yorkshire. Upon his return to Virginia in 1752, he assumed the life of a gentleman farmer. Soon, however, as would be expected as a scion of the prominent Lee family, he entered the political arena first, in 1757, as a justice of the peace in his native Westmoreland County and the next year as a member of the august House of Burgesses. Thus like most of his revolutionary compatriots, Richard Henry Lee came into manhood during propitious times— times that presented numerous opportunities for recognition and achievement by talented, well-educated, well-connected, ambitious young Virginia aristocrats.

Initially as a new young Burgess, Richard Henry observed and learned from his older, more experienced colleagues. During the 1760s and early 1770s, the Virginia House of Burgesses was truly a nursery for statesmen. Such eminent revolutionary leaders as Peyton Randolph (elected President of the First Continental Congress), George Washington (appointed Commander in Chief of the Continental Army), Thomas Jefferson, and Patrick Henry, to name only the most prominent, were members of the Virginia House of Burgesses. By 1764 Richard Henry had become associated with the younger radical faction in the House led by the young orator from Hanover County, Patrick Henry. In response to the Sugar Act (1764) and Stamp Act (1765), Lee established the Westmoreland County nonimportation association. Partly because of his aristocratic heritage and partly because of his growing radicalism, Richard Henry was elected a member of the influential Virginia delegation to the First Continental Congress.

Although overshadowed by his more well-known, experienced Virginia colleagues (Richard Bland, Benjamin Harrison, Edmund Pendleton, Peyton Randolph, and George Washington), Lee quietly allied himself with the radical faction led by Samuel Adams and John Adams of

Massachusetts, Christopher Gadsden of South Carolina, and fellow Virginian Patrick Henry. Although in the minority in the Congress, this radical clique secured endorsement of the Suffolk Resolves, defeated the conservative Joseph Galloway's Plan of Union, and supported the call for a second congress if American grievances were not addressed.

Elected to the Second Continental Congress, Richard Henry Lee became a leader of the group (often referred to as the Adams-Lee faction), who worked feverishly to convince wavering colleagues (especially the delegates from the middle colonies) of the absolute need and desirability of declaring colonial independence. Foremost among radical delegates, Lee viewed a declaration of independence as a necessary prerequisite to securing foreign recognition and much-needed foreign aid for the rebelling colonies. The Adams-Lee faction's persistent efforts to persuade, during the winter and spring of 1776, its congressional colleagues to support the idea of independence from Great Britain led directly to Richard Henry Lee's famous motion of June 7, 1776.

In ringing terms often quoted ever since, Lee offered the following motion, seconded by John Adams:

> That these United Colonies, are, and of right ought to be, free and independent States, that they are absolved from all allegiance to the British Crown, and that all political connection between them and the State of Great Britain is, and ought to be, totally dissolved. That it is expedient forthwith to take the most effectual measures for forming foreign Alliances. That a plan of confederation be prepared and transmitted to the respective Colonies for their consideration and approbation.[5]

Richard Henry Lee's major contributions to the revolutionary cause were his advocacy of independence in the spring of 1776 and his three-part motion. The first part of his famous June 7th motion led to the creation of a committee of five to draft a declaration justifying separation from Great Britain, the second led to the establishment of a committee that eventually evolved into the State Department, and the third led to the appointment of a committee that drafted the Articles of Confederation, the country's first constitution.

Serving as an active member of Congress from 1774 to 1780 and then again from 1784 to 1787 (President of Congress in 1784), Lee signed the Declaration of Independence and then worked diligently to create and to strengthen the national government under the Articles of Confederation.

In the early 1780s as a member of the Virginia House of Delegates, he was largely responsible for persuading Virginia to give up its claims to western lands, an action that convinced neighboring Maryland finally to ratify the Articles of Confederation in 1781 and thus make possible the promulgation of the country's first constitution.

Lee refused election as a delegate to the Constitutional Convention in 1787 partly because of chronic ill health, but also because of his suspicions that the nationalists gathering in Philadelphia would be crafting a document that created a government of unlimited powers. As a delegate to the Virginia Ratifying Convention, Richard Henry Lee with Patrick Henry led the anti-federalist forces in opposing ratification. In opposition to the Constitution, Lee wrote the highly acclaimed *Letters of the Federal Farmer,* in which he contended that the proposed document gave too much power to the national government in part because it did not include a bill of rights. Although losing the ratification struggle, Lee and Henry were largely responsible for getting promises of Federalist support for amendments, which would alleviate some of the concerns of the anti-federalists. With Patrick Henry's considerable encouragement and support, Lee was elected to the first U.S. Senate, where he worked for the passage and ratification of the first ten amendments to the Constitution. For these efforts, Richard Henry Lee should be rightly considered, along with Patrick Henry, George Mason, and James Madison, as one of the "fathers" of the United States Bill of Rights.

Forced to resign his senate seat in 1792 because of continued bad health, Richard Henry Lee died June 19, 1794, at his Virginia country estate "Chantilly," esteemed by all as one of the revered revolutionary leaders.

Robert Morris (1734–1806)

Robert Morris was one of the most influential, most important, and ever since his death in 1806, one of the most misunderstood or at least unappreciated of all the Revolutionary War leaders. He rightly belongs in the pantheon of Revolutionary statesmen. His major contributions to the patriot cause were not, however, in the military realm, but rather as a successful merchant, innovative banker, and creative financier. Particularly during the critical period 1781–1783 when the patriot cause appeared to be on the verge of financial collapse, Robert Morris, as Superintendent of Finance, obtained the necessary monies and equipment to carry out the

Yorktown campaign that essentially ended the military phase of the conflict. In addition, he initiated financial policies that successfully rescued the tottering financial structure of the national government under the Articles of Confederation.

It is somewhat strange, therefore, that this prominent Pennsylvania statesman is not today honored or even well known. Perhaps this historical neglect is due in part to Morris's innate political conservatism, which prompted him to oppose the Declaration of Independence initially. Also, during his tenure as Superintendent of Finance (1781–1784), he was frequently accused, probably undeservedly, of using public monies for personal gain. However, the major reason for Morris's historical obscurity was his failure in several land speculation schemes. Forced to declare bankruptcy, he spent the years 1798–1801 in debtor's prison. He was a businessman who failed in business. However, his private business failures and subsequent insolvency should not detract from his deserved reputation as one of the political and financial giants of the Revolutionary era.

Born in Britain in 1734, he migrated with his father in 1747 to Oxford on Maryland's Eastern Shore. Soon thereafter he moved to Philadelphia, where he joined, as an apprentice, the mercantile firm of Charles Willing. By 1754, the ambitious young Morris had worked his way up to being a partner with Charles Willing's son Thomas in what became the shipping and mercantile firm of Willing & Morris. Soon Willing & Morris became the leading trading company in Philadelphia. Robert Morris was always first and foremost a merchant and businessman. Even during the years spent as a state and national legislator and as Superintendent of Finance, he devoted much of his time and effort to mercantile pursuits.

Thus he often mixed public monies and transactions with his private funds and business ventures. These practices led to accusations, which have never been substantiated, of impropriety and even dishonesty.

However, the name of Robert Morris properly belongs on the list of the most conspicuous and influential public-spirited individuals not for his business acumen or business successes and/or failures. Rather, it is for his solid accomplishments as a member of the Second Continental Congress (1775–1778) and for his innovative policies as Superintendent of Finance (1781–1784) that Morris should be remembered and honored.

Although he signed a nonimportation agreement in opposition to the Stamp Act in 1765, he did not fully support the patriotic cause until 1775, when he was elected a delegate from Pennsylvania to the Second Continental Congress. As a leader, along with John Jay of New York and Joseph Galloway and John Dickinson of Pennsylvania, of a middle-colony conservative block in Congress, Morris opposed the Declaration of Independence in July 1776 claiming, like John Dickinson, that there should be yet another concerted effort at reconciliation before Congress took the irreversible step of declaring independence from the mother country. Although he voted against independence in early July 1776, he did sign the approved document in August and thereafter wholeheartedly embraced the patriot cause.

Primarily as a leading member of two of the most important congressional committees, Robert Morris rendered important, although at times inconspicuous, service to the revolutionary movement. With his worldwide mercantile connections, he was able to serve as an effective member of the Committee of Secret Correspondence—a committee that corresponded with U.S. diplomats abroad. As such, he acted as an early version of what later would become under the Articles of Confederation the Secretary for Foreign Affairs and under the Constitution of 1787 the Secretary of State. His second important committee assignment was as a member of the Committee of Commerce. Working primarily with the French but also with the Dutch and the Spanish, Morris was able to obtain much-needed monies and supplies with which to carry on the struggle with Great Britain. It was during this period that the first charges were made against Morris for allegedly using his public office for private gain. It was also in these years that Morris got involved in the notorious and unseemly Silas Deane–Arthur Lee political rift. Morris supported Deane and his patron Benjamin Franklin against the aspersions of the Adams-Lee faction. Undoubtedly his well-known opposition to the famous and well-regarded Adams-Lee faction in Congress has helped to tarnish Morris's historical reputation.

It is for his work as Superintendent of Finance (1781–1784) that Robert Morris should best be remembered and honored. He instituted a sweeping plan of financial reform at a time when the country's finances were on the verge of total collapse. As a thoroughgoing nationalist, Morris initiated economic reforms that were designed to strengthen the Confederation government. He completely revamped the currency system, he worked, unsuccessfully as it turned out, to give the national government permanent revenue, he established new procedures for supplying and equipping the army, and he was instrumental in the founding of the first national bank—the Bank of North America. Taken altogether, Morris's innovative financial reforms, as Superintendent of Finance, brought a measure of order and stability and therefore might well have saved the new republic from utter financial ruin and bankruptcy.

Elected as a delegate to the Philadelphia Constitutional Convention of 1787, Morris represented well the interests of the mercantile community in the deliberations that led to the writing of the final document. Although he was recorded as speaking rarely at the convention, his influence, and that of the several other merchant/delegates, was apparent in many of the constitutional provisions regarding trade and commerce. He signed the finished document and was elected as a U.S. Senator from Pennsylvania in the First Congress, having turned down President Washington's offer of appointment as the first Secretary of the Treasury. As a nationalist, he strongly supported most of the nationalistic Washington administration initiatives. In fact, the famous Hamiltonian fiscal program could rightly be called the Morris program because it followed in general terms the policies first introduced by Robert Morris in the early 1780s.

The years following his retirement in 1795 from the Senate were ones of continual mercantile activity and involvement in a variety of land speculation schemes, which usually ended up as failures. He reached the nadir of his financial career in 1798 when he was imprisoned for debt. At the time of his death in 1806, he was a broken man, poor and largely forgotten.

Thomas Paine (1737–1809)

Thomas Paine was the most widely read pamphleteer of the Revolutionary era. Born in Great Britain to working-class Quaker parents, Paine lived his first thirty-seven years experiencing continual failure and disappointment. Although enduring unrelenting poverty as a corset maker, tobacconist, schoolteacher, sailor, and excise officer, young Tom did manage to educate himself largely through a rigorous program of reading, especially in the natural and political sciences.

In 1774 Paine emigrated to Philadelphia with letters of introduction from Pennsylvania's London agent, the world-renowned Benjamin Franklin. In his first year in America, Paine began his publishing career by writing magazine articles and broadsides, mostly on scientific and political topics. A meeting with Philadelphia's most famous physician, Dr. Benjamin Rush, resulted in the publication of Paine's first major pamphlet. Rush convinced Paine that he should write a pamphlet that spelled out in easy-to-understand language the reasons why America should declare independence from the mother country. Published in early January 1776, the forty-seven-page *Common Sense* became an immediate best-seller, with over 100,000 copies being sold in three months.

Common Sense stated the argument for independence in logical, compelling terms. Offering "nothing more than simple facts, plain arguments, and common sense," Paine argued that reconciliation with Great Britain was an impossible dream and that independence was the only course open to Americans. Written months after the first spilling of blood at Lexington and Concord (April 19, 1775) and after the bloody encounter at Bunker Hill (June 17, 1775), *Common Sense* reflected in the language of the common people the sentiments of many Americans regarding the issue of independence. It became the most widely distributed, influential pamphlet of the "pamphlet war" being waged in the winter of 1776 between the reconciliationists and those who were leaning towards separation from the mother country. Although its impact is difficult to measure, it is known that many members of Congress and local political leaders read *Common Sense* and might well have been influenced by its call for independence from British tyranny and oppression. It is also known that the movement toward a congressional declaration of independence gained momentum in the months immediately following its publication. It was in the spring of 1776 that the radicals (led by the Adamses of Massachusetts and the Lees of Virginia) became the majority faction in Congress. Passage of Richard Henry Lee's famous motion of June 7th establishing a committee to draw up a statement justifying independence reflected this radical triumph and made almost inevitable the final July 2nd congressional vote for independence. Clearly Thomas Paine's *Common Sense* was influential in preparing the people to accept the revolutionary idea of declaring political independence.

With the publication of *Common Sense,* Paine gained the fame he had long sought. Fully convinced of the righteousness of the American cause, Paine became an active participant, first as a soldier and pamphleteer in the Continental Army and later as a politician and propagandist. While serving as a volunteer aide to General Nathanael Greene, he started writing the first of what would become a series of essays he titled *The Crisis*. In the first of these essays, which Washington had read to the army, Paine wrote, "These are the times that try men's souls. The summer soldier and the sun-shine patriot will, in this crisis, shrink from the service of his country: but he that stands it now, deserves the thanks of man and woman."[6] In subsequent essays, Paine advocated a strong national union, fiscal integrity, and a program of voluntary sacrifice for the common good. The sixteen essays in *The Crisis* series were to the war effort what *Common Sense* was to the independence movement. Paine's authorship of these engagingly written, widely read pamphlets marks him as the leading political propagandist of the American Revolution.

His short stint in the army was followed by service as secretary to the congressional committee on foreign affairs, as clerk of the Pennsylvania assembly, and as an unofficial envoy to France to obtain much-needed money and military supplies.

Paine's postwar career was spent in writing and working on his invention, an iron bridge. Praised by some for his patriotic writings, but criticized by others for his obvious and growing political radicalism, Paine lived in New Jersey and New York largely forgotten by his adopted country.

In 1787, Paine traveled to Europe where for two years he worked to sell his design of an iron bridge. Unhappily, he never realized any financial rewards for what was in fact a sound engineering design. With the outbreak of the French Revolution in 1789, Paine became a spokesman and defender of the revolution. He published *The Rights of Man* as a spirited defense of the revolution in France and as a counter to Edmund Burke's critical *Reflections on the French Revolution*. By 1792 Paine had become involved in the internal affairs of the French Revolution. He initially allied himself with the Girondin faction and when it fell from power, Paine was imprisoned as an alien. While in prison, Paine wrote his famous, some would say infamous, *The Age of Reason*. This attack on organized religion and defense of deism provoked bitter criticism, especially in America. This, along with his 1796 publication of a *Letter to George Washington* in which he attacked Washington as a military commander and as the first American president, greatly hurt his historical reputation. Saved from the guillotine in part by the intervention of American minister to France James Monroe, Paine eventually returned to America to spend the remaining seven years of his life in relative obscurity and poverty.

Although his later writings (especially *The Age of Reason* and the unseemly attack on the character and reputation of George Washington) have tarnished Paine's historical standing, he remains the leading, most oft-quoted eighteenth-century advocate of American independence and of American revolutionary patriotism. However, somewhat curiously, his death in 1809 in New York went largely unnoticed and unlamented.

Mercy Otis Warren (1728–1814)

Mercy Otis Warren combined the role of traditional wife and mother with that of intellectual and became an effective spokesperson for American independence and the principles of American rights and liberty. With a caustic pen and a ready wit, this Plymouth, Massachusetts, housewife and mother (she raised five sons) demonstrated a talent for writing that commanded the attention of the patriarchal society of the American revolutionary period. But Mercy would remain a homemaker first and only secondarily a writer, political thinker, and political activist. As she so aptly phrased it in a poem written in 1779, "Critics may censure, but if candour frowns, I'll quit the pen, and keep within the bounds, The narrow bounds, prescrib'd to female life, The gentle mistress, and the prudent wife."[7]

Born into the prominent Otis family, Mercy inherited a Puritan respectability and affluence that gave her advantages denied to most. Although not formally educated, young Mercy, with her two older brothers, James and Joseph, was tutored by her uncle, the Reverend Mr. Jonathan Russell. A Yale-trained clergyman, Uncle Jonathan imposed a rigorous program of reading for his three eager young pupils. It is because of this several-year reading program that Mercy became widely read in literature, history, theology, and the classics and gained a lifelong love of reading and scholarly discussion. At this time Mercy also came to the realization that she was the intellectual equal of men. Although opportunities for formal education and a career outside of the home were not available, she participated vicariously in the political and literary world of eighteenth-century Massachusetts, first through her favorite brother Jemmy (the mercurial James Otis, Jr.) and later through her husband, James Warren, and her close friends John and Abigail Adams.

During the 1760s Mercy became involved in the colonial protest movement, which eventually led to "the shot heard around the world" at Lexington and Concord and the War for American Independence. It was specifically her brother's (James Otis, Jr.) famous speech before the Superior

Court of Massachusetts in which he challenged the validity of Writs of Assistance (Parliamentary law that authorized general search warrants for custom officials) that drew Mercy into the political struggle between the Hutchinson/Oliver and the Otis/Warren families. Because of real and imagined political snubs from Thomas Hutchinson and the Oliver family and because the Hutchinson/Oliver faction acted as the chief defender and the major benefactor of British policies, the Otis/Warren family became the implacable foe of Hutchinson and his political cronies. For his brilliant defense of colonial rights in the Writs of Assistance controversy, Jemmy became, along with John Hancock, John Adams, Samuel Adams, and brother-in-law James Warren, a leader of the opposition party to the "English" party of Hutchinson and Oliver. Much of the planning and many of the discussions of the opposition party in fact took place in the Warren house. Thus Mercy not only met these early revolutionary leaders, but also perhaps listened in on these planning sessions and discussions, which were ultimely to lead to armed conflict and eventual political independence.

In the 1770s, despite raising five boys, Mercy found time to publish anonymously several political satirical plays that were all ill-disguised attacks on Governor Thomas Hutchinson, Lieutenant Governor Andrew Oliver, and their political henchmen. By 1775, she had become the leading "penwoman" of the revolutionary movement.

With the coming of peace in 1783, the fifty-five-year-old Mercy maintained her interest in writing and politics. During the immediate postwar period, both she and her husband viewed with dismay the growing nationalistic movement that would eventually lead to the drafting and ratification of the Constitution of 1787. In her widely circulated 1788 anti-federalist tract *Observations on the New Constitution and on the Federal Conventions,* she characterized the proposed constitution as a betrayal of the American Revolution because it would create a strong national government capable of subverting the rights and liberties of the states and of the people.

Opposed to the centralizing and nationalistic policies of Presidents Washington and Adams during the 1790s, Mercy and her husband James became virtual political exiles.

Mercy devoted her time to writing. In the 1790s, she published her first book-length manuscript, entitled *Poems, dramatic and miscellaneous* (a collection of poems, several political tracts, and two plays). The two plays reflected Mercy's growing maturity as a playwright and her emergence as an advocate of women's rights. Her not-so-subtle implication was that women were indeed the equal of men if given equal opportunities for education and career.

In 1805, Mercy finally found a publisher for what would become her most enduring published legacy, *The History of the Rise, Progress and Termination of the American Revolution interspersed with Biographical and Moral Observations.* This magnum opus established her as the first published woman historian in the United States, a fact of which she was extremely proud. As narrative history, these engagingly written volumes still command attention primarily for their biographical sketches of many of the leading protagonists of the Revolutionary era.

Mercy, however, had never enjoyed good health. Frequently bedridden for a wide variety of physical ailments and severe depression, she died in October 1814 of unknown causes at the age of eighty-six.

Mercy Otis Warren's enduring legacy was her ability to combine successfully the traditional role of wife and mother with that of respected published writer.

George Washington (1732–1799)

During the Revolutionary era, George Washington earned the title of "The Indispensable Man."[8] He played a major role in three of the most significant events of the late eighteenth century: commander in chief of the Continental Army during the War for Independence, president of the Constitutional Convention of 1787, and first president of the new American republic.

As the oldest son of Augustine Washington and his second wife, Mary Ball, Washington was born in Westmoreland County to an assured position in the patriarchal society of colonial Virginia. George took full advantage of his privileged birth and upbringing to become one of the wealthiest, most prominent members of the Virginia aristocracy—a plantation-owning, slave-owning aristocracy, which furnished a disproportionate number of revolutionary leaders.

In 1747, young George ended his formal education and embarked upon a career as a land surveyor. His appointment, in 1752, as a major in the Virginia militia launched a military career that would eventually lead to his appointment as commander in chief of the Continental Army.

As a Virginian militia officer, Washington played a significant role in the French and Indian War (1754–1763). Sent by Virginia's royal governor to the forks of the Ohio River (present-day Pittsburgh) to assert Virginia's claim to that strategic area and to the entire Ohio River valley, Washington was involved in the opening skirmishes of what eventually evolved into the Seven Years' War (1756–1763). His surrender of Fort Necessity in July of 1754 to a smaller French and Indian force and his involvement, as commander of the colonial forces, in British General Edward Braddock's ill-fated defeat in 1755, were inauspicious beginnings to what would become a distinguished military career. However, throughout even these early military setbacks, Washington displayed a courage and a fortitude that were to enhance his reputation as a military commander.

Election in 1758 to the Virginia House of Burgesses inaugurated a political career in which he would serve almost continuously until 1775 as a legislator, as a vestryman, and as a justice of the peace for Fairfax County. In the House of Burgesses ("the nursery of statesmen"), his vote, in 1769, for resolutions that asserted the right of self-taxation for Virginians and his open support of the colony's policy to prohibit the importation of British goods until the Townshend Duties were repealed marked Washington's conversion to the more radical faction that not only initially favored repeal of hated British taxes and the Coercive Acts, but also by 1776 advocated complete political separation from the mother country.

In early 1759 Washington married the wealthy widow Martha Dandridge Custis. With her vast landholdings and slaves added to his, Washington became one of the wealthiest plantation owners in Virginia.

His election as one of Virginia's seven delegates to the First Continental Congress (1774) signaled his arrival as a member of the planter elite. Election to the Second Continental Congress (1775) confirmed this status and led to his nomination and election as commander in chief of the Continental Army in mid-June of 1775. His acceptance, as a Virginian, of this command position would help to ensure Virginian and southern support for the embattled New Englanders in the months following the commencement of hostilities at Lexington and Concord in April 1775.

Washington took command of what was an ill-trained, ill-equipped, and ill-led group of New England militiamen at Cambridge, Massachusetts, on July 3, 1775. In losing many of the earlier battles and skirmishes of the Revolution, Washington was frequently outmaneuvered and out-fought by his more experienced British adversaries. His unsuccessful defense of New York City in 1776 demonstrated clearly that this Virginia planter had much to learn. The American defeat at the Battle of Brooklyn Heights almost resulted in the capture or annihilation of his entire army. At the last moment, Washington was able to transport his defeated, dispirited force across the East River to the temporary safety of Manhattan Island. By slow stages, however, the Americans were driven out of New York City by superior British forces. The decision not to abandon Fort Washington and Fort Lee was a strategic error because these two indefensible bastions were easily taken by the British, who captured 2,500 American troops and badly needed military supplies.

In late 1776 and early 1777, Washington took the initiative and captured two small Hessian and British detachments at Trenton and Princeton, New Jersey. Although relatively minor battles, these American victories gave Washington the confidence to continue the struggle and boosted American morale.

Learning from earlier blunders, Washington, by late 1777, had become an effective army commander who came to understand the "nature" of this new kind of warfare that pitted a European professional army against a nonprofessional "citizen" army composed primarily of farmers and craftsmen. Washington came to realize that he could win this War for Independence by keeping his army intact and by wearing down his British opponents. Even with the notable American victories at Saratoga (1777) and Yorktown (1781), Washington and the Continental Army did not really "win" the military struggle. Instead they did not militarily "lose" the armed conflict. Thus his army was able to exhaust the British army in America and render it ineffectual. As early as 1778 when France entered the conflict on the American side, the British began to suspect that their cause was hopeless. Although Washington "lost" more battles than he "won," he did, along with French General the Comte de Rochambeau, plan and carry out the successful last major campaign of the war, which led to Lord Cornwallis's surrender at Yorktown. Thus, it was Washington's leadership and his understanding of the "nature" of this new type of warfare that led to what is now considered by many the inevitable result of the seven-year-long military conflict. Washington was successful in leading the Continental Army in a war of attrition. On December 23, 1783, in a carefully arranged ceremony at Annapolis, Maryland, Washington voluntarily resigned his commission as commander in chief of the American army and returned to his beloved Mount Vernon.

Washington's postwar career was that of a Virginia farmer and after 1787 of a political figure and statesman. He was persuaded to accept his election to the Virginia delegation to the Constitutional Convention in 1787, and Washington's attendance and subsequent election as president of the "Grand Convention" gave the gathering legitimacy and credibility. His tactful, prudent, thoughtful leadership at the convention and his obvious and well-known support of the completed document greatly helped to secure ratification of the Constitution by the summer of 1788.

His unanimous election in 1788, and unanimous reelection in 1792, as president of the United States thrust on the somewhat reluctant Washington the task of establishing the new republic. His success in inaugurating the government, in bringing respect and legitimacy to the office of president, in implementing the Hamiltonian fiscal program, and in initiating a foreign policy of neutrality add credence to his title of father of the American Republic.

In early 1797, George Washington retired, with full honors, from public life with the heartfelt thanks of a grateful nation. His death in 1799, at age 67, was mourned by all Americans.

NOTES

1. Lyman H. Butterfield, et al., editors, *Adams Family Correspondence*. Cambridge: Harvard University Press, 1963, I, 369–70.

2. Milton E. Flower, *John Dickinson: Conservative Revolutionary*. Charlottesville, Va.: University Press of Virginia, 1983, 137.

3. *The Annals of America*. Chicago: Encyclopaedia Britannica, Inc., 1976, II, 148.

4. *The Annals of America*. Chicago: Encyclopaedia Britannica, Inc., 1976, II, 323.

5. Henry Steele Commager and Milton Cantor, editors, *Documents of American History*. Tenth Edition. Englewood Cliffs, N.J.: Prentice Hall, Inc., 1988, I, 100.

6. Mark Philp, editor, *Thomas Paine*: Rights of Man, Common Sense, *and Other Political Writings*. Oxford: Oxford University Press, 1995, 63.

7. Rosemarie Zagarri. *A Woman's Dilemma: Mercy Otis Warren and the American Revolution*. Wheeling, Ill.: Harland Davidson, Inc., 1995, 73.

8. James Thomas Flexner, *Washington: The Indispensable Man*. Boston: Little, Brown and Company, 1969.

DOCUMENTS

Document 1
Resolutions of the Stamp Act Congress (1765)

On October 7, 1765, twenty-seven delegates from nine colonies met at City Hall in New York City. They were meeting at the invitation of the Massachusetts House of Representatives, which on June 8, 1765, had sent a circular letter inviting all of the colonies to send delegates to a congress to discuss ways to oppose the almost universally opposed Stamp Act. Six colonies (Massachusetts, South Carolina, Rhode Island, Connecticut, Pennsylvania, and Maryland) sent official delegations while three colonies (New Jersey, Delaware, and New York) took no formal action, but sent unofficial delegations. Three colonies (Virginia, North Carolina, and Georgia) were prevented from participation because their royal governors refused to convene the legislatures to elect delegates. The thirteenth colony (New Hampshire) formally declined the invitation to send a delegation, but approved the Declarations of the Congress after the proceedings ended.

The congress divided into two discernible factions. Led by Timothy Ruggles of Massachusetts (elected chairman) and John Dickinson of Pennsylvania, the majority conservative faction was determined to assert its strong opposition to British taxing policies (especially the Stamp Act), but without infringing upon the royal prerogative or the traditional constitutional powers of Parliament. These conservatives favored sending dutifully worded petitions to both Parliament and the king. The minority radical group, on the other hand, supported petitioning only the crown, contending that Americans did not hold their rights from Parliament. The conservative view prevailed when on the last day of the meeting (October

19th) the Congress adopted the following declarations written by John Dickinson:

The members of this congress, sincerely devoted, with the warmest sentiments of affection and duty to his Majesty's person and government; inviolably attached to the present happy establishment of the Protestant succession, and with minds deeply impressed by a sense of the present and impending misfortunes of the British colonies on this continent; . . . make the following declarations, of our humble opinion, respecting the most essential rights and liberties of the colonists, and of the grievances under which they labour, by reason of several late acts of Parliament.

I. That his Majesty's subjects in these colonies, owe the same allegiance to the Crown of Great Britain, that is owing from his subjects born within the realm, and all due subordination to that august body, the Parliament of Great Britain.

II. That his Majesty's liege subjects in these colonies are entitled to all the inherent rights and liberties of his natural born subjects within the kingdom of Great Britain.

III. That it is inseparably essential to the freedom of a people, and the undoubted rights of Englishmen, that no taxes should be imposed on them, but with their own consent, given personally, or by their representatives.

IV. That the people of these colonies are not, and from their local circumstances, cannot be represented in the House of Commons in Great Britain.

V. That the only representatives of the people of these colonies, are persons chosen therein, by themselves; and that no taxes ever have been, or can be constitutionally imposed on them, but by their respective legislature.

VI. That all supplies to the Crown, being free gifts of the people, it is unreasonable and inconsistent with the principles and spirit of the British constitution for the people of Great Britain to grant to his Majesty the property of the colonies.

VII. That trial by jury is the inherent and invaluable right of every British subject in these colonies.

VIII. That the late Act of Parliament, entitled, An Act for granting and applying certain Stamp Duties, . . . by imposing taxes on the inhabitants of these colonies, and the said Act, and several other Acts, by extending the jurisdiction of the courts of admiralty beyond its ancient limits, have a manifest tendency to subvert the rights and liberties of the colonists.

IX. That the duties imposed by several late Acts of Parliament, from the peculiar circumstances of these colonies, will be extremely burdensome and grievous, and from the scarcity of specie, the payment of them absolutely impracticable.

X. That as the profits of the trade of these colonies ultimately center in Great Britain, to pay for the manufactures which they are obliged to take from thence, they eventually contribute very largely to all supplies granted there to the Crown.

XI. That the restrictions imposed by several late Acts of Parliament, on the trade of these colonies, will render them unable to purchase the manufactures of Great Britain.

XII. That the increase, prosperity and happiness of these colonies, depend on the full and free enjoyment of their rights and liberties, and an intercourse with Great Britain, mutually affectionate and advantageous.

XIII. That it is the right of the British subjects in these colonies, to petition the king or either house of Parliament.

Lastly, that it is the indispensable duty of these colonies to the best of sovereigns, to the mother country, and to themselves, to endeavour by a loyal and dutiful address to his Majesty, and humble applications to both houses of Parliament, to procure the repeal of the Act for granting and applying certain stamp duties, of all clauses of any other Acts of Parliament, whereby the jurisdiction of the admiralty is extended as aforesaid, and of the other late Acts for the restriction of American commerce.

Source: David C. Douglas, editor, *English Historical Documents*. London: E. Methuen, 1979, IX, 672–73.

Document 2
The Declaratory Act of March 18, 1766

The widespread colonial opposition and the influential opposition of British merchants to the Stamp Act of 1765 forced British Prime Minister Charles Watson-Wentworth, Lord Rockingham, to consider repealing the unenforceable duties. However, it was Benjamin Franklin's brilliant performance before the House of Commons on February 13, 1766, that finally convinced Rockingham to work for repeal. The highly respected American agent claimed (erroneously, as it turned out) that his fellow countrymen objected only to "internal," not to "external" (i.e., import and export taxes) duties.

However, before the Prime Minister could secure enough Parliamentary support for repeal, he had to agree to a Parliamentary act that definitively asserted Parliament's undeniable right to complete legislative authority over the colonies. The Declaratory Act of March 18, 1766, although largely ignored in America, meant that repeal of the Stamp Act did not mean that Parliament was renouncing its right to legislate "in all cases whatsoever." It also meant Great Britain might well continue on the course, started back in 1763 by Chancellor of the Exchequer George Grenville, of taxing and coercing the American colonists.

The Declaratory Act of 1766 reflected the consistent official British view that Parliament did represent the colonists and therefore did have the constitutional right to tax them. From 1766 to the outbreak of hostilities in 1775, Americans, in their declarations and broadsides, rejected totally this principle of "virtual representation" and instead advanced the doctrine of "actual representation" (i.e., only the colonial legislative assemblies in which they were represented directly could pass colonial tax laws).

Whereas several of the houses of representatives in his Majesty's colonies and plantations in America, have of late, against law, claimed to themselves, or to the general assemblies of the same, the sole and exclusive right of imposing duties and taxes upon his Majesty's subjects in the said colonies and plantations; and have, in pursuance of such claim, passed certain votes, resolutions, and orders, derogatory to the legislative authority of parliament, and inconsistent with the dependency of the said colonies and plantations upon the Crown of Great Britain: . . . be it declared . . . , That the said colonies and plantations in America have been, are, and of right ought to be, subordinate unto, and dependent upon the imperial Crown and Parliament of Great Britain; and that the King's majesty, by and with the advice and consent of the lords spiritual and temporal, and commons of Great Britain, in parliament assembled, had, hath, and of right ought to have, full power and authority to make laws and statutes of sufficient force and validity to bind the colonies and people of America, subjects of the Crown of Great Britain, in all cases whatsoever.

II. And be it further declared . . . , That all resolutions, votes, orders, and proceedings, in any of the said colonies or plantations, whereby the power and authority of the parliament of Great Britain, to make laws and statutes as aforesaid, is denied, or drawn into question are, and are hereby declared to be, utterly null and void to all intents and purposes whatsoever.

Source: Henry Steele Commager and Milton Cantor, editors, *Documents of American History.* Tenth Edition. Englewood Cliffs, N.J.: Prentice Hall, Inc., 1988, I, 60–61.

Document 3
Declaration of the Causes and Necessity of Taking Up Arms
(July 6, 1775)

When the Second Continental Congress convened on May 10, 1775, it knew that the long anticipated clash of arms had taken place just a few weeks before at Lexington and Concord. It spent its first few weeks preparing for what most hoped and expected would be a relatively short conflict. At this time, a large majority of the congressional delegates were reconciliationists (i.e., they hoped Britain would repeal the odious Coercive Acts and return to the pre-1763 policies that allowed the colonies semiautonomy within the British Empire). In the meanwhile, armed hostilities and bloodshed would, it was hoped, convince the British to abandon their recent coercive and taxing policies. Only a minority of those who gathered in Philadelphia even considered the idea of independence. Those who did consider severing the political connection with the mother country did so in private. There was virtually no public notice or discussion of the idea of independence.

Congress spent its first several weeks preparing for war. It established the Continental Army on June 14th, and the following day elected Virginian George Washington as its Commander in Chief. The bloody encounter, on June 17th, at Bunker Hill outside of Boston, now convinced many in Congress that the conflict might well be a protracted one.

Among the many congressional committees established to organize a government and prepare for continued fighting was one charged with drafting a declaration that would justify the actions taken by Congress in waging war against the mother country.

Originally this declaration was to be read only to the New England militiamen besieging Boston to boost their spirits for the coming hardships. The committee (originally composed of Benjamin Franklin of Pennsylvania, John Jay of New York, William Livingston of New Jersey, John Rutledge of South Carolina, and Thomas Johnson of Maryland) crafted a statement that was rejected. Thereupon, a new two-member committee was appointed, consisting of Thomas Jefferson of Virginia and John Dickinson of Pennsylvania, to draft an entirely new document that could be used to muster public support and bolster morale. Dickinson wrote most of the final draft with Jefferson contributing the final few paragraphs. It was approved by Congress on July 6, 1775, and sent immediately to General Washington, who had it read to the army.

Although similar to the Declaration of Independence of 1776 in that both documents listed in some detail the colonial grievances since 1763, the 1775 declaration blamed Parliament as the main culprit whereas the more famous 1776 document indicted the king alone for violating colonial rights and liberties. *The Declaration of the Causes and Necessity of Taking Up Arms* reflected the 1775 conservative colonial constitutional view of most congressmen and indeed of most Americans that Parliament was to be blamed for Britain's coercive and taxing policies, not the monarch to whom they continued to pledge allegiance.

If it was possible for men, who exercise their reason to believe, that the divine Author of our existence intended a part of the human race to hold an absolute property in, and an unbounded power over others, marked out by his infinite goodness and wisdom, as the objects of a legal domination never rightfully resistible, however severe and oppressive, the inhabitants of these colonies might at least require from the parliament of Great-Britain some evidence, that this dreadful authority over them, has been granted to that body. But a reverence for our great Creator, principles of humanity, and the dictates of common sense, must convince all those who reflect upon the subject, that government was instituted to promote the welfare of mankind, and ought to be administered for the attainment of that end. The legislature of Great-Britain, however, stimulated by an inordinate passion for a power not only unjustifiable, but which they know to be peculiarly reprobated by the very constitution of that kingdom, and desperate of success in any mode of contest, where regard should be had to truth, law, or right, have at length, deserting those, attempted to effect their cruel and impolitic purpose of enslaving these colonies by violence, and have thereby rendered it necessary for us to close with their last appeal from reason to arms. . . . .

Our forefathers, inhabitants of the island of Great-Britain, left their native land, to seek on these shores a residence for civil and religious freedom. At the expense of their blood, at the hazard of their fortunes, . . . they effected settlements in the distant and inhospitable wilds of America, then filled with numerous and warlike nations of barbarians. . . . The uninterrupted tenor of their peaceable and respectful behaviour from the beginning of colonization, . . . could not save them from the meditated innovations. Parliament was influenced to adopt the pernicious project, and assuming a new power over them, have in the course of eleven years, given such decisive specimens of the spirit and consequences attending this power, as to leave no doubt concerning the effects of acquiescence under it. They have undertaken to give and grant our money without our consent, though we have ever exercised an exclusive right to dispose of our own property; statutes have been passed for extending the jurisdiction of courts of admiralty, and vice-admiralty beyond their ancient limits; for depriving us of the accustomed and inestimable privilege of trial by jury, in cases affecting both life and property; for suspending the legislature of one of the colonies; for interdicting all commerce to the capital of another; and for altering fundamentally the form of government established by charter, and secured by acts of its own legislature solemnly confirmed by the crown; for exempting the "murderers" of colonists from legal trial, and in effect, from punishment; for erecting in a neighbouring province, acquired by the joint arms of Great-Britain and America, a despotism dangerous to our very existence; and for quartering soldiers upon the colonists in time of profound peace. It has also been resolved in parliament, that colonists charged with committing certain offences, shall be transported to England to be tried.

But why should we enumerate our injuries in detail? By one statute it is declared, that parliament can "of right make laws to bind us in all cases whatsoever." What is to defend us against so enormous, so unlimited a power? . . . The indignation of the American was roused, it is true; but it was the indignation of a virtuous, loyal, and affectionate people. A Congress of delegates from the United Colonies was assembled at Philadelphia, on the fifth day of last September. We resolved again to offer an humble and dutiful petition to the king, and also addressed our fellow-subjects of Great-Britain. We have pursued every temperate, every respectful measure; . . . Fruitless were all the entreaties, arguments, and eloquence of an illustrious band of the most distinguished peers and commoners, who nobly and strenuously asserted the justice of our cause, to stay, or even to mitigate the heedless fury with which these accumulated and unexampled outrages were hurried on. . . .

Our cause is just. Our union is perfect. . . .

Lest this declaration should disquiet the minds of our friends and fellow-subjects in any part of the empire, we assure them that we mean not to dissolve that union which has so long and so happily subsisted between us, and which we sincerely wish to see restored. Necessity has not yet driven us into that desperate measure, ... We have not raised armies with ambitious designs of separating from Great-Britain, and establishing independent states. We fight not for glory or for conquest. . . .

In our own native land, in defence of the freedom that is our birthright, and which we ever enjoyed till the late violation of it—for the protection of our property, acquired solely by the honest industry of our fore-fathers and ourselves against violence actually offered, we have taken up arms. We shall lay them down when hostilities shall cease on the part of the aggressors, and all danger of their being renewed shall be removed, and not before.

With an humble confidence in the mercies of the supreme and impartial Judge and Ruler of the Universe, we most devoutly implore his divine goodness to protect us happily through this great conflict, to dispose our adversaries to reconciliation on reasonable terms, and thereby to relieve the empire from the calamities of civil war.

By order of Congress
John Hancock, President

Source: Henry Steele Commager and Milton Cantor, editors, *Documents of American History*. Tenth Edition. Englewood Cliffs, N.J.: Prentice Hall, Inc., 1988, I, 92–95.

Document 4
Proclamation of Rebellion (August 23, 1775)

Even after the commencement of hostilities at Lexington and Concord (April 19, 1775) and the bloody battle of Bunker Hill (June 17, 1775), the reconciliationists in Congress attempted to settle the grievances with Great Britain without further bloodshed. Written by John Dickinson, the Olive Branch Petition delineated colonial grievances but also reaffirmed the colonists' allegiance to the crown. The petition then went on to plead for the restoration of harmony, and ended with an appeal to the crown to prevent further bloodshed until a reasonable and mutually acceptable reconciliation could be agreed upon. Passed by Congress on July 5, 1775, the Olive Branch Petition was carried to London by Richard Penn to be presented to King George III. Penn reached London in mid-August. The king, however, refused to see Penn or receive the petition.

Instead, angered by the news of the carnage at Lexington, Concord, and Bunker Hill, the king issued, on August 23, 1775, a proclamation for suppressing what he termed a rebellion. By late October, news of the proclamation reached America, where it was viewed as a British declaration of war against the thirteen mainland colonies.

George R.

Whereas many of our subjects in divers parts of our Colonies and Plantations in North America, misled by dangerous and ill designing men, and forgetting the allegiance which they owe to the power that has protected and supported them; after various disorderly acts committed in disturbance of the publick peace, to the obstruction of lawful commerce, and to the oppression of our loyal subjects carrying on the same; have at length proceeded to open and avowed rebellion, by arraying themselves in a hostile manner, to withstand the execution of the law, and traitorously preparing, ordering and levying war against us; And whereas, there is reason to apprehend that such rebellion hath been much promoted and encouraged by the traitorous correspondence, counsels and comfort of divers wicked and desperate persons within this realm; To the end therefore, that none of our subjects may neglect or violate their duty through ignorance thereof, or through any doubt of the protection which the law will afford to their loyalty and zeal, we have thought fit, by and with the advice of our Privy Council, to issue our Royal Proclamation, hereby declaring, that not only all our Officers, civil and military, are obliged to exert their utmost endeavours to suppress such rebellion, and to bring the traitors to justice, ...

Given at our Court at S. James's the twenty-third day of August, one thousand seven hundred and seventy-five, in the fifteenth year of our reign.

God save the King.

Source: Henry Steele Commager and Milton Cantor, editors, *Documents of American History*. Tenth Edition. Englewood Cliffs, N.J.: Prentice Hall, Inc., 1988, I, 95–96.

Document 5

Proclamation of Lord Dunmore Offering Freedom to the Slaves Belonging to the Rebels in Virginia, November 7, 1775

In the months following the Battle of Lexington and Concord (April 19, 1775), Britain concentrated its military effort in New England and upper New York state. In the south, Britain hoped to rely primarily on loyalist forces to put down the rebellion. However, by the fall of 1775, the southern patriots had gained the initiative by establishing extralegal provincial governments and forcing most of the southern royal governors to flee to the protection of nearby British warships.

In Virginia, the Royal Governor, John Murray, Lord Dunmore, attempted to rally loyalist forces. To that end, the governor issued a proclamation declaring martial law in Virginia and offering freedom to all indentured servants and slaves who would desert their masters and take up arms against the rebels. By the end of the year, several hundred slaves had deserted their colonial masters and fled to the British.

Dunmore's Proclamation, more than any other single act, persuaded many otherwise loyal subjects of the crown to embrace the patriot cause. The Proclamation was a blatant call for a slave insurrection—something the slave-owning, plantation-owning Tidewater aristocracy feared above all else.

As I have ever entertained hopes that an accommodation might have taken place between Great Britain and this colony, without being compelled by my duty to do this most disagreeable, but now absolutely necessary, duty, rendered so by a body of men, unlawfully assembled, firing on His Majesty's tenders, and the formation of an army, and an army now on its march to attack His Majesty's troops and destroy the well-disposed subjects of this colony. To defeat such treasonable purposes, and that all such traitors and their abettors may be brought to justice, and that the peace and good order of this colony may be again restored, which the ordinary course of the civil law is unable to effect, I have thought fit to issue this my proclamation, hereby declaring that, until the aforesaid good purposes can be obtained, I do, in virtue of the power and authority to me given by His Majesty, determine to execute martial law, and cause the the same to be executed throughout this colony.

And to the end that peace and good order may the sooner be restored, I do require every person capable of bearing arms to resort to His Majesty's standard, or be looked upon as traitors to His Majesty's crown and government, and thereby become liable to the penalty the law inflicts upon such offenses; such as forfeiture of life, confiscation of lands, etc.

And I do hereby further declare all indentured servants, Negroes, or others (appertaining to rebels) free, that are able and willing to bear arms, they joining His Majesty's troops as soon as may be, for the more speedily reducing his colony to a proper sense of their duty to His Majesty's crown and dignity. I do further order and require all His Majesty's liege subjects to retain their quitrents or other taxes due, or that may become due in their own custody, till such a time may again be restored to this at present most unhappy country, or demanded of them for their former salutary purposes, by officers properly authorized to receive the same.

Given under my hand, on board the ship *William*, off Norfolk, the 7th day of November, in the 16th year of His Majesty's reign.

Source: Hezekiah Niles, editor, *Principles and Acts of the Revolution in America*. Baltimore: William Ogden Niles, 1822, 373.

Document 6
Thomas Paine, *Common Sense*

By January 1776, even though the American patriots had been fighting the British for over eight months, there was little thought or talk of independence either within Congress or without. Most Americans still sought reconciliation with, not independence from, Great Britain. Thomas Paine's *Common Sense* helped to change that view.

Born in Norfolk County, England in 1737, Thomas Paine had failed as a stay-maker and as an exciseman. In October 1774 he secured letters of recommendation from colonial agent Benjamin Franklin and set sail for Philadelphia. Soon after his arrival in the City of Brotherly Love, Paine became involved in the incipient move to independence for the colonies. In early January 1776, Paine published the pamphlet *Common Sense*, which stated, in terms readily understood by all, the American case for independence. It sold over 100,000 copies in three months, and soon became one of the most influential political tracts of the revolutionary era.

Perhaps the sentiments contained in the following pages, are not yet sufficiently fashionable to procure them general favor; a long habit of not thinking a thing wrong, gives it a superficial appearance of being right, and raises at first a formidable outcry in defence of custom. But the tumult soon subsides. Time makes more converts than reason. . . .

The cause of America is in a great measure the cause of all mankind. Many circumstances hath, and will arise, which are not local, but universal, and through which the principles of all Lovers of Mankind are affected, and in the Event of which, their Affections are interested. The laying a Country desolate with Fire and Sword, declaring War against the natural rights of all Mankind, and extirpating the Defenders thereof from the Face of the Earth, is the Concern of every Man to whom Nature hath given the Power of feeling; of which Class, regardless of Party Censure, is the

AUTHOR . . .

Society in every state is a blessing, but government even in its best state is but a necessary evil; in its worst state an intolerable one; . . .

Government like dress, is the badge of lost innocence; the palaces of kings are built on the ruins of the bowers of paradise. For were the impulses of conscience clear, uniform, and irresistibly obeyed, man would need no other lawgiver; but that not being the case, he finds it necessary to surrender up a part of his property to furnish means for the protection of the rest; and this he is induced to do by the same prudence which in every other case advises him out of two evils to choose the least. Wherefore, security being the true design and end of government, it unanswerably follows, that whatever form thereof appears most likely to ensure it to us, with the least expense and greatest benefit, is preferable to all others. . . .

I know it is difficult to get over local or long standing prejudices, yet if we will suffer ourselves to examine the component parts of the English constitution, we shall find them to be the base remains of two ancient tyrannies, compounded with some new republican materials.

First. The remains of monarchical tyranny in the person of the king.

Secondly. The remains of aristocratical tyranny in the persons of the peers.

Thirdly. The new republican materials in the persons of the commons, on whose virtue depends the freedom of England. . . .

That the crown is this overbearing part in the English constitution, needs not be mentioned, and that it derives its whole consequence merely from being the giver of places and pensions, is self-evident, wherefore, though we have been wise enough to shut and lock a door against absolute monarchy, we at the same time have been foolish enough to put the crown in possession of the key.

The prejudice of Englishmen in favour of their own government by king, lords, and commons, arises as much or more from national pride than reason. Individuals are undoubtedly safer in England than in some other countries, but the will of the king is as much the law of the land in Britain as in France, with this difference, that instead of proceeding directly from his mouth, it is handed to the people under the more formidable shape of an act of parliament. For the fate of Charles the First hath only made kings more subtle—not more just. . . .

In the following pages I offer nothing more than simple facts, plain arguments, and common sense; and have no other preliminaries to settle with the reader, than that he will divest himself of prejudice and prepossession, and suffer his reason and his feelings to determine for themselves; that he will put on, or rather that he will not put off the true character of a man, generously enlarge his views beyond the present day.

Volumes have been written on the subject of the struggle between England and America. Men of all ranks have embarked in the controversy, from different motives, and with various designs; but all have been ineffectual, and the period of debate is closed. Arms, as the last resource, decide the contest; the appeal was the choice of the king, and the continent hath accepted the challenge. . . .

The sun never shined on a cause of greater worth. 'Tis not the affair of a city, a county, a province, or a kingdom, but of a continent—of at least one eighth part of the habitable globe. 'Tis not the concern of a day, a year, or an age; posterity are virtually involved in the contest, and will be more or less affected, even to the end of time, by the proceedings now. Now is the seed-time of continental union, faith and honor. The least fracture now will be like a name engraved with the point of a pin on the tender rind of a young oak; the wound will enlarge with the tree, and posterity read it in full grown characters. . . .

But Britain is the parent country, say some. Then the more shame upon her conduct. Even brutes do not devour their young, nor savages make war upon their families; wherefore the assertion, if true, turns to her reproach; but it happens not to be true, or only partly so, and the phrase parent or mother country hath been jesuitically adopted by the king and his parasites, with a low papistical design of gaining an unfair bias on the credulous weakness of our minds. Europe, and not England, is the parent country of America. This new world hath been the asylum for the persecuted lovers of civil and religious liberty from every part of Europe. . . .

I challenge the warmest advocate for reconciliation, to shew, a single advantage that this continent can reap, by being connected with Great Britain. I repeat the challenge, not a single advantage is derived. . . .

I am not induced by motives of pride, party, or resentment to espouse the doctrine of separation and independence: I am clearly, positively, and conscientiously persuaded that it is the true interest of this continent to be so; that every thing short of that is mere patchwork, that it can afford no lasting felicity—that it is leaving the sword to our children, and shrinking back at a time, when, a little more, a little farther, would have rendered this continent the glory of the earth. . . .

No man was a warmer wisher for reconciliation than myself, before the fatal nineteenth of April 1775, but the moment the event of that day was made known, I rejected the hardened, sullen tempered Pharaoh of England for ever; and disdain the wretch, that with the pretended title of Father of His People can unfeelingly hear of their slaughter, and composedly sleep with their blood upon his soul. . . .

O ye that love mankind! Ye that dare oppose, not only the tyranny, but the tyrant, stand forth! Every spot of the old world is overrun with oppression. Freedom hath been hunted round the globe. Asia, and Africa, have long expelled her—Europe regards her like a stranger, and England hath given her warning to depart. O! Receive the fugitive, and prepare in time an asylum for mankind. . . .

TO CONCLUDE, however strange it may appear to some, or however unwilling they may be to think so, matters not, but many strong and striking reasons may be given, to shew, that nothing can settle our affairs so expeditiously as an open and determined declaration of independence. Some of which are,

First. It is the custom of nations, when any two are at war, for some other powers, not engaged in the quarrel, to step in as mediators, and bring about the preliminaries of a peace; but while America calls herself the Subject of Great-Britain, no power, however well disposed she may be, can offer her mediation. Wherefore, in our present state we may quarrel on for ever.

Secondly. It is unreasonable to suppose, that France or Spain will give us any kind of assistance, if we mean only, to make use of that assistance for the purpose of repairing the breach, and strengthening the connection between Britain and America; because, those powers would be sufferers by the consequences.

Thirdly. While we profess ourselves the subjects of Britain, we must, in the eye of foreign nations, be considered as rebels. The precedent is somewhat dangerous to their peace, for men to be in arms under the name of subjects; We, on the spot, can solve the paradox: but to united resistance and subjection, requires an idea much too refined for common understanding.

Fourthly. Were a manifesto to be published, and dispatched to foreign courts, setting forth the miseries we have endured, and the peaceable methods we have ineffectually used for redress; declaring, at the same time, that not being able, any longer, to live happily or safely under the cruel disposition of the British court, we had been driven to the necessity of breaking off all connections with her; at the same time, assuring all such courts of our peaceable disposition towards them, and of our desire of entering into trade with them: Such a memorial would produce more good effects to this Continent, than if a ship were freighted with petitions to Britain.

Under our present denomination of British subjects, we can neither be received nor heard abroad: The custom of all courts is against us, and will be so, until, by an independence, we take rank with other nations.

These proceedings may at first appear strange and difficult; but, like all other steps which we have already passed over, will in a little time become familiar and agreeable; and, until an independence is declared, the Continent will feel itself like a man who continues putting off some unpleasant business from day to day, yet knows it must be done, hates to set about it, wishes it over, and is continually haunted with the thoughts of its necessity.

Source: Richard D. Brown, editor, *Major Problems in the Era of the American Revolution*. Second Edition. Boston: Houghton Mifflin Company, 2000, 155–70.

Document 7
Abigail Adams's Letter to John Adams (March 31, 1776)

During the spring of 1776 in the Continental Congress, John Adams, along with his cousin Samuel Adams, led the movement towards independence. The congressional debates between the conservatives (advocates of reconciliation) and radicals (proponents of declaring independence) were, at times, acrimonious and divisive. John Adams often would vent his frustration, in letters to his wife Abigail, over the dilatory tactics of the middle colonies' delegates (especially John Dickinson of Pennsylvania), who opposed what they considered would be a premature declaration of independence. Thus Abigail was well aware of the congressional debate, sparked in part by the January publication of Thomas Paine's *Common Sense,* over the vexing issue of independence.

Although born into a patriarchal society, this multitalented woman was, for her day, a convincing advocate for women's rights. In hundreds of letters, Abigail advocated a philosophy that rejected the notion of female inferiority. As John's intellectual partner and confidant, Abigail frequently offered unsolicited advice to the sometimes-impetuous husband regarding all manner of subjects—including congressional business.

In a March 31, 1776, letter, Abigail made her strongest appeal to her husband to "Remember the Ladies" as Congress debated whether or not to draft a declaration of independence. John's answer to this admonition was to chide his wife by writing that males knew better than to repeal the current male-oriented code.

John Adams was appointed, along with Thomas Jefferson, Benjamin Franklin, Robert R. Livingston, and Roger Sherman, to the committee that drafted the Declaration of Independence. In the Declaration of Independence finally approved by Congress on July 4, 1776, the ladies were not even mentioned, much less meaningfully remembered. It would be almost another 150 years before women were even "remembered" enough to obtain the right to vote.

Abigail Adams to John Adams

Braintree, March 31, 1776

. . . I long to hear that you have declared an independancy—and by the way in the new Code of Laws which I suppose it will be necessary for you to make I desire you would Remember the Ladies, and be more generous and favourable to them than your ancestors. Do not put such unlimited power into the hands of Husbands. Remember all Men would be tyrants if they could. If periculiar care and attention is not paid to the Laidies we are determined to foment a Rebelion, and will not hold ourselves bound by any Laws in which we have no voice, or Representation.

That your Sex are Naturally Tyrannical is a Truth so thoroughly established as to admit of no dispute, but such of you as wish to be happy willingly give up the harsh title of Master for the tender and endearing one of Friend. Why then, not put it out of the power of the vicious and the Lawless to use us with cruelty and indignity with impunity. Men of Sense in all Ages abhor those customs which treat us only as the vassals of your Sex. Regard us then as Beings placed by providence under your protection and in imitation of the Supreem Being make use of that power only for our happiness.

Source: Lyman H. Butterfield, et al., editors, *Adams Family Correspondence*. Cambridge: Harvard University Press, 1963, I, 369–70.

Document 8
Resolution for Independence (June 7, 1776)

During the spring of 1776, there were spirited debates, both in Congress and among the general population, regarding the issue of declaring independence from Great Britain. Although there had been by late April 1776 a year of fighting in which there had been a great deal of bloodshed and rancorous animosity, there were still many Americans who favored reconciliation with the mother country. These conservatives, primarily from the middle colonies of New York, New Jersey, Delaware, and Pennsylvania, had effectively prevented an official congressional declaration of independence. However, because of the effective pamphleteering of radicals such as Thomas Paine, with his widely distributed *Common Sense,* and because of the continued bloodshed (especially the unsuccessful invasion of Canada), those who favored an official declaration gained in popular support and in numbers in the Continental Congress. Finally convinced that only an official declaration of separation from Britain would entice Britain's ancient foes, France and Spain, to come to the aid of the struggling colonists, the radicals in Congress, led by Samuel Adams and John Adams of Massachusetts and Richard Henry Lee of Virginia (the Adams-Lee faction), lobbied fervently to pass a motion for independence.

Thus Richard Henry Lee offered, on June 7, 1776, his now-famous three-part motion that created three congressional committees: one to craft the Articles of Confederation (the country's first constitution), one to open negotiations with foreign countries for recognition and material and financial support (this committee evolved into the Committee of Secret Correspondence, which eventually evolved into the Department of State), and one to draft a statement that would justify the colonies in declaring their independence from Great Britain. The passage of this motion was a major step leading to the formal declaration of independence of July 2, 1776, and to the congressional approval of the document now famously known as the Declaration of Independence of July 4, 1776.

RESOLVED, That these United Colonies are, and of right ought to be, free and independent States, that they are absolved from all allegiance to the British Crown, and that all political connection between them and the State of Great Britain is, and ought to be totally dissolved.

That it is expedient forthwith to take the most effectual measures for forming foreign Alliances.

That a plan of confederation be prepared and transmitted to the respective Colonies for their consideration and approbation.

Source: Henry Steele Commager and Milton Cantor, editors, *Documents of American History*. Tenth Edition. Englewood Cliffs, N.J.: Prentice Hall, Inc., 1988, I, 100.

Document 9
Declaration of Independence (July 1776)

After months of debate, frequently heated, the Continental Congress accepted, on June 7, 1776, Richard Henry Lee's three-part motion urging a declaration of independence and the creation of two committees, one to form foreign alliances and the other to prepare a plan of confederation. The first part of the motion calling for a declaration of independence was debated for two days, and then it was decided to postpone a vote on the all-important issue of independence until July 1st. In preparation for the momentous July 1st vote, Congress appointed, on June 11th, a committee to draft a document that would state persuasively and unequivocally the reasons for declaring independence from Great Britain. Composed of Roger Sherman of Connecticut, Robert R. Livingston of New York, Benjamin Franklin of Pennsylvania, John Adams of Massachusetts, and Thomas Jefferson of Virginia, this committee got down to work the following day. At the urgent prompting of John Adams, the work of crafting the initial draft of the document was given to Thomas Jefferson. This thirty-three-year-old Virginian had already gained a deserved reputation as an effective writer with his 1774 publication of *A Summary View of the Rights of British America*.

For the next fifteen days, Jefferson labored over his writing table in his Philadelphia rooming house writing the original rough draft of what would become America's charter of liberty. Often quoted, but not so often fully understood, the Declaration of Independence is the best statement of America's revolutionary philosophy. Espousing a natural rights philosophy and also drawing heavily on his own *A Summary View,* his 1776 draft of a state constitution for Virginia, and the writings of English political philosopher John Locke, Jefferson advanced a radical philosophy of government that has been, ever since, the model not only of revolutionaries and political idealists, but also of people worldwide. "That all men are created equal," that governments are instituted to secure the "unalienable rights of life, liberty, and the pursuit of happiness," that governments derived "their just powers from the consent of the governed," and that "whenever any form of government becomes destructive of these ends, it is the right of the people to alter or to abolish it, and to institute new government, . . . " are radical concepts not enjoyed by a majority of the world's population even today. The Declaration of Independence offers a philosophy that people everywhere still strive to have implemented.

On June 28th, the committee presented Jefferson's initial draft (with a few minor changes made by Adams and Franklin) to Congress. On the following Monday, July 1st, Congress resumed debate of Lee's motion of June 7th urging independence. John Adams successfully led the debate for a declaration of independence. The final formal vote for American independence came on Tuesday, July 2, 1776. Congress then took up the matter of the committee's draft of a statement that justified the decision for independence. Deleting about a fourth of the committee's verbiage (including, at the behest of the delegates from South Carolina and Georgia, the provision that censured the king for promoting the slave trade), the Congress approved the final Declaration of Independence on July 4, 1776.

The Unanimous Declaration

of the Thirteen United States of America

When, in the course of human events, it becomes necessary for one people to dissolve the political bonds which have connected them with another, and to assume among the powers of the earth, the separate and equal station to which the laws of nature and of nature's God entitle them, a decent respect to the opinions of mankind requires that they should declare the causes which impel them to the separation.

We hold these truths to be self-evident, that all men are created equal, that they are endowed by their Creator with certain unalienable rights, that among these are life, liberty and the pursuit of happiness. That to secure these rights, governments are instituted among men, deriving their just powers from the consent of the governed.

That whenever any form of government becomes destructive to these ends, it is the right of the people to alter or to abolish it, and to institute new government, laying its foundation on such principles and organizing its powers in such form, as to them shall seem most likely to effect their safety and happiness. Prudence, indeed, will dictate that governments long established should not be changed for light and transient causes; and accordingly all experience hath shown that mankind are more disposed to suffer, while evils are sufferable, than to right themselves by abolishing the forms to which they are accustomed. But when a long train of abuses and usurpations, pursuing invariably the same object evinces a design to reduce them under absolute despotism, it is their right, it is their duty, to throw off such government, and to provide new guards for their future security.

Such has been the patient sufferance of these colonies; and such is now the necessity which constrains them to alter their former systems of government. The history of the present King of Great Britain is a history of repeated injuries and usurpations, all having in direct object the establishment of an absolute tyranny over these states. To prove this, let facts be submitted to a candid world.

He has refused his assent to laws, the most wholesome and necessary for the public good.

He has forbidden his governors to pass laws of immediate and pressing importance, unless suspended in their operation till his assent should be obtained; and when so suspended, he has utterly neglected to attend to them.

He has refused to pass other laws for the accommodation of large districts of people, unless those people would relinquish the right of representation in the legislature, a right inestimable to them and formidable to tyrants only.

He has called together legislative bodies at places unusual, uncomfortable, and distant from depository of their public records, for the sole purpose of fatiguing them into compliance with his measures.

He has dissolved representative houses repeatedly, for opposing with manly firmness his invasions on the rights of the people.

He has refused for a long time, after such dissolutions, to cause others to be elected; whereby the legislative powers, incapable of annihilation, have returned to the people at large for their exercise; the state remaining in the meantime exposed to all the dangers of invasion from without, and convulsions within.

He has endeavored to prevent the population of these states; for that purpose obstructing the laws for naturalization of foreigners; refusing to pass others to encourage their migration hither, and raising the conditions of new appropriations of lands.

He has obstructed the administration of justice, by refusing his assent to laws for establishing judiciary powers.

He has made judges dependent on his will alone, for the tenure of their offices, and the amount and payment of their salaries.

He has erected a multitude of new offices, and sent hither swarms of officers to harass our people, and eat out their substance.

He has kept among us, in times of peace, standing armies without the consent of our legislature.

He has affected to render the military independent of and superior to civil power.

He has combined with others to subject us to a jurisdiction foreign to our constitution, and unacknowledged by our laws; giving his assent to their acts of pretended legislation:

For quartering large bodies of armed troops among us:

For protecting them, by mock trial, from punishment for any murders which they should commit on the inhabitants of these states:

For cutting off our trade with all parts of the world:

For imposing taxes on us without our consent:

For depriving us in many cases, of the benefits of trial by jury:

For transporting us beyond seas to be tried for pretended offenses:

For abolishing the free system of English laws in a neighboring province, establishing therein an arbitrary government, and enlarging its boundaries so as to render it at once an example and fit instrument for introducing the same absolute rule in these colonies:

For taking away our charters, abolishing our most valuable laws, and altering fundamentally the forms of our governments:

For suspending our own legislatures, and declaring themselves invested with power to legislate for us in all cases whatsoever.

He has abdicated government here, by declaring us out of his protection and waging war against us.

He has plundered our seas, ravaged our coasts, burned our towns, and destroyed the lives of our people.

He is at this time transporting large armies of foreign mercenaries to complete the works of death, desolation and tyranny, already begun with circumstances of cruelty and perfidy scarcely paralleled in the most barbarous ages, and totally unworthy of the head of a civilized nation.

He has constrained our fellow citizens taken captive on the high seas to bear arms against their country, to become the executioners of their friends and brethren, or to fall themselves by their hands.

He has excited domestic insurrections amongst us, and has endeavored to bring on the inhabitants of our frontiers, the merciless Indian savages, whose known rule of warfare, is undistinguished destruction of all ages, sexes, and conditions.

In every stage of these oppressions we have petitioned for redress in the most humble terms: our repeated petitions have been answered only by repeated injury. A prince, whose character is thus marked by every act which may define a tyrant, is unfit to be the ruler of a free people.

Nor have we been wanting in attention to our British brethren. We have warned them from time to time of attempts by their legislature to extend an unwarrantable jurisdiction over us. We have reminded them of the circumstances of our emigration and settlement here. We have appealed to their native justice and magnanimity, and we have conjured them by the ties of our common kindred to disavow these usurpations, which, would inevitably interrupt our connections and correspondence.

We must, therefore, acquiesce in the necessity, which denounces our separation, and hold them, as we hold the rest of mankind, enemies in war, in peace friends.

We, therefore, the representatives of the United States of America, in General Congress, assembled, appealing to the Supreme Judge of the world for the rectitude of our intentions, do, in the name, and by the authority of the good people of these colonies, solemnly publish and declare, that these united colonies are, and of right ought to be free and independent states; that they are absolved from all allegiance to the British Crown, and that all political connection between them and the state of Great Britain, is and ought to be totally dissolved; and that as free and independent states, they have full power to levy war, conclude peace, contract alliances, establish commerce, and to do all other acts and things which independent states may of right do. And for the support of this declaration, with a firm reliance on the protection of Divine Providence, we mutually pledge to each other our lives, our fortunes and our sacred honor.

Source: Henry Steele Commager and Milton Cantor, editors, *Documents of American History*. Tenth Edition. Englewood Cliffs, N.J.: Prentice Hall, Inc., 1988, I, 100–103.

Document 10
Articles of Confederation (March 1781)

In the June 7, 1776, resolutions, introduced by Richard Henry Lee and seconded by John Adams, that declared "these United Colonies are, and of right ought to be free and independent States" and "that it is expedient forthwith to take the most effectual measures for forming foreign Alliances," there was a third resolution that proposed "That a plan of confederation be prepared and transmitted to the respective Colonies for their consideration and approbation."[1] Pursuant to that resolution, Congress, on June 12, 1776, appointed a committee of thirteen to draft what would become the first national constitution. As chairman of the committee, John Dickinson of Pennsylvania wrote the initial draft of what would be designated as the Articles of Confederation and Perpetual Union.

In moving towards independence and drafting a national constitution simultaneously, Congress was taking the middle course between conservatives and radicals. The radicals, led by Samuel Adams, John Adams, and Richard Henry Lee, advocated an immediate declaration of independence whereas the conservatives, led by John Dickinson, James Wilson, and Robert R. Livingston, favored the creation of a union before possible separation from the mother country.

After desultory debate, Congress, on July 8th, rejected Dickinson's original draft. Thereafter, Congress took up in more leisurely fashion the issue of creating a viable union. After many months of debate during which numerous amendments were proposed to the Dickinson draft, Congress, on November 15, 1777, accepted the amended document as the final Articles of Confederation and Perpetual Union. Because ratification of the document required the approval of all thirteen states, the Articles were not officially promulgated until March 1, 1781, when Maryland ratified after Virginia finally agreed to give up to Congress its claims to lands north and west of the Ohio River.

The Articles of Confederation created the weak national government most Americans thought they wanted. In the midst of a bloody war against a strong imperial British government, the colonists did not want to create for themselves a central government capable of duplicating the tyranny and oppression they perceived they were experiencing from Great Britain.

In the allocation of political power, the Articles reserved most power to the individual states. What the Articles created was "a firm league of friendship" in which "each state retains its sovereignty, freedom and independence." Because the one-branch government (a national legislature in which each state had one vote) was established by the states, not by the people, it turned out to be little more than a debating society. To ensure that the national government would not become too powerful, Congress was denied the power to tax, the power to regulate trade and commerce, and the power to enforce its laws. As a result of the requirement that amendments to the document had to obtain the approval of all thirteen states, the Articles were never amended. This inflexibility made almost inevitable the Constitutional Revolution of 1787 when the Articles were overthrown in favor of the Constitution of 1787. Experience soon demonstrated that the relatively weak national government created by the Articles could not deal successfully with the manifold problems that confronted the young American republic after the conclusion of the Revolutionary War in 1783.

To all to whom these Presents shall come, we the undersigned Delegates of the States affixed to our Names send greeting.

Whereas the Delegates of the United States of America in Congress assembled did on the fifteenth day of November in the Year of our Lord One Thousand Seven Hundred and Seventy-seven, and in the Second Year of the Independence of America agree to certain articles of Confederation and perpetual Union between the States of Newhampshire, Massachusetts-bay, Rhodeisland and Providence Plantations, Connecticut, New York, New Jersey, Pennsylvania, Delaware, Maryland, Virginia, North-Carolina, South-Carolina and Georgia in the Words following, viz.

Articles of Confederation and perpetual Union between the States of Newhampshire, Massachusetts-bay, Rhodeisland and Providence Plantations, Connecticut, New-York, New-Jersey, Pennsylvania, Delaware, Maryland, Virginia, North-Carolina, South-Carolina and Georgia.

Article I. The stile of this confederacy shall be "The United States of America."

Article II. Each State retains its sovereignty, freedom and independence, and every power, jurisdiction and rights, which is not by this confederation expressly delegated to the United States, in Congress assembled.

Article III. The said States hereby severally enter into a firm league of friend-ship with each other, for their common defence, the security of their liberties, and their mutual and general welfare, binding themselves to assist each other, against all force offered to, or attacks made upon them, or any of them, on account of religion, sovereignty, trade or any other pretence whatever.

Article IV. The better to secure and perpetuate mutual friendship and intercourse among the people of the different States in this Union, the free inhabitants of each of these States, paupers, vagabonds and fugitives from justice excepted, shall be entitled to all privileges and immunities of free citizens in the several States; and the people of each State shall have free ingress and regress to and from any other State, and shall enjoy therein all the privileges of trade and commerce, subject to the same duties, impositions and restrictions as the inhabitants thereof respectively, provided that such restrictions shall not extend so far as to prevent the removal of property imported into any State, to any other State of which the owner is an inhabitant; provided also that no imposition, duties or restriction shall be laid by any State, on the property of the United States, or either of them.

If any person guilty of, or charged with treason, felony, or other high misdemeanor in any State, shall flee from justice, and be found in any of the United States, he shall upon demand of the Governor or Executive power, of the State from which he fled, be delivered up and removed to the State having jurisdiction of his offence.

Full faith and credit shall be given in each of these States to the records, acts and judicial proceedings of the courts and magistrates of every other State.

Article V. For the more convenient management of the general interests of the United States, delegates shall be annually appointed in such manner as the legislature of each State shall direct, to meet in Congress on the first Monday in November, in every year, with a power reserved to each State, to recall its delegates, or any of them, at any time within the year, and to send others in their stead, for the remainder of the year.

No State shall be represented in Congress by less than two, nor by more than seven members; and no person shall be capable of being a delegate for more than three years in any term of six years; nor shall any person, being a delegate, be capable of holding any office under the United States, for which he, or another for his benefit receives any salary, fees or emolument of any kind.

Each State shall maintain its own delegates in a meeting of the States, and while they act as members of the committee of the States.

In determining questions in the United States, in Congress assembled, each State shall have one vote.

Freedom of speech and debate in Congress shall not be impeached or questioned in any court, or place out of Congress, and the members of Congress shall be protected in their persons from arrests and imprisonments, during the time of their going to and from, and attendance in Congress, except for treason, felony, or breach of the peace.

Article VI. No State without the consent of the United States in Congress assembled, shall send any embassy to, or receive any embassy from, or enter into any conference, agreement, alliance or treaty with any king, prince or state; nor shall any person holding any office of profit or trust under the United States, or any of them, accept of any present, emolument, office, nor title of any kind whatever from any king, prince or foreign state; nor shall the United States in Congress assembled, nor any of them, grant any title of nobility.

No two or more States shall enter into any treaty, confederation or alliance whatever between them, without the consent of the United States in Congress assembled, specifying accurately the purposes for which the same is to be entered into, and how long it shall continue.

No State shall lay any imposts or duties, which may interfere with any stipulations in treaties, entered into by the United States in Congress assembled, with any king, prince or state, in pursuance of any treaties already proposed by Congress, to the courts of France and Spain.

No vessels of war shall be kept up in time of peace by any State, except such number only, as shall be deemed necessary by the United States in Congress assembled, for the defence of such State, or its trade; nor shall any body of forces be kept up by any State, in time of peace, except such number only, as in the judgment of the United States, in Congress assembled, shall be deemed requisite to garrison the forts necessary for the defence of such State, but every State shall always keep up a well regulated and disciplined militia, sufficiently armed and accoutred, and shall provide and constantly have ready for use, in public stores, a due number of field pieces and tents, and a proper quantity of arms, ammunition and camp equipage.

No State shall engage in any war without the consent of the United States in Congress assembled, unless such State be actually invaded by enemies, or shall have received certain advice of a resolution being formed by some nation of Indians to invade such State, and the danger is so imminent as not to admit of a delay, till the United States in Congress assembled can be consulted: nor shall any State grant commissions to any ships or vessels of war, nor letters of marque or reprisal, except it be after a declaration of war by the United States in Congress assembled, and then only against the kingdom or state and the subjects thereof, against which war has been so declared, and under such regulations as shall be established by the United States in Congress assembled, unless such State be infested by pirates, in which case vessels of war may be fitted out for that occasion, and kept so long as the danger shall continue, or until the United States in Congress assembled shall determine otherwise.

Article VII. When land-forces are raised by any State of the common defence, all officers of or under the rank of colonel, shall be appointed by the Legislature of each State respectively by whom such forces shall be raised, or in such manner as such State shall direct, and all vacancies shall be filled up by the State which first made the appointment.

Article VIII. All charges of war, and all other expenses that shall be incurred for the common defence or general welfare, and allowed by the United States in Congress assembled, shall be defrayed out of a common treasury, which shall be supplied by the several States, in proportion to the value of all land within each State, granted or surveyed for any person, as such land and the buildings and improvements thereon shall be estimated according to such mode as the United States in Congress assembled, shall from time to time direct and appoint.

The taxes for paying that proportion shall be laid and levied by the authority and direction of the Legislatures of the several States within the time agreed upon by the United States in Congress assembled.

Article IX. The United States in Congress assembled, shall have the sole and exclusive right and power of determining on peace and war, except in the cases mentioned in the sixth article—of sending and receiving ambassadors—entering into treaties and alliances, provided that no treaty of commerce shall be made whereby the legislative power of the respective States shall be restrained from imposing such imposts and duties on foreigners, as their own people are subjected to, or from prohibiting the exportation or importation of and species of goods or commodities whatsoever—establishing rules for deciding in all cases, what captures on land or water shall be legal, and in what manner prizes taken by land or naval forces in the service of the United States shall be divided or appropriated—of granting letters of marque and reprisal in times of peace—appointing courts for the trial of piracies and felonies committed on the high seas and establishing courts for receiving and determining finally appeals in all cases of captures, provided that no member of Congress shall be appointed a judge of any of the said courts.

The United States in Congress assembled shall also be the last resort on appeal in all disputes and differences now subsisting or that hereafter may arise between two or more States concerning boundary, jurisdiction or any other cause whatever; which authority shall always be exercised in the manner following. Whenever the legislative or executive authority or lawful agent of any State in controversy with another shall present a petition to Congress, stating the matter in question, and praying for a hearing notice thereof shall be given by order of Congress to the legislative or executive authority of the other State in controversy, and a day assigned for the appearance of the parties by their lawful agents, who shall then be directed to appoint, by joint consent, commissioners or judges to constitute a court for hearing and determining matter in question; but, if they cannot agree, Congress shall name three persons out of each of the United States, and from the list of such persons each party shall alternately strike out one, the petitioners beginning, until the number shall be reduced to thirteen; and from that number not less than seven, nor more than nine names, as Congress shall direct, shall, in the presence of Congress, be drawn out by lot; and the persons whose names shall be so drawn, or any five of them, shall be commissioners or judges, to hear and finally determine the controversy, so always as a major part of judges who shall hear the cause shall agree in the determination; and if either party shall neglect to attend at the day appointed, without shewing reasons which Congress shall judge sufficient, or, being present, shall refuse to strike, the Congress shall proceed to nominate three persons out of each State, and the secretary of Congress shall strike in behalf of such party absent or refusing; and the judgment and sentence of the court to be appointed, in the manner before prescribed, shall be final and conclusive; and if any of the parties shall refuse to submit to the authority of such court, or to appear or defend their claim or cause, the court shall nevertheless proceed to pronounce sentence or judgment, which shall, in like manner, be final and decisive, the judgment or sentence and other proceedings being, in either case, transmitted to Congress, and lodged among the act of Congress for the security of the parties concerned: provided, that every commissioner, before he sits in judgment, shall take an oath, to be administered by one of the judges of the supreme or superior court of the State where the cause shall be tried, "well and truly to hear and determine the matter in question, according to the best of his judgment, without favour, affection, or hope of reward:" provided, also, that no State shall be deprived of territory for the benefit of the United States.

All controversies concerning the private right of soil, claimed under different grants of two or more states, whose jurisdictions, as they may respect such lands and the states which passed such grants, are adjusted, the said grants, or either of them, being at the same time claimed to have originated antecedent to such settlement of jurisdiction, shall, on the petition of either party to the Congress of the United States, be finally determined, as near as may be, in the same manner as is before prescribed for deciding disputes respecting territorial jurisdiction between different states.

The United States, in Congress assembled, shall also have the sole and exclusive right and power of regulating the alloy and value of coin struck by their own authority, or by that of the respective states; fixing the standard of weights and measures throughout the United States; regulating the trade and managing all affairs with the Indians not members of any of the states; provided that the legislative right of any State within its own limits be not infringed or violated; establishing and regulating post offices from one State to another throughout all the United States, and exacting such postage on the papers passing through the same as may be requisite to defray the expences of the said office; appointing all officers of the land forces in the service of the United States, excepting regimental officers; appointing all the officers of the naval forces, and commissioning all officers whatever in the service of the United States; making rules for the government and regulation of the said land and naval forces, and directing their operations.

The United States, in Congress assembled, shall have authority to appoint a committee to sit in the recess of Congress, to be denominated "a committee of the States," and to consist of one delegate from each state, and to appoint such other committees and civil officers as may be necessary for managing the general affairs of the United States, under their direction; to appoint one of their number to preside; provided that no person be allowed to serve in the office of president more than one year in any term of three years; to ascertain the necessary sums of money to be raised for the service of the United States, and to appropriate and apply the same for defraying the public expences; to borrow money or emit bills on the credit of the United States, transmitting, every half year, to the respective states, an account of the sums of money so borrowed or emitted; to build and equip a navy; to agree upon the number of land forces, and to make requisitions from each State for its quota, in proportion to the number of white inhabitants in such State; which requisition shall be binding; and, thereupon, the legislature of each State shall appoint the regimental officers, raise the men, and cloathe, arm, and equip them in a soldier-like manner, at the expence of the United; and the officers and men so cloathed, armed, and equipped, shall march to the place appointed and within the time agreed on by the United States, in Congress assembled; but if the United States, in Congress assembled, shall, on consideration of circumstances, judge proper that any State should not raise men, or should raise a smaller number than its quota, and that any other State should raise a greater number of men than the quota thereof, such extra number shall be raised, officered, cloathed, armed, and equipped in the same manner as the quota of such State, unless the legislature of such State shall judge that such extra number cannot be safely spared out of the same, in which case they shall raise, officer, cloathe, arm, and equip as many of such extra number as they judge can be safely spared. And the officers and men so cloathed, armed, and equipped, shall march to the place appointed and within the time agreed on by the United States, in Congress assembled.

The United States, in Congress assembled, shall never engage in a war, nor grant letters of marque and reprisal in time of peace, nor enter into any treaties or alliances, nor coin money, nor regulate the value thereof, nor ascertain the sums and expences necessary for the defence and welfare of the United States, or any of them: nor emit bills, nor borrow money on the credit of the United States, nor appropriate money, nor agree upon the number of vessels of war to be built or purchased, or the number of land or sea forces to be raised, nor appoint a commander in chief of the army or navy, unless nine states assent to the same; nor shall a question on any other point, except for adjourning from day to day, be determined, unless by the votes of a majority of the United States, in Congress assembled.

The Congress of the United States shall have power to adjourn to any time within the year, and to any place within the United States, so that no period of adjournment be for a longer duration than the space of six months, and shall publish the journal of their proceedings monthly, except such parts thereof, relating to treaties, alliances or military operations, as, in their judgment, require secrecy; and the yeas and nays of the delegates of each State on any question shall be entered on the journal, when it is desired by any delegate; and the delegates of a State, or any of them, at his, or their request, shall be furnished with a transcript of the said journal, except such parts as are above excepted, to lay before the legislatures of the several states."

Article X: The committee of the states, or any nine of them, shall be authorized to execute, in the recess of Congress, such of the powers of Congress as the United States, in Congress assembled, by the consent of nine states, shall, from time to time, think expedient to vest them with; provided, that no power be delegated to the said committee, for the exercise of which, by the articles of confederation, the voice of nine states, in the Congress of the United States assembled, is requisite."

Article XI: Canada acceding to this confederation, and joining in the measures of the United States, shall be admitted into and entitled to all the advantages of this union; but no other colony shall be admitted into the same, unless such admission be agreed to by nine states."

Article XII: All bills of credit emitted, monies borrowed and debts contracted by, or under the authority of Congress before the assembling of the United States, in pursuance of the present confederation, shall be deemed and considered as a charge against the United States, for payment and satisfaction whereof the said United States and public faith are hereby solemnly pledged."

Articles XIII: Every State shall abide by the determination of the United States, in Congress assembled, on all questions which, by this confederation, are submitted to them. And the articles of confederation shall be inviolably observed by every State, and the union shall be perpetual; nor shall any alteration at any time hereafter be made in any of them, unless such alteration be agreed to in a Congress of the United States, and be afterwards confirmed by the legislatures of every State.

These articles shall be proposed to the legislatures of all the United States, to be considered, and if approved of by them, they are advised to authorize their delegates to ratify the same in the Congress of the United States; which being done, the same shall become conclusive."

Source: James D. Richardson, editor, *A Compilation of the Messages and Papers of the Presidents, 1789-1903*. New York: Bureau of National Literature and Art, 1903, I, 9–18.

[1]Henry Steele Commager and Milton Cantor, editors, *Documents of American History*. Tenth Edition. Englewood Cliffs, N.J.: Prentice Hall, Inc., 1988, I, 100.

Document 11
Treaty of Paris, 1783

The Treaty of Paris (1783) was a remarkable American diplomatic triumph. By its terms, Great Britain not only recognized American independence, but she also gave to the newly created American republic generous geographic boundaries. The United States was able to secure such an advantageous treaty for two main reasons. Foremost, after the humiliating defeat at Yorktown, Virginia, in October 1781, Great Britain finally became convinced that she could not win the military conflict in America. Also, credit for negotiating such a favorable treaty should be given to the three major American negotiators. In Benjamin Franklin, John Jay, and John Adams, the United States had three diplomats who were able to participate successfully in the intricate and at times Machiavellian diplomatic games played by Europeans.

Because Adams and Jay mistrusted French intentions, the Americans negotiated separately with the British, thus violating their Treaty of Alliance with France, which mandated joint negotiations with their common enemy. At the conclusion of the long, drawn out negotiations, Benjamin Franklin was able, however, to convince the French Foreign Minister Comte de Vergennes that it was in France's best interest to approve the drafted treaty rather than prolong the negotiations.

In granting generous terms to the rebellious colonies, Great Britain was acknowledging that the Bourbon Powers of France and Spain were still her primary enemies. In giving up political control over the thirteen colonies, she could and indeed would try to continue to exploit them economically. The Treaty of Paris (1783) gained for the United States its political independence from Great Britain while the Treaty of Ghent (1814), which ended the War of 1812, secured for the fledgling American republic its economic independence from the former mother country.

. . . Article I. His Britannic Majesty acknowledges the said United States, viz. [*vi de li cet*], New Hampshire, Massachusetts Bay, Rhode Island and Providence Plantations, Connecticut, New York, New Jersey, Pennsylvania, Delaware, Maryland, Virginia, North Carolina, South Carolina, and Georgia, to be free, sovereign and independent States; that he treats with them as such, and for himself, his heirs and successors, relinquishes all claims to the Government, propriety and territorial rights of the same, and every part thereof.

Article II. And that all disputes which might arise in future, on the subject of the boundaries of the said United States may be prevented, it is hereby agreed and declared, that the following are, and shall be their boundaries, viz.; from the northwest angle of Nova Scotia, viz: that angle which is formed by a line drawn due north from the source of Saint Croix River to the Highlands; along the said Highlands which divide those rivers that empty themselves into the river St. Lawrence, from those which fall into the Atlantic Ocean, to the northwesternmost head of Connecticut River; thence down along the middle of that river, to the forty-fifth degree of north latitude; from thence, by a line due west said latitude, until it strikes the river Iroquois or Cataraquy; thence along the middle of said river into Lake Ontario, through the middle of said lake until it strikes the communication by water between that lake and Lake Erie; thence along the middle of said communication into Lake Erie, through the middle of said lake until it arrives at the water communication between that lake and Lake Huron; thence along the middle of said water communication into Lake Huron; thence through the middle of said lake to water communication between that lake and Lake Superior; thence through Lake Superior northward of the Isles Royal and Phelipeaux, to the Long Lake; thence through the middle of said Long Lake, and the water communication between it and the Lake of the Woods, to the said Lake of the Woods; thence through the said lake to the most northwestern point thereof, and from thence on a due west course to the river Mississippi; thence by a line to be drawn along the middle of the said river Mississippi until it shall intersect the northernmost part of the thirty-first degree of north latitude. South, by a line to be drawn due east from the determination of the line last mentioned, in the latitude of thirty-one degrees north of the Equator, to the middle of the river Appalachicola or Catahouche; thence along the middle thereof to its junction with the Flint River; thence straight to the head of St. Mary's River; and thence down along the middle of St. Mary's River to the Atlantic Ocean. East, by a line to be drawn along the middle of the river St. Croix, from its mouth in the Bay of Fundy to its source, and from its source directly north to the aforesaid Highlands, which divide the rivers that fall into the Atlantic Ocean from those which fall into the river St. Lawrence; comprehending all islands within twenty leagues of any part of the shores of the United States, and lying between lines to be drawn due east from the points where the aforesaid boundaries between Nova Scotia on the one part, and East Florida on the other, shall respectively touch the Bay of Fundy and the Atlantic Ocean; excepting such islands as now are, or heretofore have been, within the limits of the said province of Nova Scotia.

Article III. It is agreed that the people of the United States shall continue to enjoy unmolested the right to take fish of every kind on the Grand Bank, and on all the other banks of Newfoundland; also in the Gulph of Saint Lawrence, and at all other places in the sea where the inhabitants of both countries used at any time heretofore to fish. And also that the inhabitants of the United States shall have liberty to take fish of every kind on such part of the coast of Newfoundland as British fishermen shall use (but not to dry or cure the same on that island) and also on the coasts bays and creeks of all other of His Britannic Majesty's dominions in America; and that the American fishermen shall have liberty to dry and cure fish in any of the unsettled bays, harbours and creeks of Nova Scotia, Magdalen Islands, and Labrador, so long as the same shall remain unsettled; but so soon as the same or either of them shall be settled, it shall not be lawful for the said fishermen to dry or cure fish at such settlements, without a previous agreement for that purpose with the inhabitants, proprietors or possessors of the ground.

Article IV. It is agreed that creditors on either side shall meet with no lawful impediment to the recovery of the full value in sterling money, of all bona fide debts heretofore contracted.

Article V. It is agreed that the Congress shall earnestly recommend it to the legislatures of the respective States, to provide for the restitution of all estates, rights and properties which have been confiscated, belonging to real British subjects, and also of the estates, rights and properties of persons resident in districts in the possession of His Majesty's arms, and who have not borne arms against the said United States. And that persons of any other description shall have free liberty to go to any part or parts of any of the thirteen United States, and therein to remain twelve months, unmolested in their endeavors to obtain the restitution of such of their estates, rights and properties as may have been confiscated; and that Congress shall earnestly recommend to the several States a reconsideration and revision of all acts or laws regarding the premises, so as to render the said laws or acts perfectly consistent, not only with justice and equity, but with that spirit of conciliation which, on the return of the blessings of peace, should universally prevail. And that Congress shall also earnestly recommend to the several States, that the estates, rights, and properties of such last mentioned persons, shall be restored to them, they refunding to any persons who may be now in possession, the bona fide price (where any has been given) which such persons may have paid on purchasing any of the said lands, rights or properties, since the confiscation. And it is agreed, that all persons who have any interest in confiscated lands, either by debts, marriage settlements or otherwise, shall meet with no lawful impediment in the prosecution of their just rights.

Article VI. That there shall be no future confiscations made, nor any prosecutions commenced against any person or persons for, or by reason of the part which he or they may have taken in the present war; and that no person shall, on that account, suffer any future loss or damage, either in his person, liberty or property; and that those who may be in confinement on such charges, at the time of the ratification of the treaty in America, shall be immediately set at liberty, and the prosecutions so commenced be discontinued.

Article VII. There shall be a firm and perpetual peace between His Britannic Majesty and the said States, and between the subjects of the one and the citizens of the other, wherefore all hostilities, both by sea and land, shall from henceforth cease; All prisoners on both sides shall be set at liberty, and His Britannic Majesty shall, with all convenient speed, and without causing any destruction, or carrying away any Negroes or other property of the American inhabitants, withdraw all his armies, garrisons and fleets from the said United States, and from every post, place and harbour within the same; leaving in all fortifications the American artillery that may be therein; And shall also order and cause all archives, records, deeds and papers, belonging to any of the said States, or their citizens, which, in the course of the war, may have fallen into the hands of his officers, to be forthwith restored and deliver'd to the proper States and persons to whom they belong.

Article VIII. The navigation of the river Mississippi, from its source to the ocean, shall forever remain free and open to the subjects of Great Britain, and the citizens of the United States.

Article IX. In case it should so happen that any place or territory belonging to Great Britain or to the United States, should have been conquer'd by the arms of either from the other, before the arrival of the said provisional articles in America, it is agreed, that the same shall be restored without difficulty, and without requiring any compensation. . . .

Source: Henry Steele Commager and Milton Cantor, editors, *Documents of American History*. Tenth Edition. Englewood Cliffs, N.J.: Prentice Hall, Inc., 1988, I, 117–19.

ANNOTATED BIBLIOGRAPHY

Alden, John Richard. *A History of the American Revolution*. New York: Alfred A. Knopf, 1969. One of the more informative one-volume surveys of the entire revolutionary period.

——. *The American Revolution, 1775–1783*. New York: Harper & Brothers, 1954. A volume in the *New American Nation* series written by a noted military historian.

Annals of America, The. Chicago: Encyclopaedia Britannica, Inc., 1976. This twenty-one-volume set contains hundreds of valuable primary documents on American history from 1493–1986. Volume II contains 147 of the more important documents for the period 1755–1783.

Bailyn, Bernard. *The Ordeal of Thomas Hutchinson*. Cambridge: Harvard University Press, 1974. A sympathetic portrayal of the trials and tribulations of the much-maligned, fifth-generation American Governor of Massachusetts Bay who suffered grievously for his loyalty to the British crown.

Becker, Carl L. *The Declaration of Independence: A Study in the History of Political Ideas*. New York: Vintage Books, 1959. An easy-to-read analysis of the political concepts in the famous Declaration.

Beeman, Richard R. *Patrick Henry: A Biography*. New York: McGraw-Hill Book Company, 1974. The best single-volume biography of Virginia's gifted orator and wartime governor.

Bemis, Samuel Flagg. *The Diplomacy of the American Revolution*. Bloomington: Indiana University Press, 1957. The standard, although somewhat outdated, study of the successful American diplomacy that led to the French Alliance (1778) and the Treaty of Paris (1783).

Billias, George Athan, ed. *George Washington's Generals*. New York: William Morrow and Company, 1964. A highly readable collection of biographical essays on America's top twelve revolutionary generals.

────. *George Washington's Opponents: British Generals and Admirals in the American Revolution.* New York: William Morrow and Company, 1969. Informative essays on the British generals and admirals who were asked to conduct the war in America against what are now generally considered to be impossible odds.

Boatner, Mark Mayo III. *Encyclopedia of the American Revolution.* New York: David McKay Company, Inc., 1966. An extremely useful reference tool for obtaining detailed information on battles, people, and events.

────. *Landmarks of the American Revolution.* Harrisburg, Penn.: Stackpole Books, 1973. An excellent state-by-state guide to most of the revolutionary war battlefields and historic sites to be found east of the Mississippi River.

Bonwick, Colin. *The American Revolution.* Charlottesville: University Press of Virginia, 1991. An excellent study of the War of American Independence and the accompanying "internal revolution" by a well-regarded English historian.

Brandt, Clare. *The Man in the Mirror: A Life of Benedict Arnold.* New York: Random House, Inc., 1994. A highly readable, somewhat overly sympathetic biography of America's most famous and most maligned military hero/traitor.

Brown, Richard D., ed. *Major Problems in the Era of the American Revolution, 1760–1791.* Second Edition. Boston: Houghton Mifflin Company, 2000. A useful collection of the most significant primary documents of the revolutionary era plus thirty short interpretive essays by such distinguished scholars as Jack P. Greene, Pauline Maier, Don Higginbotham, Linda K. Kerber, Jack N. Rakove, and Edward Countryman.

Burnett, Edmund Cody. *The Continental Congress: A Definitive History of the Continental Congress from its Inception in 1774 to March, 1789.* New York: W. W. Norton & Company, Inc., 1964. The classic detailed survey of the First and Second Continental Congresses through their fifteen-year history. Extremely useful for an understanding of the political history of the revolutionary era.

Butterfield, Lyman H., et al., eds. *Adams Family Correspondence.* Cambridge: Harvard University Press, 1963. Volume I of this superb edition contains most of the extant letters between John and Abigail Adams. The informative editorial commentary makes this a valuable source for the study of the last quarter of the eighteenth century.

Commager, Henry Steele and Milton Cantor, eds., *Documents of American History.* Volume 1 to 1898. Tenth Edition. Englewood Cliffs, N.J.: Prentice Hall, 1988. A valuable compilation, with accompanying informative commentary, of 345 of the most significant primary documents of the early half of United States history.

Conway, Stephen. *The War of American Independence, 1775–1783.* London: Edward Arnold, 1995. A British historian's contention that the American Revolution was only part of a worldwide military and naval conflict between the Bourbon powers (France and Spain) and Great Britain.

Cunliffe, Marcus. *George Washington: Man and Monument*. New York: New American Library, 1958. In this well-written brief biography, the author separates the real Washington (Man) from the mythological Washington (Monument). It remains the best brief single-volume biography of the first president.

Douglas, David C., ed., *English Historical Documents*. London: E. Methuen, 1979. Vol. IX. An indispensable research tool for the serious student of colonial and revolutionary America.

Dull, Jonathan R. *A Diplomatic History of the American Revolution*. New Haven, Conn.: Yale University Press, 1985. The best brief, single volume introduction to the complexities of American revolutionary diplomacy.

Ellis, Joseph J. *American Sphinx: The Character of Thomas Jefferson*. New York: Alfred A. Knopf, 1997. The most recently published first-rate interpretive biography of the enigmatic author of the Declaration of Independence.

Ferguson, E. James. *The American Revolution: A General History, 1763–1790*. Homewood, Ill.: The Dorsey Press, 1974. An informative general survey of the entire revolutionary era that stresses the effect of internal social, political, economic, and intellectual unrest on the emerging American republic.

———. *The Power of the Purse: A History of American Public Finance, 1776–1790*. Chapel Hill: The University of North Carolina Press, 1961. The best general survey of public finance during the Revolution, with particular emphasis on the valuable contributions of financier Robert Morris.

Ferling, John. *John Adams: A Life*. New York: Henry Holt and Company, 1992. An informative full-length biography that places the often-quarrelsome Adams in the first rank, along with Benjamin Franklin, George Washington, and Thomas Jefferson, as a revolutionist and nation builder.

Fleming, Thomas, ed. *A Narrative of a Revolutionary Soldier: Some of the Adventures, Dangers, and Sufferings of Joseph Plumb Martin*. New York: Penguin Putnam, Inc., 2001. A highly readable firsthand account of the trials and tribulations experienced by a private in the Continental Army.

Flexner, James Thomas. *Washington: The Indispensable Man*. Boston: Little, Brown and Company, 1969. The best single-volume biography of the one man who was truly "indispensable" to the American cause.

Flower, Milton E. *John Dickinson: Conservative Revolutionary*. Charlottesville: University Press of Virginia, 1983. In this long-overdue, full-length biography of one of the most influential revolutionary figures, Professor Flower has resurrected his subject's historical reputation.

Gipson, Lawrence Henry. *The Coming of the Revolution, 1763–1775*. New York: Harper & Brothers, 1954. A volume in the *New American Nation* series by a renowned proponent of the "imperial" school who claimed that the War for American Independence was the inevitable consequence of what he called the "Great War for the Empire" (Seven Years' War or French and Indian War, 1754–1763).

Gruber, Ira D. *The Howe Brothers and the American Revolution*. New York: W. W. Norton & Company, 1972. The author claims that the Howe brothers were not to be blamed for failing to subdue the rebellion in America. They did not have, he asserts, the full support of the British ministry or fellow officers.

Higginbotham, Don. *The War of American Independence: Military Attitudes, Policies, and Practice, 1763–1789*. New York: The Macmillan Company, 1971. A volume in *The Macmillan Wars of the United States* series. An excellent examination of the organization and practices of the American military during its formative years.

Jameson, J. Franklin, *The American Revolution Considered as a Social Movement*. Princeton, N.J.: Princeton University Press, 1926. An early and now classic interpretation that stressed the broad social impact of the American Revolution on American society.

Jensen, Merrill. *The Articles of Confederation: An Interpretation of the Social-Constitutional History of the American Revolution, 1774–1781*. Madison: University of Wisconsin Press, 1959. A classic study that stresses the "internal revolution" aspects of the Revolution.

———. *The Founding of a Nation: A History of the American Revolution, 1763–1776*. The best single-volume survey of the tempestuous prewar years.

Kaminski, John P. *George Clinton: Yeoman Politician of the New Republic*. Madison, Wis.: Madison House, 1993. With this well-researched monograph, Kaminski has admirably fulfilled the need for an up-to-date biography of this pivotal, but relatively unknown early American politician and New York governor.

Kurtz, Stephen G. and James H. Hutson, eds. *Essays on the American Revolution*. New York: W. W. Norton & Company, 1973. Eight interpretive essays by nine distinguished scholars on the causes and consequences of the American Revolution.

Labaree, Benjamin Woods. *The Boston Tea Party*. London: Oxford University Press, 1964. Detailed study of the famous Tea Party, an event that greatly changed the course of subsequent prewar history.

McCullough, David. *John Adams*. New York: Simon & Schuster, 2001. A majestic, Pulitzer Prize–winning, full-length narrative biography of John Adams, who has heretofore been somewhat neglected by biographers.

Middlekauff, Robert. *The Glorious Cause: The American Revolution, 1763–1789*. New York: Oxford University Press, 1982. A volume in *The Oxford History of the United States* series. A lengthy, detailed survey of the entire revolutionary era. Narrative history at its best.

Morgan, Edmund S. *The Birth of the Republic, 1763–89*. Chicago: University of Chicago Press, 1956. An excellent brief survey of the events of the last quarter of the eighteenth century, which witnessed the transformation of thirteen disunited colonies into the united American republic.

Morgan, Edmund S. and Helen M. Morgan. *The Stamp Act Crisis: Prologue to Revolution.* New York: Collier Books, 1962. A superbly written narrative and interpretation of the "crisis" brought about by Parliament's passage of the universally hated Stamp Act.

Morison, Samuel Eliot, ed. *John Paul Jones: A Sailor's Biography.* Boston: Little, Brown, 1959. A Pulitzer Prize–winning biography of the colorful, legendary, but often unjustly criticized American naval hero.

———. *Sources and Documents Illustrating the American Revolution, 1764–1788.* London: Oxford University Press, 1965. An indispensable one-volume collection of the most significant primary sources.

Morris, Richard B. *The American Revolution Reconsidered.* New York: Harper & Row, Publishers, 1967. In these four provocative interpretive essays by a leading diplomatic historian of the revolutionary period, the author offers a new conservative interpretation of the American Revolution.

———. *Seven Who Shaped Our Destiny: The Founding Fathers as Revolutionaries.* New York: Harper & Row, Publishers, 1973. Seven highly interpretive biographical sketches of the most prominent founders of the American republic.

———, ed. *The Era of the American Revolution.* New York: Harper & Row, Publishers, 1965. In this collection of eleven interpretive articles, of particular interest and value are the essays dealing with the navigation acts as a possible cause of the Revolution and the Sons of Liberty.

Nagel, Paul C. *The Adams Women: Abigail and Louisa Adams, Their Sisters and Daughters.* New York: Oxford University Press, 1987. In this entertaining and informative portrayal of the remarkable Adams family women, the author writes convincingly that Abigail, her sisters, and their daughters were intellectually the equal of their more famous husbands, sons, and brothers.

———. *The Lees of Virginia: Seven Generations of an American Family.* New York: Oxford University Press, 1990. A well-written, informative portrayal of one of America's most distinguished families. This is a particularly useful source for information on the four famous revolutionary-generation Lee brothers: Richard Henry Lee, Francis Lightfoot Lee, William Lee, and Arthur Lee.

Namier, Lewis B. *England in the Age of the American Revolution.* London: Macmillan and Co., 1930. In this thorough examination of domestic politics in Great Britain during the 1760s and 1770s, Sir Lewis Namier asserts that the political instability in pre-1775 Great Britain was one of the causes for the estrangement with the American colonies.

———. *The Structure of Politics at the Accession of George III.* London: Macmillan & Co., 1965. The author maintains that, in the absence of the two traditional political parties (i.e., Whig and Tory), several powerful political factions emerged in Great Britain during and immediately after the Seven Years'

War (1756–1763). The political infighting among these factions for patronage and political advantage resulted in the pursuance of policies, which helped to precipitate the American War for Independence.

Nelson, William H. *The American Tory*. Boston: Beacon Press, 1964. The best brief study of American Toryism.

Niles, Hezekiah, ed. *Principles and Acts of the Revolution in America*. Baltimore, Md.: William Ogden Niles, 1822. A valuable collection of letters, acts, declarations, and broadsides. This is a readily accessible source for many primary documents not otherwise available.

Onuf, Peter S. *Jefferson's Empire: The Language of American Nationhood*. Charlottesville: University Press of Virginia, 2000. A highly interpretive portrayal of Thomas Jefferson as the apostle of American liberty, freedom, and democracy.

Palmer, Robert Roswell, *The Age of the Democratic Revolution*. Princeton, N.J.: Princeton University Press, 1959, 1964. This noted French Revolution scholar argues that the American Revolution and the French Revolution were part of the same general democratic movement of the late eighteenth century and early nineteenth century.

Peckham, Howard H., ed. *The Toll of Independence: Engagements & Battle Casualties of the American Revolution*. Chicago: University of Chicago Press, 1974. A listing of virtually every military engagement with the most accurate available casualty figures. An essential source for the study of the military aspects of the War of American Independence.

Perica, Esther. *The American Woman: Her Role During the Revolutionary War*. Monroe, N.Y.: Library Research Associates, 1981. An excellent, brief, informative survey of the role of women during the American Revolution gleaned chiefly from primary sources.

Philp, Mark, ed. *Thomas Paine*: Rights of Man, Common Sense, *and Other Political Writings*. Oxford: Oxford University Press, 1995. The best recent edition of Paine's major writings. The informative introduction and the chronology of Paine's life make this volume an excellent reference for the study of this international revolutionary.

Quarles, Benjamin. *The Negro in the American Revolution*. Chapel Hill: University of North Carolina Press, 1961. The standard, but somewhat outdated, monograph on the role and contributions to both sides of Black Americans.

Rhodehamel, John, ed. *The American Revolution: Writings from the War of Independence*. New York: The Library of America, 2001. Contains over a hundred items drawn from diaries, newspaper articles, and letters. Also includes a detailed chronology of the major events between 1774 and 1783. A valuable reference.

Richardson, James D., ed. *A Compilation of the Messages and Papers of the Presidents, 1789–1897*. New York: Bureau of National Literature and Art, 1903. This twenty-volume set is particularly valuable to students of the American presidency. It contains many valuable primary sources not otherwise accessible.

Schlesinger, Arthur M. *The Colonial Merchants and the American Revolution, 1763–1776*. New York: Atheneum, 1968. The classic study of the role played by colonial merchants in leading the early movement toward American independence.

Schoenbrun, David. *Triumph in Paris: The Exploits of Benjamin Franklin*. New York: Harper & Row, Publishers, 1976. A somewhat overly sympathetic, but engagingly written narrative of Franklin's diplomatic and political achievements in Paris, 1776–1785.

Stokesbury, James L. *A Short History of the American Revolution*. New York: William Morrow, 1991. An excellent brief one-volume military history of the American War for Independence.

Triber, Jayne E. *A True Republican: The Life of Paul Revere*. Amherst: University of Massachusetts Press, 1998. In this full-length biography, Triber has gone beyond the mythological hero of Henry Wadsworth Longfellow's "Paul Revere's Ride" to give a scholarly portrayal of a significant revolutionary artisan, entrepreneur, and patriot.

Van Doren, Carl. *Secret History of the American Revolution*. New York: Viking Press, 1941. Although primarily an engagingly written, informative, although somewhat outdated, treatment of Benedict Arnold's treasonous conspiracy, it does include several other spy stories not usually related in general histories of the American Revolution.

Ver Steeg, Clarence L. *Robert Morris: Revolutionary Financier*. Philadelphia: University of Pennsylvania Press, 1954. An informative, sympathetic biography of the somewhat forgotten "Financier of the Revolution."

Wallace, Willard M. *Appeal to Arms: A Military History of the American Revolution*. Chicago: Quadrangle Books, 1951. The author assigns credit and blame to both sides in this valuable one-volume appraisal of the military aspects of the Revolution.

Ward, Harry M. *The American Revolution: Nationhood Achieved, 1763–1788*. New York: St. Martin's Press, Inc., 1995. A volume in the *St. Martin's Series in U.S. History*. A well-written, informative survey that examines all major aspects of the period from the Treaty of Paris (1763) to the promulgation of the Constitution (1788).

Wood, Gordon S. *The American Revolution: A History*. New York: The Modern Library, 2002. An excellent synthesis of the entire revolutionary era by a Pulitzer Prize–winning historian.

————. *The Radicalism of the American Revolution.* New York: Alfred A. Knopf, 1992. An authoritative study that emphasizes that the American Revolution "transformed a monarchical society into a democratic one."

Wood, William J. *Battles of the Revolutionary War, 1775–1781.* New York: Da Capo Press, 1995. Author contends that the Americans won the war on the battlefield and did not merely outlast the British.

Zagarri, Rosemarie. *A Woman's Dilemma: Mercy Otis Warren and the American Revolution.* Wheeling, Ill.: Harland Davidson, Inc., 1995. An excellent, brief cradle-to-grave biography of the foremost female intellectual of the new American Republic.

Zobel, Hiller B. *The Boston Massacre.* New York: W. W. Norton & Company, 1970. The definitive revisionist study of the misnamed event that sparked bitter colonial opposition and British countermeasures.

Electronic Resources

Historical Text Archive. *Http://www.msstate.edu/Archives/History.* Large collection of significant primary documents including sections on the Declaration of Independence and U.S. Constitution.

History Channel. *Http://www.historychannel.org.* Excellent introduction to numerous links dealing with all aspects of the discipline of history.

Index of Resources for Historians. *Http://www.ukans.edu/history.* Over a thousand links to historical sites, arranged alphabetically by general topic.

Internet Archive of Texts and Documents. *Http://history.hanover.edu/texts.html.* Listing of primary sources arranged chronologically, geographically, and by subject.

Internet Modern History Sourcebook. *Http://www.fordham.edu/halsall/mod/modsbook12.html.* Collection includes information about events leading to the American Revolution.

Military Actions in the American Revolution. *Http://www.sar.org/history/docsbatt.htm.* Contains synopses of the major battles of the American Revolution.

National Archives and Records Administration (NARA). *Http://www.nara.gov/.* The official depository for United States government documents.

Films

Founding Fathers. 2000. Produced by Susan Werbe, MPH Entertainment for the History Channel. Four hours. A somewhat overly sympathetic portrayal of the contributions of the major revolutionary figures. It features the roles of George Washington, John Adams, Samuel Adams, Thomas Jefferson, and Thomas Paine.

Liberty: The American Revolution. 1997. Produced by Catherine Allan, KTCA-TV, Twin Cities Public Television, Inc. Six hours. A colorful pictorial overview of the American Revolution with informative commentary by several noted Revolutionary historians.

INDEX

Privy Council (British), 12
Proclamation of Lord Dunmore
  Offering Freedom to the Slaves
  Belonging to the Rebels in Virginia,
  79; text, 172–173
Proclamation of Rebellion (including
  text), 170–171
Proprietary colonies, 4–5; Pennsylvania
  founded as, 7
Provisions, foraging, 80
Prussia, 93
Pulaski, Casimir, 64
Puritans, 6
Putnam, Israel, 44

Quakers, 3, 7; and slavery, 3, 79
Quartering Act, 33
Quebec, 13, 18, 33, 40, 44, 46; *see also*
  Canada
Quebec Act, 33, 35
Queen Anne's War, 13
Quincy, Josiah Jr., and Boston Massacre,
  29

Rall, Johann, 50
Randolph, Edmund, 5
Randolph, Peyton, 5; and the Quebec
  Act, 33; First Continental Congress, 34
Ranger (ship), 74
Rangers, John Butler's Loyalist, 62
Read, George, and First Continental
  Congress, 34
Reconciliationists, 34
Reed, Joseph, 95
Repayment of war debts, issue of, 97
Republic, established, 3, 4, 77
Republicanism, 84, 104–105
Resolution for Independence (including
  text), 179–180
Revere, Paul, 42; *The Bloody Massacre*
  (engraving), follows page 76
Revolution, American, *see* American
  Revolution
Revolution, defined, 1

Revolution, right of, 104
Rhode Island, 6, 30, 33, 43, 64, 71,
  83; and taxation, 25; state constitu-
  tion, 4, 85
Ridicule, as punishment, 83
Rochambeau, Jean Baptiste, 70, 71, 72
Rockingham, Marquis of, 24
Roderique Hortalez and Company, 90
Roman Catholics, and Maryland, 7;
  see also Catholics
Russian Revolution, 101
Rutledge, Edward, and Carlisle
  Commission, 95
Rutledge, John, 23

Salary, Anglican ministers, 19
Salutary neglect, 34; and First
  Continental Congress, 34; concept
  of, 11–14, 15
Saratoga, Battle of, 51, 53*ff.*, 87, 92
Savannah, Georgia, 62, 64, 73, 74
Schuyler family, 6
Schuyler, Philip, 44, 46, 55
Scotch-Irish settlements, 5, 7
Scottish settlements, 4
Search warrants, 25, and state
  constitutions, 86
Second Hundred Years' War, 13, 90
Secretary of State for the Southern
  Department (British), 12
Self-incrimination, and state constitu-
  tions, 85
Selkirk, Lord, 75
Seneca Indians, 78
Separation of Powers, 84
Serapis (ship), 75
Seven Years' War, 13, 18, 53–54, 98;
  map of North America after, xviv
Sevier, John, 67
Shelby, Isaac, 67
Sherman, Roger, 91
*Signing of the Treaty of Amity and
  Commerce and of Alliance* (paint-
  ing), follows page 76

About the Author

JOSEPH C. MORTON is Professor of History, Emeritus, at Northeastern Illinois University.